Tides of Resilience:
Beyond The Wave

Paperback ISBN: 979-8-9934285-1-2
eBook ISBN: 979-8-9934285-0-5
US Copyright Registration Number: TXu 2-509-221

This is a work of nonfiction. Some names and identifying details have been changed to protect privacy. This book may include brief quotations or references to copyrighted material used under fair use for commentary and cultural context. All rights remain with the original copyright holders.

Cover design by John Bromfield using Publisher 2
Interior design by Footsteps Press

Printed in USA
First Edition: October 2025

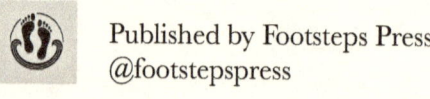

Published by Footsteps Press
@footstepspress

Disclaimer

This is a work of nonfiction based on the author's personal experiences, memories, and reflections. Events are portrayed to the best of the author's recollection; however, some timelines, locations, and details have been adjusted for narrative clarity. The thoughts, feelings, and dialogue presented reflect the author's perspective at the time and may not represent the views or experiences of others.

To respect the privacy of individuals and protect their identities, certain names and identifying details have been changed. Composite characters have occasionally been used, and some events have been condensed or restructured. Any resemblance to actual persons, living or dead, is coincidental and unintentional unless explicitly stated.

This book includes references to popular music, films, books, and cultural figures. All such references are used under the principles of fair use for commentary, criticism, and cultural context. All copyrights and trademarks remain the property of their respective owners.

The author does not intend to cause harm or distress to any person or organisation, and has made every effort to present events truthfully and respectfully.

Content Note

This memoir contains references to trauma, grief, addiction, natural disasters, and mental health challenges, which may be distressing to some readers. These stories are shared in the spirit of honesty, resilience, and healing.

For Mum
For always believing

Author's Note

This book began as a therapy exercise—a way to make sense of what I'd buried and what I couldn't forget. I never intended to write a memoir. But as the pages accumulated, so did the memories, the questions, the ghosts, and eventually, the clarity.

Tides of Resilience is my attempt to piece together what it means to survive—not just a disaster, but the slow, invisible aftermath. If you've ever carried something heavy in silence, I hope this story reminds you: you're not alone, and you're not broken.

Prologue

On 26th December 2004, at 07:58:53 local time (UTC+7), a 9.3-magnitude earthquake struck beneath the Indian Ocean near Sumatra, Indonesia.

The earthquake generated a massive tsunami that devastated coastal regions across 14 countries. Waves towering up to 100 feet claimed the lives of over 225,000 people, leaving countless others to grapple with unimaginable loss and destruction.

Now known as the Boxing Day tsunami, it remains one of the deadliest natural disasters in recorded history.

For me, it marked a day that would change my life forever.

This is my story.

'It may seem difficult at first but everything is difficult at first.'
Miyamoto Musashi

One

The Help

15th July 2021
London

The waiting room was empty. Through the glass, the security guard stared at me—expressionless—and told me to wait outside until my allotted time. It pissed me off. Immensely.

It had been a long day. The rain was relentless, each droplet gnawing at my nerves. Fluorescent lights flickered inside the empty room. Just five minutes early—but it felt like the guard was being deliberately difficult. I felt the familiar fire rise, but forced myself to walk away.

This was life now—post-pandemic. Rules followed to the letter, no matter how arbitrary. People were still emerging from lockdown: cautious, scared, clinging to the protocols.

I got it. I'd been militant about the rules too. Distancing, sanitiser, masks—even stupidly humming 'Happy Birthday' as I washed my hands. If there was guidance, I stuck to it. But now, after months of overkill and misinformation, I was tired of the pointless restrictions.

The drizzle cooled my face as I wandered through the residential complex flanking the Docklands. Towering skyscrapers loomed overhead—a far cry from its days as the world's largest port.

The walk did the trick. My temper faded with each step as I lost myself in history. Lately, this had become my strategy: when I felt the burn, I'd take photos—googling facts to distract my mind. It worked a treat. So well, in fact, it had become a kind of therapy.

Frustrations set aside, I re-focused on the mission. Calmer, I made my way back and pressed the buzzer. The same guard glanced up, checked his watch, and gave a little shake of his head. He got up, opened the door, and told me—reluctantly—to wait on the sofa.

"Thanks," I muttered, sarcasm lacing the word. 'Deep breaths, John. Don't get dragged into this nonsense.'

The mask didn't help my mood. I'd gone overboard, buying a clunky filtered contraption that felt more like a muzzle than protection. It was hot, damp, itchy—and made breathing a chore.

I inhaled with difficulty, closed my eyes. Focus. 'Why am I here?'

19:59. Almost time.

I'd always had a problem with anger—at least that's what my friends told me. I didn't see it. Self-awareness had never been my strong suit. But lockdown changed that. It gave me time. Time to pause, reflect, strip away the distractions and ask: Who am I? How did I get here? What's wrong with me?

The anger was the first red flag—too frequent, too intense to ignore. It flared mostly behind closed doors. But I couldn't control it. Often, I didn't even realise it was happening. An involuntary reflex that rarely matched the moment. If I didn't let it out, it built into aggression. Sometimes worse.

One incident at work started the chain of events that brought me here. A simple email request from my boss. The tone of it—the assumption—set me off. Stress was high, and I snapped. Fired off a ridiculous reply. Walked away from my laptop, convinced I'd have to quit.

Life over.

Then the absurdity hit me. 'What are you doing? Calm the fuck down.' My boss had been great. And here I was, imploding. But reason wasn't enough. The fear still clouded everything. So I grabbed my shoes and walked out the front door.

One benefit of lockdown. When I lost control, I could step away—no one had to see the 'meltdown.' I headed into the woods behind my house. The air, the stillness, the trees—anything to ground me. 'Time to be honest,' I thought. 'Be brave, John. Nothing to lose, mate.'

9

As I wandered through the trees, my mind began to draft the response: "I'm so sorry. My last message was completely uncalled for...I've recently been diagnosed with PTSD..."

It was the most honest thing I'd ever composed. An apology, yes—but also an admission. A turning point.

Sitting on a bench in a sunlit clearing, I felt the warmth seep into my skin. For the first time, I let it in: this wasn't just stress. This was something deeper. Something I had to stop ignoring.

The apology didn't come easy. I'd barely accepted the news myself, and now I was about to invite judgement. My last job had been brutal. The kind of place where 'stress' came with air quotes and eye rolls.

I told them about my diagnosis—and two weeks later, I was a goner. That memory made me hesitate. But things were getting worse anyway.

Time to own it.

I hit 'send,' slammed the laptop shut, and ran for cover—literally. Straight to bed. Ashamed. Panicked. Frozen under the duvet, limbs locked in place. Breath shallow.

Petrified flesh, frantic brain. One shut down so the other could spin. Like a Cyberdyne T-800, my mind looped through every possibility. Because anything really can happen. I knew that all too well.

My body slowly returning to normal, I found the courage to check the reply. To my surprise—it was kind. In a way I hadn't expected. I needed that. More than I realised.

And in that moment, I knew: there was no turning back. There were people who wanted to help—resources in place. Now it was up to me.

"John?" A voice snapped me back.

"Yes, that's me," I muttered through the mask—instantly regretting the involuntary Bane impression.

"You can come through—and feel free to take off your mask."

Yes!

The office was small and bright. Pastel walls, soft furniture. Cheery and calming. I pulled off the mask and finally breathed.

"Please, take a seat," she said, gesturing to a purple couch under the window.

"Thanks," I replied, assuming the position.

It wasn't what I pictured. No leather chair. No antique desk. No chaise lounge. No "Tell me about your mother…"

'This is a mistake. There's nothing wrong with me. I'm fine. This is a waste of time.' I'd told myself those lies for years. 'Quiet!'

High-functioning. In control. No drama. But not this time. I know something's off.

"So John, would you like to tell me why you're here?" Her eyes bored into mine.

Good question. 'Help!' echoed through my mind as I tried to let go of denial long enough to speak.

"I don't really know," I lied. "Bit stressed at work. My boss suggested I come see someone." Half-truth. Still hiding. Still scared to say it out loud.

Her name was Rada. Open, direct, with piercing blue eyes that contradicted her kind smile. She spent time trying to make me feel at ease. It worked. I liked her. A straight shooter. I respect that. 'Maybe this time will be different,' I thought.

Not my first rodeo.

"A few years ago I had a rough time at work. Took a kind of redundancy package. Was told I had PTSD… but I'm not sure really."

I exhaled. It was out.

Forty-four, diagnosed with a serious mental illness—and still living in complete denial. 'Help!'

"Why were you diagnosed?" she asked, eyes narrowing slightly.

"Well I had a bit of a... meltdown. Or a breakdown, I suppose. I left my job and had some counselling," I said, nervously.

"And that gave you PTSD?" she asked, brow raised.

I exhaled. "No... A long time ago I was in *the* tsunami." I let that hang for a beat. "The work thing just triggered some bad memories."

She stayed silent, waiting.

"It was the Boxing Day one. Not Fukushima. I was on an island in Thailand—me, my best mate Barry, and my girlfriend Tina. We all survived. But it was... bad. Really bad." That's all I could manage. Even saying it out loud stirred monsters I preferred to keep buried.

"That sounds pretty awful, John—and no doubt incredibly traumatic," she said, matter-of-factly.

In that moment, I decided: she was the help I desperately needed. I'd spent years hoping someone would tell me it wasn't true. That PTSD was just a mistake. That I was normal. But now? I wanted the truth.

I was ready to face it—whatever it meant.

"Before we go into it," she said gently, "I'd like to understand more about the breakdown, and your earlier counselling sessions. Let's start there, please John."

Here we go!

'Anger is like a fire. It can cook your food or burn down your house.'
Charlotte Kasl

Two

Anger Management

May 2018
England

The year began like so many others—paying for the excesses of the last. My body, mind, and spirit were spent. No resolutions. No hopeful plans. Just a crushing, colourless exhaustion.

On the surface, I had it all—loving wife, decent job, nice house, great mates. I moved through the motions with people who said, "John's doing well, isn't he?"

In quiet moments, I fantasised about retirement. Ridiculous. I'd only just turned forty. Still, I clung to the fantasy. If I could stop working, maybe everything else would fall into place.

I couldn't see the real issue. Work wasn't the enemy—my lifestyle was.

Every day felt like a high-wire walk—one bad decision from plunging into a darkness I wasn't sure I could crawl out of.

I'd been on the job twenty five years, climbing the corporate ladder. Still several rungs from the top, but for a working-class kid, not too shabby.

I still remember my interview. I waited nervously beside another lad, Joey. We both landed apprenticeships and became best mates. Full-time work, full of promise. I was hungry—nerdy, even.

Those were the early days when anything seemed possible. Now, decades later, I felt utterly trapped.

Was this the infamous mid-life crisis? Probably.

In the blink of an eye, I'd gone from fresh-faced teenager to alcohol-ravaged, drug-dependent, depressed adult.

'Surely there's more to life than this?' I'd tasted more in my youth—backpacking the world with my best friends—but that felt like a lifetime ago. 'Was this now it?'

The cracks were forming.

I was middle management now—responsible for everything, rewarded for nothing. Most days were spent on the road. Long hours. Little productivity. No satisfaction.

And always—always—traffic.

I was systematically losing my mind. A car cut me up? White-hot fury. Reckless lane change? Idiots risking my life. I'd scream behind the wheel, fists clenched, chest tight.

The anger consumed me. Left me breathless.

The cracks from the road soon fissured into the workplace, threatening the façade I'd carefully built. I felt something dark pressing forward.

The mask was slipping.

Then the crack became a chasm: my job was suddenly at risk of redundancy. I couldn't believe it. For all my angst, the job had always been my safety net. Now, I could be toast.

Fuck!

I was told I'd be fine. "Don't fret, John," my manager said, with a wink. "It won't be you."

Still, the news hit hard. I had debts, commitments… habits to feed. Those hours behind the wheel began to feel like solitary confinement. At home my drinking escalated as I tried to mask the panic.

It didn't work.

I'd arrive at work hungover, exhausted, irritable—barely coping. I was pissed off. Fear had buddied up with anger, and the two of them were having a jolly-up in my head.

Eventually, the façade crumbled.

One morning we were gathered in a meeting room. A little white projector sat on the table, spitting heat into the already oppressive air.

It was too warm. Too cramped.

'Come on, what the fuck are we waiting for?' I checked the clock. Delayed. We were waiting for one person. Still, I wound myself up. 'Where the fuck is he?'

As time ticked on my irritation twisted into something more visceral. The room seemed to shrink. For a second, I imagined us in the Death Star's garbage compactor—steel walls closing in, squeezing my lungs.

I yanked at my tie, loosened my collar. Still couldn't breathe.

The conversations faded into white noise. All I could hear was the bloke next to me—chewing. Loudly. Open-mouthed.

Chomp. Slurp. Chomp.

Every bite felt weaponised. I edged away, turned my back, tried to block him out. Couldn't. Someone handed me water. I gulped half, hoping to reset. But something was seriously wrong.

Short gasps. Face burning.

Munch. Slurp. Munch.

Rage rising.

I wanted to shove the other half of his egg salad sandwich, complete with plastic packaging, right down his throat.

I clenched my jaw so hard it hurt. I stared at him, hoping he'd notice the fury in my eyes. Instead, he laughed—loud—spitting flecks of bread onto the table in front of me.

That did it.

"This is fucking ridiculous! Where the fuck is he?" I shouted, kicking my chair back and storming to the toilets.

In the mirror, I barely recognised myself. The anger had fused with fear, condensing into something radioactive. I imagined a dark blue ball of energy glowing in my chest, desperate to burst out— obliterating my Primark shirt and incinerating the gobbling prince where he sat.

I splashed cold water on my face. 'Just breathe, John. This is all fucking stupid.'

Back in the corridor, I got the update: our missing colleague had called in sick. The meeting could start.

Good. I needed to shine. Maybe it was just nerves.

But then I heard what actually happened. He'd gone out on the razz. Strip club until 4 a.m. Pissed up. Coked up.

'What the actual fuck?' Whatever fragile control I had left evaporated.

Missing a divisional review to get wasted? Taking the piss out of the rest of us? I hadn't missed one of these in twelve years. And this guy— this absolute numpty—was lying on a bathroom floor while I'd just battled the M1 for three straight hours.

The anger... oh, the anger.

It glowed under my sweat-soaked shirt. Everyone else found it hilarious—like he was some kind of legend. That only made it worse. I sat there in silent fury, tussling with my mutant gene—fierce, unstable. Alex Summers mode. I could feel the blast building inside me, every muscle focused on containment.

I don't remember the next part. I came to in the car. I just needed to get home. To vent. To breathe.

'What the hell was that?' White-hot anger. A new kind of rage.

I should clarify—I was no stranger to big sessions. That'll become obvious later. Our motto had always been work hard, play hard, but that was boozy pub crawls, not class A's and strippers.

This isn't *Goodfellas*. It's facilities management in Milton Keynes, you mug.

In the workplace, I maintained a slimmed-down replicant persona. My Nexus-7 model. Professional, composed, measured. So seeing him act like that? It felt personal. Like he was mocking me.

My mind was unravelling. Chasms forming, widening.

I was in no state for what came next: the annual company conference, held at a fancy London hotel.

I'd been stewing, still raging at our very own Henry Hill. 'Who does that sort of thing on a Monday night? Dickhead.'

Maybe it was a sign. Take the redundancy. Fuck off, and Re-evaluate.

The thought passed through like a cold wind—always followed by fear. I was institutionalised. Scared of the unknown. "These walls are funny. First, you hate them. Then you get used to them..." Morgan Freeman's voice echoed as I rounded the final corner, lost in conflict.

"John! Just the man I need!" I looked up. HR manager. On the steps. Gesturing. "We need someone to go on stage...."

"You can FUCK RIGHT OFF!"

The words burst out before she could finish. She froze—mouth agape, shocked.

"I'm not doing it! I could be out of a job next week and you expect me to jump on stage and be all smiles? Not fucking happening!"

"What? I... I don't understand?"

I brushed past her into the foyer, made a beeline for the coffee. Downed it. Refilled it—hands shaking. She followed and gently touched my shoulder.

"C'mon—lets have a chat," she said softly. Calm. Sincere.

As we made our way to a private table, I realised something: I didn't care anymore. The barrier was gone. The gate unmanned.

"What's going on with you then, mate?" Her thick Mancunian accent danced across my eardrums.

"Are you having a laugh?" I snapped. "What d'ya think's going on? Last month I was told my job was safe. A day later I'm at risk of redundancy—and since then, nothing. Not one fucking word."

She looked genuinely confused, but I kept going. "The only letter I've had says I'm done next week—so yeah, I'm fucked off. It's all bollocks!"

Deep breath. 'Get a grip, John… you're losing it.' The rage was hard to contain—like *Cujo*, clawing up my throat, frothing at the mouth.

"I'm sorry for the language," I added, trying to reclaim some decorum. "It's not directed at you, Eve. I'm just really pissed off."

"That's okay, I get it," she said gently. "But I think there's been a misunderstanding. We'd never want to lose you. We assumed you knew that."

"Am I a mind reader then, mystic fucking John?" I shot back. The rabid dog snapping at the leash. "How hard is it to pick up the phone?"

PLEASE MAKE YOUR WAY BACK TO THE MAIN ROOM. The tannoy cut through, putting a muzzle on it.

"Look," she said, standing. "Leave this with me. We'll catch up later, okay?"

"Thanks," I said. "I appreciate your help," I added, softer now.

18

My voice cracked. Emotion caught in my throat. How quickly I'd gone from fury to welling up was terrifying.

My emotions were a rollercoaster—and I was hurtling blindly down the track. No matter how much I tried to ignore it, something wasn't right.

The conference closed and the crowd surged toward the nearest pub. It was a typical London boozer. Inside, warm lighting bathed worn leather booths and a polished bar.

I took a seat and tried to distance myself from the obnoxious prick that had inhabited my skin all day.

The drinking, as always, started at a voracious pace. Soon, Eve updated me. "Don't worry," she said. "Ignore the letter—your job is safe."

Great. It was the reassurance I'd craved but the outburst haunted me. I was sure they were all talking about it. About me. Determined to show my better side, I started to mingle. The nice guy. Not the psycho that had let loose on an innocent young lady.

Somehow, the mask held.

An hour later, coming back from the bogs, one of the lads pulled me aside. "You want a sniff?"

Now, I've hinted—I was no angel. And saying "yes" was a lifelong weakness. Several double vodkas deep, my response was swift.

"Yeah alright then."

Too late. No thought. Just instinct. Two-footed, head first.

Back upstairs, I felt the surge. I scanned the room, avoiding eye contact with the directors. 'Is my jaw giving me away?'

I leaned on the bar, ordered another vodka. 'Play it cool, Trig. Nice and cool.'

"Did Griff sort you out?" My manager leaned in, grinning, arm around my shoulder.

"Yeah," I said, trying to hide my surprise.

Ringleader?!

"Good stuff, innit? There's more if you want in—just give Griff the money." He winked and disappeared into the crowd.

My brain, wired and spiralling, started calculating. 'Get the fuck out of here. Don't get pulled deeper into this shit.'

I slipped out the side exit.

I weaved through the crowd like a paranoid android, the buzz fading fast, leaving only shame.

When I got home, I felt a flicker of pride for slipping away—but no peace. I stayed up drinking, alone, trying to organise my thoughts.

A habit that would soon get much much worse.

'It's not the weight that crushes us, but how we carry it.'
Anonymous

Three

Falling Down

June 2018
England

I spent the next two days in bed wrestling demons. Mind strangled with disgrace. Hating the way I'd blown off steam.

Doing gear at work? It felt wrong. Out of place. Was I really any better than our Goodfella, Henry Hill?

By Sunday, I dragged myself to the sofa, cocooned in the bedspread. Battered. Physically and mentally wrecked.

Not sick—just not well.

By evening, I finally showered.

There was a new *Star Wars* film out. After everything, seeing my mates felt like a glimmer at the end of a torrid tunnel. Steve—one of my closest friends—was supposed to be there. I hadn't seen him in a few months, and I'd been looking forward to catching up.

The night started well. A few pints deep and venting to Jarrod, the biggest Star Wars nerd among us. And then…

"Life's mental sometimes, John. Don't worry, you can get a job anywhere. Just look at Steve's son. Tragic. You can't wait for life to happen…"

"Sorry? What are you talking about?"

Jarrod blinked. "What? You don't know?" He leaned in. "His son topped himself last week."

Wallop.

The words hit like a hammer. No wonder Steve had been a no show.

The world spun. I tried to make sense of what I'd just heard. It felt like gossip—dirty and careless. I hated how it had been delivered. Not Jarrod's fault, just bad timing and worse framing.

My mind, already frayed, couldn't handle it. Rage flared. I wanted to punch him in his fat throat and watch him spit up his Camden Hells.

I came around, sitting. Motionless. Staring at the screen.

John Williams' trumpets blared. But I felt a million light-years from my own galaxy.

Lost in grief, guilt, and sadness.

Seventeen. He was just a kid. My god. The pain consumed me.

Life's cruel synchronicities flicked past at warp speed.

Three of our best friends had died in a car crash at the same age. Same time of year. Almost to the day.

Sudden death—stirred everything in me. Especially when it came to children.

Fear. Guilt. Anger.

I lived expecting the worst. Not because I was negative, but because of what I'd seen. What I'd survived.

That day on Koh Phi Phi.

That wave. Unannounced. It decimated everything in its path—including the children.

So many children.

I hadn't seen Steve in so long. Why was I hearing it like second hand news? What kind of friend was I? 'Fucking wanker John.'

The truth? I'd been pulling away from people ever since that day. Not deliberately. Just… changed.

Thailand changed me.

I was living on the edges of my own galaxy—angry, scared, ashamed. Lost and alone, somewhere out beyond the Dagobah System.

Sleep didn't come. I drank vodka to drown out the pain. But it only summoned darker memories.

Lost friends. Screams. Children. Guilt. And then the blackout came— as it always did.

The next morning, I felt worse than usual. Like my gut had been torn out. How could I be so angry about my own life when there was so much pain elsewhere? It felt selfish. 'Get a fuckin' grip, mate.'

The journey to work was hell. A truck had jackknifed on the M25. Road closed. Air ambulance called in.

I sat on the central reservation. Car abandoned. Sun beating down on the tarmac. My chest tightened. Breath turned shallow.

The chopper was the trigger.

I hadn't seen one since that day on Phi Phi. The rhythmic thrum of the blades. The way it hovered over devastation. The memory punched through—vivid, unwelcome, unstoppable. My mind locked into a loop. A trilogy of trauma played back to back:

A woman on a stretcher. Blood pooling beneath her. A red air ambulance at the end of the beach, a lifeline against despair.

A car, crushed against a tree. Bonnet curled like a tin can. Flames roaring. Faces behind glass. Screaming. Trapped. Melting.

A boy. Small. Still. Standing beneath a tree. Silent. Alone. Afraid.

23

Three scenes. Different timelines. Same thread of anguish—sewn together in my head.

I sat shaking as the chopper rose and disappeared into the sky.

Too young to die.

I arrived three hours late—dishevelled, broken, and in no state to work. But I opened my laptop anyway. Tried to teleport back to the present.

A soft chime. New email. Nothing major. But enough. The words blurred. My chest clenched. Hands trembled.

The room dissolved into white noise. I gripped the table. The anger surged. Hot. Primal. Black dots freckled the edge of my vision.

'Stay calm.' But I couldn't. Not this time.

"Who the fuck do you think you're talking to? Who the fuck do you think I am, you fucking cunt?"

The snap came without warning. I slammed the laptop shut. The table shook.

Heads turned. Conversations died.

I didn't care.

Heart thundered in my ears.

I stood so fast the chair crashed behind me.

I stormed out—out of the meeting, out of the building, into my car. Hands locked around the wheel. Knuckles bone white. Whole body shaking.

I stared at the dashboard. Vision blurred. Tears threatened.

I leaned back, staring through the windscreen. Grappling with my inner Ferrigno. Trying to push him back down—face twisted, breath shallow—desperate to avoid that moment when, like Dr. Banner, my eyes would go white and the green monster would take over.

"I'm done," I whispered. "I'm fucking done."

I didn't know it then, but I was already in the middle of a breakdown.

There was no going back. Not to the meeting. Not to the job. Not to the life I'd spent so long pretending to be okay in.

Game over, man.

'It is often safer to be in chains than to be free.'
Franz Kafka

Four

The Game

July 2018
London

It felt like a huge weight had been lifted. Walking out was abrupt, but it felt right. As I put distance between myself and the meeting I'd stormed out of, I knew I couldn't go back.

It was over.

Stuck in traffic at Junction Ten, I rang my work mate Joey.

"Good for you!" he replied. "Just play the game pal, and you'll be laughing."

I knew what he meant. Their botched redundancy process had given me leverage, and I had a plan. A safety net. Something to ensure a decent payout if the worst ever happened. I hadn't planned the meltdown—nobody does—but now that it had occurred, I had to follow through.

Call in sick with "stress" and play the game.

Easier said than done. I was bricking it. I'd always been told stress wasn't a "real" illness—just weakness. The idea of pretending to be sick made me even more anxious—except I wasn't pretending. The symptoms were already there. I just didn't know how to name them.

Looking back, I wish I'd understood how serious stress could be. It wasn't weakness—it was carrying too much, for too long. But at the time, I was just trying to survive.

I acted fast. Called my manager. Kept it short. Then switched off my phone. Next: book a GP appointment and get a sick note. But first, I needed my back looked at. All those hours hunched in my car had taken a toll, and the chronic pain wasn't helping my already fragile mood.

The chiropractor's waiting room was sweltering. The sun blazed through the windows. People sat wiping brows, fanning themselves with magazines, exchanging weary glances. I didn't wait long. A woman called me through.

After the usual questions, she asked me to remove my T-shirt and lie face down on the padded bed. I wasn't expecting much—just some light relief—but I got much more than I bargained for.

As she worked along my spine, she spoke about mindfulness, meditation, and the body's natural ability to heal itself. Sounded like mumbo jumbo, but her touch was gentle, and I was too sore to argue. I let her talk as I drifted in and out, trying to distract myself from the discomfort.

She asked about the pain. Somehow, I ended up mentioning the tsunami. Not in detail—just the sanitised version I'd rehearsed for years. A script I could recite without activating the memories.

When I finished, silence.

Then, softly: "You should talk to someone. Someone trained to listen."

"Maybe," I muttered, still face down, my mind spinning.

"Has anyone ever suggested you might have PTSD?"

The words hit hard. PTSD? Me? I thought that was for soldiers. Not someone like me. 'I wasn't crazy... was I?'

I mumbled something about not usually telling people. Especially strangers.

"Thank you for trusting me," she said. "That was really personal."

"I didn't mean to," I replied. "It just came out."

"I think you should look into it," she said gently.

It had never even occurred to me that I'd walked away from the tsunami with more than a few bruises. But now I wondered—had I been carrying something all this time?

My recent behaviour—the anger, the explosion at work—it was seriously out of character. I'd blamed it on a midlife crisis. But what if it wasn't?

What if something was really wrong with my mind?

I left reception with my back slightly better—but my head now full of new problems. I didn't know it yet, but that session would be the catalyst for everything that followed.

The next day, I was up early—groggy, emotional. Walking out of work had felt right, but now the fear crept in. I technically had a job, but I was teetering on the edge of unemployment for the first time in my life.

No income. Dependent on my wife. And now this new thought: PTSD?

At the doctors I sat far from the others. Distracting myself with posters about flu jabs and stroke symptoms—anything to avoid rehearsing my explanation.

"Mr Bromfield?" I looked up. A young doctor stood at the door.

"That's me," I said, standing to follow her.

"How can I help today?"

I took a breath. "I'm not sure where to begin… I haven't been able to go into work for the past week." Then, piece by piece, I laid it out. The redundancy. The insomnia. The chronic pain. The suicide. And, quietly, the word: PTSD.

"PTSD?" she repeated. "Why would you think that?"

I gave her the cliffs notes version of the tsunami. It skipped the horror, just enough to explain.

Then I noticed: I was crying. Not sobbing. Just silent tears, trickling down. I hadn't even felt them fall. I just tasted the salt on my lips.

Embarrassed, I laughed and took the tissue she offered.

"I don't usually cry. Not sure where that came from."

It was true. The car crash in my teens—the one that took The Lads—had shattered something in me.

"That's okay. Please don't apologise," she said, sliding her chair a little closer.

"I'm going to do a few things today. First, a prescription—something for the insomnia, the back pain, and your mood."

"Thank you," I said, relieved she was taking me seriously.

"Second, I'll refer you to a mental health specialist. Based on what you've shared, PTSD is a likely."

She typed away. The printer whirred into life behind her.

"Here you go, Mr Bromfield," she said, handing over an envelope. "There's a note for four weeks' rest. Come back if things don't improve."

I walked out feeling ten times lighter. The diagnosis hadn't sunk in yet, but knowing I didn't have to face work gave me a huge lift.

The short walk home was a daze. I filled the prescription—though I had no plans to take the pills. Just wanted them there—just in case.

I couldn't believe I'd cried. I always prided myself on being in control. Of everything. But now I wasn't so sure. 'Maybe you just wanted that sick note real bad?'

'But the tears were real, weren't they, John?'

At home, I had to explain everything to my wife. One of the hardest conversations of my life.

I felt like a failure—ashamed.

"Hey, you know the guy you married? Well, he just cried at the doctor's, might be on the dole, and apparently has a serious mental illness. Please don't leave me."

I didn't say those exact words, but that's what I felt.

The following week, things got worse. Depression tightened its grip— fear, shame, isolation. Panic would surge without warning. I'd be breathless. Nauseous.

And then the tsunami returned.

The memories—long buried—bubbled up. The potential diagnosis had cracked something open. For the first time, I started to connect the dots:

The sleepless nights. The rage. The emptiness.

Maybe it wasn't burnout. Or a midlife crisis. Maybe it was something deeper.

I still had hope. I'd worked at the company for donkeys years. Built a good rep. Surely they'd support me. I wasn't crazy—just—not quite myself.

I sat down and wrote an email to the HR Director. Told him everything. The diagnosis. The meltdown. The suicide. The Lads. The tsunami.

It was raw. Maybe too raw. But it was honest. I wasn't playing games anymore. I just needed time. I hoped they'd understand.

A few hours later, I got a reply. Concerned. Suggesting a meeting. It gave me hope. A chance to explain. I felt a flicker of energy. Maybe things could go back to normal.

I didn't think of myself as unwell. Not really. But I was beginning to realise: The tsunami hadn't ended on that beach. I'd carried it with me for years. I just hadn't noticed the scar.

The day came. Nervous, I headed to a local coffee shop for the meeting.

Shane, the divisional HR director, showed up late. He was a young, brash, Australian lad. Flaming red hair. Smug as they come.

He sat down. "So, how are you doing?"

I took a breath and launched into it—the meltdown in a nutshell. I anchored it all to the tsunami. Still vague. Still sanitised. But enough to show the weight of it.

When I finished, I grabbed my cup, mostly to stop myself from talking. I peered at him over the rim, searching for empathy.

Instead, Shane pulled out a letter and slid it across the table. Inside: a compromise agreement. Some money, to leave quietly.

No questions. No fuss.

"Have a lawyer look it over, mate. We'll cover the cost. You won't get a better offer than that mate."

"Okay… thanks," I said flatly. "I'll have to find one first—don't exactly keep one on retainer."

"We can help with that too mate. Just make sure it's independent. It's a good deal, mate. You should take it."

That word—mate—grated more each time he said it. He looked too much like the Sherminator from *American Pie* to take seriously. I half-wondered if he'd been sent back in time just to fuck with my future.

I was devastated. I'd reached out hoping for help. Instead, they found out I had a mental illness and moved to cut me loose—efficiently, quietly.

I'd been playing the game.

They'd outplayed me.

Only difference was—I wasn't bluffing anymore. I was sick. I didn't know what I was doing—but I knew I couldn't fall apart in a Caffè Nero.

So I told myself it was a win. The money was decent. The sophisticated sex robot was right—it was a good deal.

I clung to that thought as I walked out. "Thanks *mate!*"

I don't want to be anywhere I'm not wanted. 'Fuck him. Fuck them.'

But the second I hit the street, the rollercoaster dropped. 'You'll get another job... What if I don't? What if I can't work? What if this... spreads?'

My chest tightened. Thoughts raced. I could barely breathe. I couldn't move. Hands locked on the steering wheel like I'd fall apart without it. The world blurred. My brain sprinted through catastrophe. Time bent around the fear.

Eventually—I rode out the storm. Shaky. Spent. A little more broken.

Afraid of another public meltdown, I withdrew. Hid with my illness. I drank. When that didn't work, I smoked weed and took painkillers.

Numbness helped. It didn't solve anything, but it dulled the edge. The anxiety became background noise. I internalised everything. Tried to iron out the creases in private.

It wasn't healthy. But it was survival.

After two weeks, I steadied the ship. Hold tight. Stay true. I convinced myself this wasn't a breakdown—it was a midlife awakening.

A big reset.

The plan was simple: get a new job, while sorting my head out. And before I could figure out the logistics my phone rang. A mental health nurse.

A slot had opened up early with a local charity.

I almost said no. But maybe I owed myself at least this much. One hour. Every Friday. Six weeks. Easy Peasy.

I told myself the worst was over. Knock out the therapy and start interviewing. This was just a blip. A minor episode.

I'd played the game and got a result. But I didn't feel like a winner.

It had exposed something sinister. Something I didn't want to own.

It wasn't over. Not by a long shot. The real game was just beginning.

"We'll call it a draw."

'You can't change the past, but you can change the way you think about it.'
Buddhist Proverb

Five

Analyse This

August 2018
London

I'd been in a bad way for weeks—low, restless, out of sorts. But the news that I'd secured a place with Mind, the mental health charity, gave me something to focus on. In my head, it was going to be a quick fix. In, out, and resume life as normal.

The introductory assessment caught me off guard. I was halfway through breakfast and had to excuse myself upstairs for privacy. It was supposed to be a quick check-in—but it dragged.

I found myself awkwardly answering personal questions in hushed tones. The nurse was kind and professional, working through the usual script—did I smoke, exercise, take any medication. Routine stuff.

Just as I thought we were wrapping up, she mentioned something deeper. She warned it might be unsettling. Not exactly what you want to hear while sitting on your bedroom floor in Marvel pyjamas, vulnerable as hell.

"Err, yeah sure, let's do it," I said, bracing for impact.

"Okay, thank you. Could you answer the following questions using: 1 - Not At All; 2 - Several Days; 3 - More Than Half The Days; or 4 - Nearly Every Day. Did you get that, John? Want to write it down?"

"Yeah, give me a sec." I grabbed an old envelope from the bedside table and scribbled down the options. Barely legible, but enough. "Ready."

"Let's begin. Over the last two weeks, how often have you been bothered by the following problems?"

34

The questions started off easy, but almost every answer was the same
—4: Nearly every day.

1.   Little interest or pleasure in doing things? None.
2.   Feeling down, depressed, or hopeless? Completely.
3.   Trouble sleeping? Barely sleep.
6.   Feeling like a failure or letting your family down? Yep.
7.   Trouble concentrating? Constantly.

But then came the last question hit hard, dropped casually:

10.   Thoughts that you'd be better off dead, or of hurting yourself
in some way? What? No. Absolutely not. Never.

"Thank you for your honesty, Mr Bromfield. Someone will call later
today to confirm your appointment."

That final question haunted me. I'd answered honestly, but now I was
questioning everything. 'What did those answers mean? Were my
scores normal? Was suicide linked to PTSD?'

Was this where it was heading?

I dropped the phone and let myself fall back onto the carpet. Soft
beneath me. I stared at the ceiling, eyes glazed, trying to empty my
mind. A wave of tiredness hit—but so did the images.

'Suicide? What the fuck?'

Eventually, I shook it off. Let the thought dissolve. Lying on the floor
all day wasn't going to help. But staying in my pyjamas? That felt
right. Just moments ago I'd felt hopeful. But after that call, I'd hit a
new low.

This was supposed to be a game. Now it felt way too serious.

The following week I found the local Mind office. I lingered outside in
the sun, stalling. The sky was nearly flawless—just one blemish of
cloud drifting by. I let the warmth touch my face, soaking it in before
stepping up to face the music.

There were no banners, no signs saying 'lunatics this way.' Just an intercom. I pressed it, gave my name, and was buzzed in.

The receptionist smiled and handed me a clipboard. I sat down, nerves already frayed. The waiting room was designed to feel safe— soft colours, worn-in chairs, a cheap coffee table scattered with dog-eared magazines. Plastic plants filled the corners, their glossy leaves pretending to be alive. They were calm. Peaceful. It helped.

My eyes darted around the room, subtly scanning the others. Wondering if their inner turmoil mirrored my own. I blinked and refocused on the clipboard. Name. Date of birth. Address. Then the same damn questionnaire. Again finishing with the suicide question.

'Hadn't I already done this?'

The irritation simmered. These questions were planting thoughts I didn't want. 'Was I a nutter? Was I in the right place?' I didn't feel like I fit this model.

Part of me wanted to walk out. But another part wondered—what if this was the lifeline I didn't know I needed?

Too late for second thoughts.

A woman appeared in front of me, smiling warmly. "Hi John, I'm Gita. Shall we head upstairs?"

I followed her up to an underwhelming office. Small desk, two chairs, one broken AC unit.

"I'm sorry about the heat," she said as I shrugged off my jacket.

I wanted to take off more, to deal with the sweat box. But stripping down to my underpants might confirm my status as a whack-job. So I sat, already uncomfortable. Opposite a stranger. Convinced she wasn't qualified to fix what might be broken inside me.

Trying to break the tension, she started with routine intake questions —alcohol, drugs, sleep.

"I drink a bit at weekends and don't do drugs," I flat-out lied. It was none of her business.

"That's good," she said gently. "I do need to let you know—if you're drinking more than six units a week, we'll have to end the sessions."

"What!?" A fire erupted inside me. "That's ridiculous. Don't addiction and mental health go hand in hand? You just cut people loose when they need help? Unbelievable."

The anger surged, hot and immediate. My hands trembled, but I forced a deep breath, choking back the rant building in my throat.

I do six units a day. Easy.

She flinched slightly. "I'm really sorry. It's an NHS rule. We have to ask weekly and record your response."

Great. So I'll lie every time.

The divide between us grew.

The next twenty minutes dragged. Gita outlined the tools we'd use, how I'd develop coping mechanisms, and what to expect. I nodded along, barely listening. I was locked in my own discomfort.

"The Boxing Day tsunami? I remember it vividly—it was all over the news. You were there? Wow. I've never met someone who went through that." She paused, softening her excitement. "Over the coming weeks, we'll revisit it in detail and process the event. Is that okay?"

"I suppose. I've never really talked about it. Not properly.... but I'll try."

"I do have to warn you, the techniques we use may open up painful memories. It can be traumatic in the short term, but over time, we aim to help you reprocess them—change the way you feel, so you can cope more effectively."

That day, I learned about grounding—using physical sensations to

37

anchor myself in the present when things got overwhelming. I couldn't help but think of John McClane, barefoot in Nakatomi Tower, making fists with his toes just moments before Hans Gruber so rudely interrupted his grounding efforts.

Oddly comforting.

Something I'd use to pull me out when I went too deep. Yippee-ki-yay.

The following week, I returned, beginning with an apology. My abrupt behaviour had been playing on my mind.

A fresh start.

Again, I had to fill out the dreaded questionnaire. A weekly exercise to track progress. Gita collected it without comment and led me upstairs to the same claustrophobic room.

I closed my eyes, took several deep breaths. Seconds stretched into minutes. Then, slowly, the story began to leave my lips—one word at a time, one terrifying moment after the next.

It was the first time I'd let it out. And as I spoke, the images became vivid and clear, like the words were casting a spell. My skin prickled—senses sharpened—as I tried to relive the worst day of my life.

My chest tightened. Breathing went shallow. But I kept going, guided only by the sound of my own voice—and the presence of someone willing to listen.

Over the next few weeks, I told my story in full. Bit by bit. Like sketching out a graphic novel—each panel more intense than the last. From how I got to Thailand, to the day everything changed, and the struggle to get home.

Small doses. Still explosive.

Gita barely interrupted. Just nodded and took notes while I sat with eyes closed, damp cheeks, voice shakier by the week. My mind projected the memories like a film. I could see it all in Technicolor.

At the end of the penultimate session, she asked, "Am I right in thinking there was a movie made about the tsunami?"

"Yes. *The Impossible*. I bought it years ago but never watched it. Still have the DVD somewhere."

"You should. Think of it as homework. I know it's hard, but avoiding reminders only gives them more power. If something triggers you— don't turn away. Watch. Feel it. You need to stop keeping it locked up." She paused. "Can you try please John?"

I said I would. But I wasn't thrilled. I usually obsessed over films. But this one had sat in my loft, still in its cellophane, for nearly a decade.

That night though, I found it, peeled off the wrapper, and slid the disc in.

Here we go again.

The movie transported me instantly—sights, sounds, even the tension in the air. Too familiar. A kaleidoscope of emotion.

I had to remind myself to breathe—sometimes I forgot.

Several times I paused, walked around, tried to collect myself. But eventually, I finished it.

It was harrowing—raw, honest, too close. A reminder of the nightmare so many lived through that day. And how lucky I was to still be here.

To live to tell the tale.

Except I hadn't told my tale. Not properly. Not until now. And only under the duress of therapy. Matchsticks in my eyes.

I still hadn't spoken to my mum. Or my wife, Meg. Or even to the friends who were there with me. How do you even start that conversation?

Instead, I stayed silent.

The following week I was back in the same uncomfortable chair.

"PTSD is often fuelled by repression," Gita said, pushing me to talk to my family. "You've kept that box sealed for fourteen years. Talking through it, processing it—that's how we start to heal."

"I'll try." I knew I wouldn't.

"Thank you. Before we wrap up—one more assignment. I'd like you to write it all down—everything you've shared. Use the recordings to guide you."

I'd recorded every session on my phone—her idea—though the idea of replaying it all was too much.

"Alright," I said as we shook hands.

"Oh—before I forget, I need you to fill out the form again," Gita said as she left to fetch the dreaded kill yourself survey.

I'd learned the scoring system. First time, I'd probably landed on Severe. But now—knowing the game—I could manipulate the answers to show progress. Just enough to pass.

I handed it over. Gita looked pleased.

And just like that, I was done. Process complete. Tick the box. File away the notes.

But I wasn't convinced. Reopening every wound hadn't made me feel better—just sharpened the memories. Still, I'd done my part. That was enough.

The denial came roaring back the moment I walked out.

I told myself I was fine. That I'd been fine all along. This was just something I'd done to play the game.

Nothing more.

I jumped in the car and breathed a huge sigh of relief. My autopilot engaged, driving me to my usual spot on a rough estate in Woolwich.

Whatever it took to keep the memories at bay.

Game on.

'There are some faults which men readily admit, but others not so readily.'
Epictetus

Six

Half Baked

24th August 2018
London

I only smoked in small doses—never too much—just enough to take the edge off. It wasn't a problem.

Getting it, however, was a complete ball ache. Unreliable dealers, vague instructions, awkward handoffs in dodgy places. Every meet-up was a gauntlet—but I needed it. And yeah, ducking into shadowy corners only added to the anxiety I was trying to silence—but what choice did I have?

To me, weed was a remedy. The antidepressants sat untouched in my bedside cabinet. I'd tried therapy, and it only made things worse. Thoughts I didn't even know existed had bubbled up—murky and mean.

So I leaned back into my tried and tested solution.

I'd read that in the US, veterans with PTSD were being treated with THC, MDMA, even psilocybin. The stats were impressive. That was all the validation I needed. I'd been micro-dosing for years—long before I had any inkling of trauma.

In a weird way, I'd been ahead of the curve.

Sure, there were other studies warning about psychosis, schizophrenia, the usual scare stories—but I ignored those. Kidding myself that it was fake news.

So before the ink was dry on that final survey, I was already thinking about my next hit. All I wanted was silence. And weed delivered that in droves.

My usual guy wasn't answering—typical—so I scrambled for a backup. A new number. A new risk.

"Across the road. Black hoodie," the text read.

I tried to look casual as I crossed over, toward the man in the black hoodie. Forty quid balled up in my sweaty right fist.

I walked up, shoved the cash into his midriff like we were old mates. Looked him in the eye. Waited.

"You got the wrong person, fam." His voice was low. Sharp. And for a second, everything stopped.

Panic. I realised my mistake instantly. My heart pounded as I stammered an apology and backed away, face burning. Jesus. I'd just shoved dosh into a random bloke's stomach. In broad daylight.

Lucky I didn't get jumped.

Back in the car, my hands trembled as I fumbled with my phone. Why was it always like this? Just once, I wanted a pick-up without the adrenaline, without the gamble. Strangers in shady spots. Cryptic messages. Always wondering if I'd get caught.

This time, I approached the right geezer slower. The exchange, in a piss-stained stairwell, was swift. No words—just a nod. I made a quick exit, hoping I didn't look as rattled as I felt.

Every time I got back in the car, I'd roll down the windows, trying to clear the stench before it soaked into the seats. But the fear gnawed at me—what if I got pulled over?

Once, I had been. A few months earlier, just past midnight, picking Meg up from the station. I was stoned, of course, and nudging just over the limit. Empty roads. Barely a mile from home. Then—bang—speed gun.

I slammed the brakes, heart hammering. Rolled down the window. Tried to stay calm. "Evening, officer."

"You were going pretty fast. Where are you headed?"

"Just picking up my wife—she's been working late."

"Had a drink tonight?"

"No officer.

"Any weed?"

That one hit like a slap.

"Never." Too fast. Too defensive.

He studied me for a beat, then waved me on.

Just like that.

I eased forward, hands still shaking, watching the speedometer like a hawk. My eyes flicked to the mirror—nothing. He hadn't caught a whiff. Or maybe he had and didn't care. Middle-aged white guy, middle of suburbia. Probably not worth the paperwork.

I'd dodged a bullet.

I survived the gauntlet again that day. Once home, I rolled myself a joint. The ritual itself helped. Rolling grounded me. A few careful licks, a twist at the end—I was calm before I even sparked it.

One small joint could last hours. A few tokes to start, then a few more every thirty minutes. Just enough to stop the gears grinding. The creative cogs turned freely. But the consequence was inertia. All imagination, no execution.

That day, I revisited something Gita had said. "Find something you used to enjoy."

I'd enjoyed plenty once upon a time, but for as long as I could remember, I hadn't had the will. It wasn't the weed. It went deeper. Like someone had drained all desire from me.

Therapy. I showed up, nodded along, but never really believed in it. Who were they to tell me what was wrong? I wasn't mental. Or maybe I was—but not in the way they thought. I kept things hidden. Guarded. Treated it like community service. Did my time.

I never truly accepted the diagnosis.

I didn't engage with the techniques. In my head, I was fine. Sure, I'd lived through something enormous—but the trainee therapist hadn't exactly inspired confidence. If anything, I walked away convinced my own methods were better than anything the "professional" had to offer.

I had to find something though. "What did I used to love?" Nothing came. Smoking and streaming were the only things I looked forward to.

Maybe that was my hobby?

I remembered loving music back when *Top of the Pops* was still a thing —did listening count? Movies? Used to love them. But now? Couldn't be arsed. I had hundreds of DVD's, but they all lived in the loft— relics of another time.

My body sat still while my brain rummaged through the attic of my past—and found nothing.

So I decided my hobby would be TV. More weed. More booze. More screens. I told myself it was balanced. Vodka and Lilt in one hand, remote in the other, I started scrolling. As luck would have it, a *Harry Potter* movie marathon was starting that night.

This was my sweet spot: full story arc, evolving characters, immersive world.

And I didn't need to get off my arse. Result.

Meg joined me on the Hogwarts Express. The film was great—magic, ghosts, comedy—a perfect escape. I felt a flicker of joy, that old spark for storytelling.

45

Then it hit me.

A scene I'd seen before—harmless—but this time it landed different.

Water. Not just on screen. In my lungs.

I was back there. Tumbling. Drowning. No air. Panic surged through me.

I gripped the armrests, frozen, sinking deeper into the chair.

The world warped—like that scene in *A Nightmare on Elm Street III* when Nancy's pulled through the armchair into the abyss. That was me.

Except I wasn't dreaming. I was drowning.

The harmless wizard duel twisted into horror. Water everywhere. It rushed the corridor. Swallowed them. Swallowed me.

"Are you okay?" Meg's voice—distant, then louder. "John. Look at me."

All I could do was nod.

This was a kids' movie. How could it hit so hard?

But it did.

My body thought it was real. My mind knew it wasn't. Instinct didn't care. Fight. Flight. Freeze.

I froze.

I started my grounding techniques—breathe, touch, sound. Pull back from the dark. Bruce Willis it… 'Welcome to the party, pal!'

Finally. Back in the room…

"I'm sorry," I said, head bowed.

"Don't be silly," she replied. "But that was intense. I've not seen you like that before."

"I'm okay now," I lied, offering a shaky explanation of grounding techniques like I was reading a weather report.

"Maybe you shouldn't watch stuff like this."

"I'm not meant to avoid triggers. I'm supposed to work through them. Anyway, how could I know? It's only Harry bloody Potter!"

That was the first time I realised what a flashback really felt like. Maybe I'd had them before, but I hadn't noticed—too drunk, too stoned, too numb.

Maybe they'd never surfaced because I'd buried the worst of it.

This one didn't just tap me on the shoulder—it dragged me under and kicked me in the bollocks.

And I blamed therapy.

Before, I thought I was winning. Holding it together. Sure, I was self-medicating, but it worked. Now, thanks to digging into the past, I was unraveling. Therapy had opened the box, stirred the silt at the bottom —and now I had to swim through it.

All I'd gained were fresh triggers and old wounds. My habits weren't just reinforced—they were amplified. Now they came with emotional landmines.

Shortly after that rude awakening, I was offered a new job. I hadn't even interviewed but somehow landed on my feet. 'See? Just a blip.'

A burnout after twelve years of busting my nuts? Understandable.

The tsunami? Ancient history. It had never really affected me—until Gita forced me to look.

No, what I needed wasn't talking. It was change.

Done. Problem solved.

Instead of recovering, I retreated.

But deep inside, something had started ticking. Faint at first. Louder each day.

I wasn't listening. Not yet.

New job. New people. New game.

Same me. I'd just reset the clock.

Tick...Tick...Tick...

'To be yourself in a world that is constantly trying to make you something else is the greatest accomplishment.'
Ralph Waldo Emerson

Seven

Fight Club

15th July 2021
London

So, I'd been to therapy, sort of. But the anger always bubbled back up, dragging fear in its wake. This time, though, I'd caught it early—and for the first time, I was facing it head-on with a kind of maturity I didn't know I had.

"It's good that you've had some experience, John." Rada said, scribbling furiously into her notebook. "I must say, you don't seem like an angry person."

"Thank you," I replied. "I'm better than I was, but it's still there."

Anger, Rada explained, is a key sign of PTSD—a hyperarousal symptom that can tip you over the edge before you realise you're falling. I'd learned that the hard way. The rage would surge out of nowhere—blinding, consuming.

Most of the time, it turned outward. But sometimes, it turned inward. And that, I learned, was often more dangerous. Self-destructive behaviour. Self-harm.

Even suicide.

There it was again—that damn word.

It had felt misplaced when I first heard it. But now, I was beginning to understand the relevance. In that context, my outbursts felt almost like a relief. Regretful, yes. Shameful, absolutely. But definitely the lesser of two evils.

"How have you managed it—tell me," Rada continued.

"It's hard. Everything pisses me off," I admitted with a nervous laugh.

"I try to avoid situations where I might blow up. I've been taking photos, posting on Instagram… just something to distract me from the noise."

"Is it working?"

"I think so. I haven't had a fight in a few years—so that's a good sign." I laughed at the ridiculousness of my own words.

I wasn't built for fighting, and honestly, I hated it. It was like a switch I couldn't control. The moment I felt threatened, I'd lash out, swing for the fences, and get my retaliation in first.

A survival tactic handed down early by my nutty uncle.

It's why I hated confrontation. Arguments always felt like the precursor to a tear-up.

But the last time still sickens me.

My final outburst—when my fist connected with a stranger's head. It all happened so fast. An old man pushed to the floor as he made his way through the turnstiles, then surrounded by a gang in London Bridge station.

I was hammered—of course—adrenaline surged, and suddenly, I couldn't stop myself. "What the fuck are you playing at… you fucking wankers…."

Bang!

Next thing I knew, I was at the far end of the platform, clutching my hand. I'd entered some kind of fugue state—like the Gamma monster had taken over.

'What just happened?' My hand felt broken. It looked broken. It was broken. A classic boxer's fracture: fifth metacarpal smashed, pinkie knuckle gone, sunken and throbbing.

I tried to justify it: 'bad things happen when good people do nothing.' That was a saying, right? I was defending someone. That had to count for something?

But anxiety shut that train of thought down sharpish. There'd be CCTV. What if they came looking for me? What if I'd hurt someone? What if I got caught up in a police incident?

Full panic mode. Heart racing. Fear storming my organs. I boarded the midnight express, hand stuffed into my suit jacket like a makeshift sling, gasping for breath.

Meg was livid—understandably so. She'd seen this side of me before and was running out of patience.

Neither of us knew then that something deeper was fuelling my volatility. I wasn't just a hothead. But to the outside world? I was a classic South Londoner.

Little man syndrome. Boisterous, fiery, especially after a few sherberts.

The next morning, I drove myself to A&E with Meg's disappointed face lingering. My thoughts ping-ponged between her expression and the fear of repercussions.

'Time to stop this shit.' I couldn't lose her—the one good thing in my life. My anchor. My home base.

I was putting myself in harm's way for no reason. London's streets weren't safe. You never knew who had a chiv in their back pocket. It had nearly happened to me once upon a time...

Fuck! I can still feel the cold steel when I think back to that night...

Not yet, John. Stay on point.

I wasn't a skilled fighter either—far from it. I was slight of build, weak, and clearly brittle. Every time I threw a punch, something broke. I'd become fluent in the medical terms for the tiny bones in the hand. "It's the scaphoid, Mr Bromfield—you'll be in a cast for nine months!"

I can now see how my abrasive behaviour was linked to my upbringing. Growing up in 1980s London was a constant battle for survival. You didn't go looking for fights—but they found you anyway, so you'd better be ready.

I grew up on a rough housing estate. If you weren't hard, the place shaped you fast—and we were tested regularly.

I still remember my introduction to the hierarchy. I was only six.

The woods behind the estate were our favourite place to play—our wilderness—but sometimes, a battlefield. One day, someone called me over to the big weeping willow.

As I ducked inside, it was like stepping into an arena. The drooping branches shut out most of the world, leaving just enough light to cast long, eerie shadows. The dirt floor was well-trodden and dry from the long, hot summer, and there—scattered around the pit and perched on branches like vultures—were a dozen or so boys.

Waiting. Watching.

In the centre stood another boy, shirtless and staring me down. He looked scrappy, with streaks of dirt marking his face and chest. Red welts covered his arms and legs—this wasn't his first fight of the day.

He was the reigning gladiator, and I was the latest victim.

"You two are fighting each other," a voice called down from the top branch.

I looked across at my opponent. The grime made him look like a battle-hardened warrior. He seemed ready. I had no idea what I was doing. But there was no way out. Too many boys, too many eyes. Running would only invite more trouble later.

So I did the only thing I could: stepped to the centre and squared up. We were evenly matched—same height and build—but he was clearly more 'up for it' than I was.

We rolled around in the dirt while cheers and jeers echoed all around. I don't remember the intricate details of my first ever brawl—only that I walked away with minimal damage and a smidge more respect than when I had walked in.

Those skirmishes soon became more regular than I wanted. Over the years, that same boy would seek me out. I think my unexpected resilience bruised his ego. A rivalry was born—one I never asked for.

No one should have a nemesis at six, right?

He'd sneak up on me in the school yard or the scout hall, jumping me whenever I wasn't looking. And every time, I stood my ground. Part of me always wanted to scarper—but something deeper refused to back down.

I'm just not built that way.

In hindsight, maybe he wasn't a nemesis at all. Maybe he was my very own Cato—like the bumbling inspector's unpredictable sparring partner in *The Pink Panther*, always ready to pounce when I least expected it. "Every day, in every way, I'm getting better and better— thanks to Cato's surprise attacks!"

Back in those days it wasn't just kids you had to worry about. I've just recalled another surprise attack—and looking at it through today's lens, it seems outrageous. You be the judge.

I was eleven, cycling through the school playground like I always did. Out of nowhere, someone yanked me backwards by my backpack. I flew off the bike and hit the concrete hard, scraping my knee. When I looked up, a man was standing over me, furious.

Ratty beard, foul breath, cheap brown suit.

"What the bloody hell do you think you're doing? You can't cycle through here!" he shouted in my face.

"Fuck off. Let go of me!" I yelled, squirming in his grip.

"How dare you swear at me," he snapped—and then yanked me by the scruff of the neck and slapped me. Hard. Right across the face.

I swallowed back tears, shit scared but trying to save face in front of a crowd. I pulled myself free, grabbed my bike, and bolted.

At home, my Mum and Dad were fuming and they called the police straight away. Two officers showed up and sat in our front room questioning me.

But the fallout was worse than the slap.

"Well, you shouldn't have been cycling there, should you?"

"Oh, so you did swear at him then…"

They took turns finding fault with me—a child on the receiving end of a back-hander.

My mum eventually kicked them out in disgust. The man? A well-respected local doctor. Me? I was just a mouthy estate kid who should respect his elders.

So nothing happened.

Imagine that. A grown man assaults someone else's child in front of a playground full of parents—and it's the child that gets reprimanded.

Madness.

I felt ashamed. I ran upstairs to hide my tears, only to hear my mum roaring downstairs: "He thinks he can hit my boy and get away with it? He can fucking think again!"

My mum was a small but ferocious woman. Tightly coiled and always ready to go. "Get your coat. You're gonna show me who did it."

That was life for us back then. Handle things yourself.

This is the way!

Not long after, I got the talk from my Uncle Frank. Part warning, part lesson. Don't let anyone take the piss, no matter how big or old they are. Mum's family were East End through and through, and Frank made no bones about his villainous past.

So before I'd hit puberty, I was schooled in violence. Where to hit. How to take on more than one opponent. Even the dark arts like eye gouging and biting—tactics outlawed in the Octagon but apparently fair game on the streets of London.

Now, I'm pretty sure it's not standard parenting to teach a child street warfare—but it did serve me well. In dicey situations that could've gone either way, I reacted first. And lived to tell the tale.

And never once had to bite anyone's ear off!

So as I grew up, I wasn't purposely angry. I could be violent, but only because of what was drilled into me—reactions that kicked in the moment I felt threatened. It was all driven by fear—fear of being hurt, of not standing up for myself or my family. And especially of the consequences if I didn't.

When the doctor re-set my broken finger after that fight at London Bridge, I made a quiet promise to myself: I wouldn't let it happen again. I wouldn't risk everything I held dear over a moment of misplaced rage.

The fear that once kept me alert had grown unchecked—had become the very thing I now needed to protect myself from.

Meg was the most amazing thing that had ever happened to me. I was determined to be a better man than the one regularly in the fracture clinic.

Meg knew what she was getting into. That became painfully clear on one of our first dates.

Christmas Eve 2011. Another punch, another train station.

Before she even knew what was happening, I was in a half-nelson hold under a citizen's arrest—pinned to the wall on platform five by a giant of a man who'd witnessed the lash-out.

I thought I'd blown it. My chance at happiness—gone in a flash of rage.

I narrowly avoided arrest that night, and on the train home, I bared my soul and quietly begged for a second chance.

It was the first time I told her I loved her. Full truth. Double panic.

Somehow, she saw something in me. Something worth fighting for. And yes, I see the irony in that.

As I sat across from Rada, ashamed of who I used to be, she explained something that hit me hard: fight or flight. It kicks in to save lives. Mine had activated on that island, exactly when I needed it. That involuntary response was meant to keep me alive—preparing me to deal with mortal danger. And it did.

But after the tsunami, it stayed switched on—constantly pumping out stress hormones. My amygdala, that tiny cluster of cells at the base of my brain, had been hijacked. It was misfiring, sensing danger where there was none. The smallest fear, the faintest anxiety—and wallop. My rational brain was overridden, and I'd go straight to an irrational response.

Attack mode. Survival Mode.

Then came the shame. The crushing regret. The bone-deep fatigue.

"I've probably painted a terrible picture of myself," I said. "I wasn't out fighting all the time. Sometimes it just found me. I haven't come close to anything like that in a long time. I feel better. A lot better."

Rada looked up, and waited.

"I've also started Jiu-Jitsu. It's been a game changer."

I'd had lessons when I was a kid. Me and my best mate Nick joined a local club after that first showdown with Cato in that dusty colosseum.

I'd forgotten all about that—until my first class sparked a warm, dormant memory back to life. From my first step onto the mat, something clicked. Control, balance, discipline—everything I lacked.

"How was it?" Meg asked when I got home.

"It was so good. Honestly, I loved it," I said, launching into a full spiel about Japanese martial arts history.

She smiled. "I haven't seen you this excited about something in a long time."

"Funny thing," I added. "Me and Nick used to do it. Some of the moves came straight back to me."

It felt amazing. Like I'd uncovered something meaningful—something that belonged to me before the trauma. Before the tsunami.

Something I had once enjoyed.

I just wanted to get fit again, not be a liability, maybe even learn how to get out of a half-Nelson—but this was becoming more than that.

"I've been doing it a while now," I told Rada. "Haven't missed a single lesson."

"And Meg?" she asked. "How's she finding this new you?"

"She's been great. Nothing but supportive."

"Your wife sounds like a wonderful person," Rada said.

"She's put up with so much. Without her… I don't think I'd be here."

Before her, I was on a one-way track to oblivion. My dark passenger steering me straight toward self-destruction.

She wasn't just my compass—she'd been quietly holding me together all along.

'New beginnings are often disguised as painful endings.'
Lao Tzu

Eight

Love Actually

November 2011
London

I'd been alone for almost a year. Thirty-four and separated from my wife, Tina—the one who'd been through the tsunami with me. The marriage had been a disaster from day one. Bonded by catastrophe, not love.

I was relieved to be out of it, but I still felt like a failure. I became a hermit—drinking, smoking, doing absolutely nothing. The decline was slow, but something inside me had changed. I worried I was over the hill, doomed to live out my days at the bottom of a Smirnoff bottle.

Friends tried to pull me out of my funk, but I made excuse after excuse. Most days were spent alone in front of the TV, staring blankly at the screen, racing toward the next blackout.

Loneliness consumed me.

I craved companionship—I always had. I hated going out and had zero confidence to meet anyone new. Dating apps were becoming normal but still carried a lot of stigma. I hovered at the edges, browsed a few sites but never made a profile. I pictured those old-school dating videos: "Hi, I'm John. I like long walks and dining out..."

It felt like a Del Boy sketch. Rose in the lapel, waiting under the clock at Waterloo. No thanks.

Tina bailed on day one of the new year, leaving me with the house, the bills, and commitments that had been hard enough for two—impossible alone. To keep a roof over my head, my parents took out a second mortgage. That left me with two mortgages and a house worth less than the debt I was accumulating.

That summer was brutal, but I pulled myself together long enough to give the best man's speech at Bobby's wedding. I stayed sober for it, determined not to be an embarrassment. I was proud to play a part in their big day—especially since Bobby and his fiancée had been my lifeline. They'd let me crash on their sofa for months. I was the permanent third wheel, but they never made me feel unwelcome. Always fed, included, looked after.

So standing up to speak felt like the least I could do.

I met Bobby at my new school in Eltham, just after we moved from the estate in '91. His look—later compared to Harry Potter—masked his naughty streak. On my first day, I sat next to this lanky, bespectacled kid who wouldn't shut up. I had no idea he'd become one of the best people I'd ever meet. A real good egg, as he liked to say. The kind of mate who makes your life better just by being in it.

We bonded quickly, but it was that first summer that sealed it. Bobby convinced me to come to summer school. I thought he was prepping for exams—turns out he was doing detention, sentenced by his parents after a shoplifting incident. He'd duped me into keeping him company. But I didn't mind. That summer changed my life.

I needed to be off the streets as much as he did.

When Bobby's Vegas 'buddymoon' came around, I could barely function. He'd travelled after uni and met LA native Mike, who became part of our inner circle of friends. He'd planned the 'buddymoon' just so Mike could join in the celebrations.

The trip was wild—a proper celebration. We partied hard and laughed our arses off. But underneath the fun was a hollow feeling. Everyone had their partners. I was alone.

Drugs and booze blurred the nights—but the days were razor-sharp with loneliness. I smiled through it, played the part, then collapsed in private.

Back home, the sadness returned with a vengeance. I came back to silence. The emptiness clung to me. I drank more to numb the ache, but it only magnified the pain. Everything felt like it was unravelling.

Then November came—and with it, an unexpected lifeline. Mike invited me to his wedding in San Francisco.

At first, I dismissed it. No money. No leave. No energy. Too many excuses. But a week before the wedding, something clicked. I'd spent the whole year saying 'no.' No to friends. No to joy. No to life. But I remembered what happened when I used to say yes. Adventures. Growth. Moments I'd never have experienced otherwise.

So I said it: "Fuck it. Yes."

Out Friday morning, back Sunday night. A 48-hour blitz. Just hitting "confirm" on the booking lifted something in me.

The first challenge was work. No holiday left, so I winged it. Took my laptop to London, showed my face in the office, schmoozed just enough, then made my escape before lunch.

I caught a glimpse of Meg before I left—we hadn't spoken in a while, but when our eyes met, something shifted. My heart thudded.

Then I was off. Onto the Tube, through Heathrow, working from the terminal until my flight. As the plane lifted off, I felt alive again. Impulsive. Free. I was chasing something. I didn't know what—but it felt like hope.

The flight was exhilarating. I felt untethered—free to take chances, to move forward. I'd wasted enough time letting the breakup define me.

This was a reboot. A declaration.

I'd wanted out of that marriage, but I'd let the aftermath break me. Now, I was taking back control.

But it wasn't just the thrill of flying across the Atlantic that filled my mind.

It was Meg.

She was all I could think about. We'd worked together for five years but had always been taken. Still, I don't mind admitting—from the moment I saw her, I thought she was the most beautiful girl in the world, and completely out of my league.

She had these huge hazelnut eyes flecked with jade that changed colour in the light. Mesmerising. (Pop culture break: "Rare, like leather bucket seats that cost double the price!"—Classic Jack Burton, *Big Trouble in Little China*. Sorry, I digress. Splintered, PTSD-soaked brain and all.)

As the plane droned through the sky, I wondered if the stars were finally aligning. Both of us single. Could it be more than timing?

I landed in San Fran late afternoon and went straight to the wedding. The weekend was exactly what I needed: laughter, reconnection, old faces, new stories. My body didn't have time to catch up before I was already on a red-eye home. But even as I mingled, danced, and toasted the happy couple, one thought stayed with me: Meg.

How would I ask her out? Could I find right moment? Would she say yes?

On the flight back, I was brimming with confidence. That spontaneous escape had revived something in me.

Mojo partially restored. Groovy baby.

But as soon as I landed, London sucked all the hope right out of me— back to grey skies, damp suits, and the heavy weight of self-doubt. I went straight to the office from the airport, soaked from a downpour, still in the same suit I'd left in. Played it cool. Small talk. Smiles. I'd pulled it off. Score one for Bromfield.

The Yes Man returns.

A week passed. Maybe two. Every day, I convinced myself I had no chance with Meg. Too stunning. Too smart. Too funny.

Then came a leaving party—Meg would be there. As soon as I arrived, she walked straight over. We started chatting, drinking. She ordered Sambuca shots. I necked mine, grimacing through the fire. A few drinks later, I leaned in.

"Let's ditch these losers?"

"Yeah, let's go." I could hardly believe it.

But the more time I spent with her alone, the louder the doubts grew. 'She's not going to go for you. You're old, mate. Who do you think you are?'

My toilet breaks got longer. I'd stand at the mirror, pep-talking myself like a schizo Don Logan. "No no no no no, no fucking way. Not on your nelly!"

Back at the table, fresh from my self-berating, she leaned close. "I need to tell you something."

"Oh yeah? What's that?" I asked, feigning casual.

"I like—"

The chorus of a song drowned the rest.

"You like who?"

"I like YOU."

I blinked. "Me?"

"Yeah, you."

My head spun. Was this real? Or had I smoked a rogue Jeffrey and was still in the bathroom stroking a furry wall?

She leaned in. We kissed. A group of girls at the bar burst into cheers, giving Meg the thumbs up.

This was real!

And just like that, my whole life changed.

I had hope. I wasn't going to mess this up.

Looking back now, those years with Meg were the best I've ever had. She might say the same—but I still can't believe my luck.

We shared so many interests, but travel was our glue. Our first big adventure came just months after we got together: a three-week road trip across the U.S. We landed in Minneapolis and flew home from L.A., with little more than a rental car and a vague plan to head west.

On day one, barely a few miles in, I slammed on the brakes.

"Is that... a castle?"

It was. An actual White Castle. Just like the one from *Harold and Kumar*.

Barry and I had watched that film during our world trip in 2004—the fun part, before everything fell apart. Before the wave.

That ridiculous building stopped me cold. A trigger before I knew what a trigger was. Forgotten memories crashed in—Barry laughing, our stupid in-jokes, the ease of those days.

Then the water. The devastation. The death.

For a moment, I gripped the wheel tightly, overwhelmed. I focused on Meg, tried to stay present. Not now. Don't go there.

"Want me to drive?" Meg asked, sensing my tension.

"No, I've got it," I said, my smile glazing over a secret pain.

The flashback lingered—silent but present. I couldn't lose control. Not of the car, not of myself. Not in front of Meg.

Thankfully, I managed to navigate the three weeks without melting down. We ended in neon-drenched Las Vegas.

"Who are we meeting here again?" Meg asked as we pulled into Planet Hollywood.

"Mike and Keisha. They're flying in for the weekend. You'll love them."

I'd witnessed pure joy and love at their wedding. Being around that again was a reminder that it did exist. It was the catalyst for my re-birth.

A full-circle moment.

For the first time in my life, I was truly in love. With Meg, I'd found something real—friendship, trust, adventure, and a future worth fighting for. She'd stolen my heart.

And I was determined to prove I was worthy of it.

'Those who are devoid of purpose will make the void their purpose.'
Friedrich Nietzsche

Nine
Groundhog Day

22nd July 2021
London

The first step in any recovery system is admitting you have a problem. I wasn't following a set program, but I'd finally accepted that I had one. Maybe not full-blown dependency, but definitely a pull. A need for escape. Alcohol, drugs, anything to take the edge off.

I'd lived in denial for years, telling myself I wasn't that bad. But something shifted as the new year rolled in. Not a lightbulb moment—more a slow burn, inching toward something that might resemble wellness.

For years, I justified my behaviour by comparing myself to the people around me. I don't go as hard as them, so I must be fine, I told myself. My circle covered the full spectrum—daily drinkers, bingers, coke heads, weekend warriors, stoners, chain-smokers, the 'Frank the Tanks' of this world. On that scale, I was average, right?

I didn't drink every day—just smashed it on weekends. I smoked weed daily, but that was self-medication, better than pills. I rarely bought coke or mandy, but if it was there, I said yes. Always yes.

Wrong. I had to stop measuring myself against my so-called peers and start doing what was right for me—and more importantly, for Meg.

I didn't have to keep repeating the same cycle: getting high, crashing low. That wasn't living. The root cause had to be addressed. I didn't need rest; I needed recovery.

I wasn't tired. I was in turmoil.

As I stepped onto the escalator, I felt a flicker of pride. I was finally getting help—and this time, I was determined to be honest. But as the clinic neared, my mood dipped. I was early again, and the thought of dealing with the guard sparked a wave of anxiety, snuffing out that brief moment of progress.

I veered left, looping the complex with my AirPods in. I checked my phone: 17:28. Almost perfect.

Like last week, the waiting room was empty, but the same locked door and disgruntled security guard were waiting for me.

He cracked the door an inch. "What do you want?"

"Same as last week, mate—my appointment?"

"Does she know you're here? Call her and wait outside," he said, flicking his wrist dismissively.

My mood flatlined—was this guy serious?

Before I could let him have it, Rada appeared behind him, waving me in.

"What's wrong?" she asked, sensing the tension.

"Him! He's doing my nut in. I'm bang on time and he still won't let me in!"

She chuckled. "He's like that with everyone, John. Just ignore him."

Her calm defused my irritation. We shared a laugh at his expense, and just like that, I was back in the zone—ready to engage, maybe even open up.

"So nice to see you!" she said warmly as we took our seats. "Since our last session, I looked into the tsunami a bit more. I didn't know much beyond the headlines—but wow. It must've been terrifying."

Terrifying? Understatement of the year. And I hadn't even taken my jacket off.

"Relax, John," she said. "I'm not asking you to relive anything—not yet. We'll focus on how you're feeling, and get there when you're ready. I just wanted you to know that I've done my homework."

Relief. Just hearing the word tsunami made my chest tighten. Last session had been about the breakdown, Now she was laying the groundwork—building trust before diving into the real cerebral invasion.

"How has the pandemic been for you?" she asked, gently shifting gears.

"Surprisingly good," I blurted—then winced. "Sorry, that probably sounds awful. I know it's been horrific for so many. I don't mean to sound insensitive." But the truth was, lockdown had been transformative. Time to think. To take stock. It felt like a weird kind of gift.

"That's okay," she said. "It's not an uncommon response. What made it feel that way for you?"

"Well, I've been clean for six months," I said, surprising even myself. I hadn't meant to reveal that—at least not yet. But once it was out, there was no taking it back.

"Good for you," she said, smiling. And then she let the silence do its work.

I sat a little taller, her praise giving me a small boost.

"I've been a binge drinker for as long as I can remember. I started at fourteen—maybe thirteen. I honestly don't remember. Went straight for the hard stuff—vodka, whiskey, rum—whatever we could get from the off-license. Downing it straight from the bottle."

I paused, letting the memory wash over me. There was always someone to buy it for us. A stranger. A mate with a fake ID. We'd take the loot to the park and drink until we couldn't stand.

"I hated the taste. Drank just to get drunk—just like everyone else back then. Eventually, it became automatic. Get home, pour a vodka. I was going through bottles like they were going out of fashion." I

66

chuckled.

This had to be the most recycled story therapists ever heard.

I'd wanted to quit for years, but there was always a reason. Birthday. Wedding. Shit day at work. Any excuse. But this year I did Dry January—and by the end of the month, I felt so good I decided to keep going.

"That's excellent, John. I hope you can keep it up," she said, prompting me on. "Does your wife drink too?"

"Yeah, we're as bad as each other. But she's been supportive—did Dry Jan with me and stuck it out. But here's the best bit," I grinned. "I haven't touched weed in almost a year."

One eyebrow lifted—Roger Moore style. "Really? I wouldn't have pegged you as a stoner—you don't look the type." She jotted something in her notepad.

"Thanks," I laughed, appreciating the backhanded compliment. "I never really saw myself as one either. I started later in life, but it turned into a daily thing I just couldn't kick."

This was it. Full honesty. For the first time, I laid it bare.

My favourite side effect? It shut off my dreams. Boom. Nighty-night. I hadn't dreamt in over a decade. Sounds mad, I know, but it's true.

When your nights are haunted by the worst moment of your life, you welcome the blank slate.

Before the tsunami, drugs were rare. Booze was the real issue. But after the wave, alcohol wasn't enough to silence the chaos. That was the moment—the line I crossed.

Rada listened, her expression neutral, but I could feel her urging me on.

"I wasn't chain-smoking it," I continued. "Just enough to simmer down. Helped me sleep. Shut off the worry. Honestly? I didn't care about much else. The problem was, I couldn't be bothered to do anything either. But back then, that felt like a fair trade-off."

"How are you feeling now?" she asked gently.

"Weird," I replied, without thinking.

"Weird?" she pressed, curious.

"Yeah. I've been drenched in substances for so long, I'd forgotten what a clear head felt like. It's unbelievable. Like... the fog has lifted. My organs finally dried out and are operating at full capacity."

She nodded thoughtfully. "What made you change? You sound like you're in a good place—but most people don't get here on their own."

"Like I said, the pandemic gave me the gift of time. I had two options —locked up at home, getting on it, or try switching it up."

Fear won in the end. The virus scared the shit out of me. I genuinely thought we were all going to die. I started reading, researching, trying to figure out what I could actually do about it. And everything pointed to the same truth—Be healthy.

My *Groundhog Day* lifestyle was already killing me slowly. The virus could finish the job.

Quitting booze and weed wasn't even at the top of the list—I had a dozen other things to fix first to become a healthier, happier version of myself.

Whoever that is.

But for the first time in years, I actually wanted to find out.

'Well-being is realised by small steps, but is truly no small thing.'
Zeno

Ten
Stir Crazy

2020 - 2021
London

The start of 2020 was strange, to say the least. Coronavirus had rapidly spread across the globe. Stay-at-home orders were in place, and social distancing was on everyone's lips.

I remember the eerie silence in the city centre—no cars, no planes, no sound. It was straight out of *28 Days Later*, wandering through deserted streets. The resemblance was uncanny.

Ironically, this was what I'd always wanted—more time at home with Meg, no commute, no pointless office routine. But I hadn't accounted for the danger of isolation with my unacknowledged addictions.

The gravity of my situation hit within the first month. Work had all but stopped. By 3 p.m., I'd spark up, pour a glass of wine, and wait for the 5 p.m. update, hoping Boris might offer a glimmer of hope. Soon enough, that routine became my new normal.

I realised something had to change. I was heading down a dark path— and I needed something to stop me going full Skip Donahue. "Harry, I don't think I'm going to make it!"

I knew myself too well—anything requiring too much effort would be a fleeting obsession. I had to keep it simple. Sustainable habits that might, eventually, create a new man.

First up: exercise. My output? Zero. Shamefully out of shape. So we extended our daily walks—longer, faster—until five kilometres became standard. It was easy. Fresh air and movement as we meandered through the neighbourhood.

Then I stumbled on a thirty-day yoga challenge—Yoga with Ari. Not a yogi by any stretch of the imagination, but watching him wobble through poses gave me permission to fail. Some days I nailed it. Some days I was too hungover to even contemplate a downward dog. But I kept going. By the end, I had enough confidence to create my own simple daily routine.

And it made me wonder—could I redirect my addictive personality? Get hooked on something good?

I'd seen it happen. Against all odds, a schoolmate of mine flipped his life completely. While banged up, he hit the weights. Inmates mocked him as he lapped the yard—called him "He-Man." But he didn't give a shit. When he got out, he doubled down—training, dieting, studying trends, completely transforming his lifestyle. Eventually, he became a world champion bodybuilder—the spray-tanned, speedo-wearing kind, popping poses like the real Prince of Eternia.

Now he runs his own PT business, helping others change their lives. A true inspiration. I wasn't aiming for He-Man—but if he could channel his compulsions into purpose, maybe I could too.

Nutrition was obviously key, but my diet had always been a farce— crisps, chocolate, takeaways, fizzy drinks, alcohol. Veg? Forget it. I was a meat-and-potatoes man all day long. What was the point of fixing everything else if I was still fuelling myself with filth?

But this journey wasn't just about fitness—it was about reconnecting with a part of myself I'd lost. Gita's voice echoed: "Find something you used to love."

One evening, scrolling through my playlist, I realised how much music had once meant to me. I also realised something more profound: I was stuck looping the tracks I'd played on my first iPod. Songs frozen in time. The same ones I'd played the weeks before…

Don't think about it. That fuckin' wave.

From a young age, music was everything. For my eighth birthday, my dad gave me a Walkman. Bulky silver casing, oversized buttons, fuzzy orange headphones—cutting-edge at the time. But more than anything, it meant freedom. I could take music anywhere.

70

1985 was a golden year for a newbie like me. In the UK, it was Wham!, Duran Duran, and Culture Club—battling for top spots and Just Seventeen covers.

Then came 19 by Paul Hardcastle. A game-changer. I remember standing frozen, letting that electro-synth beat thump through me. I didn't fully grasp its anti-war message, but the rhythm and samples stuck deep. Even now, that opening riff sends me straight back to that cramped bedroom, staring at peeling wallpaper, dreaming of a world bigger than the one I knew.

Like many kids, I was obsessed with Jacko. Reconciling that now is complicated—but at the time, he was a cultural juggernaut. I'd roam the estate playing Thriller on loop, stopping only to flip the tape. I'd catch myself singing out loud, trying not to dance too much in public. In those days, that kind of extroversion could earn you a beating—and Cato was usually lurking behind a tree, waiting to pounce.

The ability to retain lyrics has stayed with me. But now, thanks in part to PTSD, my memory has become unreliable. I can't always remember what I did last weekend, but play me an 80s hit and the words come tumbling out.

During lockdown, I noticed it for the first time. It started with a question from Bobby: "Remember that night we saw Arctic Monkeys at Wembley?"

"No," I replied. "Are you sure I was there?"

"Of course," he said, showing me photos as proof.

I had no recollection. Until that moment, I'd have sworn blind I'd never seen them. It shook me—how could I forget something like that? My once-loyal memory now felt like a stranger. I joked that it was probably the booze—but it wasn't. It was deeper. I just couldn't admit it.

A few weeks later, it happened again. Different friend. Different gig. Same blank space. I tried to laugh it off. "Maybe it was a parallel universe. COVID must've split the timelines."

It was easier to joke than admit I was scared.

Dementia, Alzheimer's—that's where my mind went. That's when I realised something was broken.

One of the lesser-known effects of PTSD is its impact on memory. Traumatic memories can fragment or distort—but I hadn't realised how much it could erode general memory. Fourteen years had passed since the tsunami, and I'd done everything to avoid dealing with it. Now I was facing the cost. Whole chunks were missing. Sometimes, with a nudge, I could recall moments—but the details were hazy.

It was embarrassing. And terrifying.

Oddly, memories from before 2004 remained vivid. The music from that time looped endlessly. It was like the needle had jammed—each note tied to a mental slideshow, until the needle slipped off the vinyl and all that was left was static.

Then one afternoon it hit me: I had to break free. There was so much incredible music I hadn't even begun to explore—and I'd been carrying a portal to it in my pocket the whole time.

What a waste. It was time to shake things up. To challenge myself. To replace the haunted loop with something new.

I felt a flicker of excitement—something I hadn't felt in a long time.

I needed a guide, so I turned to Rolling Stone's 500 Greatest Albums of All Time. It felt like the perfect roadmap.

Over the next few months, I rediscovered my first love—and with it, something more valuable: a doorway to hidden memories.

Some songs transported me back to moments I thought I'd lost. Like that time Mike introduced me to *Kings of Leon*. Big Bear Lake. The truck bursting with snow gear, snacks, and *Aha Shake Heartbreak*. *Caleb Followill's* voice rasped in sync with the terrain.

Then I fell from the ski lift. Mike's laugh echoed across the mountain.

Fragments I feared were gone forever. Restored. These songs became a tether to a version of myself I barely recognised but deeply missed.

I wasn't going to sit back and fear the gaps in my memory. I would resurrect them. Rewire the neurones, spark the synapses—whatever magic lay buried in the grey matter—I'd call it back to life. I'd make my brain an ally again.

A new beginning. Music and me.

With my new routine taking hold, I noticed subtle improvements. My mood lifted. My fitness increased. My general wellbeing slowly stabilised. It wasn't monumental—but it was progress. For the first time in ages, I felt mentally strong enough to confront my addictions head-on.

I'd flirted with the idea of quitting weed for years, but never seriously. So I came up with a plan: I'd run out and go cold turkey. I hoped that after a few weeks, the cravings would ease and I could finally move on.

I didn't tell anyone—not even Meg.

The first few nights were brutal. I lay wide awake, delirious, every muscle twitching with frustration. The bed felt like a prison. I tossed and turned, sweating, desperate for sleep that never came. And during the day, I was a nightmare—snapping at Meg over the smallest things.

Classic withdrawal: sleeplessness, irritability, restlessness.

On the worst nights, I caved. Took painkillers to take the edge off. Trading one vice for another wasn't smart, but my body felt like it was in open revolt. The pills numbed the pain just long enough for a few hours' rest. Each time I reached for them, I reminded myself it was temporary.

If I could ride it out, maybe I wouldn't need anything to sedate myself at all.

The cravings didn't vanish. Sometimes they hit like a freight train. But I had a strategy: one day at a time. I didn't think about forever. Just not today. And that, I could manage.

As the 'not todays' piled up, the cravings lost their power. I wasn't cured by any means—but I was finding my way back to a version of myself I could be proud of.

Things were going well—too well. Like the eerie calm before a storm.

And then, without warning, the nightmares returned. Full-on horror movie scenes I couldn't escape. That's when I remembered why I'd started smoking in the first place—to silence the onslaught.

Each night, I woke up drenched in sweat, heart racing, dragged under by a force I couldn't control. My instinct screamed: block it out, light up, make it stop! But I couldn't go back—not after coming this far.

So I made a deal with myself. If I couldn't escape the dreams, I'd face them head-on. I forced myself to do the breathing exercises and grounding techniques I barely believed in. Sometimes they helped. Mostly they didn't. But trying felt like progress. At least I wasn't running anymore.

I was standing my ground—even if I was terrified.

The thought of bedtime filled me with anxiety, knowing that closing my eyes meant another round with the wave. It was harder than I'd ever imagined. The progress I'd made crumbled under exhaustion. Each night dragged me back to the worst day of my life—relived in vivid detail.

Some days, the urge to drink was overwhelming. I'd quit weed—but quitting alcohol at the same time? Maybe that was stupid. Cravings crept in, whispering promises of relief: Just one drink. Take the edge off. The old habit, always waiting.

But this time I had a secret weapon. Accountability.

A support group, sort of. I was on this wellbeing journey with my best friends: Mike, Bobby, Wiggy and Barry. We checked in on our WhatsApp group—The Breakfast Club—constantly, confronted challenges, celebrated milestones, kept each other honest. It wasn't some big system—but it worked. A quick message when things got tough. That connection gave me a reason to hold on.

And slowly, I realised: alcohol and drugs had never helped. They'd only masked symptoms. They hadn't solved a goddamn thing.

Not only did I make it through October—I kept going. Into November. Then December.

There's a truth to dependency: once you start to clear it from your system, you genuinely feel incredible. I felt more alert, more engaged. And for the first time, I fully accepted it: I'm an addict.

A real one. With real consequences.

The idea of making it through the holidays sober? It was no longer terrifying. It was exciting. I could hit the new year clear-headed. I got this!

I was excited for the life I was creating.

Then life, as I'd come to expect, threw another shitty curveball.

Mike died. Stage 4 pancreatic cancer.

He'd kept it hidden from everyone—even his family. We only found out when he was admitted into palliative care. By then, he could no longer speak. Nine days later, he was gone. At forty-six.

The news hit like a sledgehammer. Sudden. Merciless. A real sucker punch. I had no idea how to process it. Just when I thought I was getting my shit together, my world collapsed.

All the progress crumbled. The demons I'd fought so hard to bury came roaring back. What was the point in trying to live well, to do the right thing, if life could be snatched away so abruptly?

This wasn't the first time I'd lost a friend without warning... and it destroyed me all over again.

Why not drown it all out? Give in to my demons?

So that's exactly what I did.

I hit the bottle—hard. If I'd had access to weed, I would've spiralled there too. I drank myself into oblivion. Tears flowed. Rage bubbled. The futility of it all wrapped around me like a straitjacket.

All the barricades I'd built were obliterated.

For the first time in what felt like decades, the emotions swelled—and I didn't even try to hold them back. I let the floodgates open. And it wasn't just Mike. It was everything I had refused to confront. Everything I had locked away.

Mike messaged daily during lockdown—a thread of connection, helping us survive the isolation and stay on the path to wellness. They're all still on my phone. But I can't listen. Not yet.

The last one still haunts me. At the time, I missed it—the crack in his voice. The weight behind the words. He wanted to tell me. But he couldn't.

"John, uh... I've got something I need to tell you. Maybe we can FaceTime this weekend..."

I listened. But waited to respond.

By the time I realised what he was trying to say, it was too late.

Life can be brutal. Mine feels like an endless road of loss. Tragedy after tragedy, with only sparse glimpses of sunshine.

Mike's death was a blow I didn't see coming.

And it pulled me straight back into the clutches I thought I'd escaped.

'With life as short as a half-taken breath, don't plant anything but love.'
Rumi

Eleven
Dazed & Confused

22nd July 2021
London

I attended the funeral via livestream—a cold, digital bridge stretched across continents. As the link loaded, it hit me how surreal it all was. The emotional distance felt even greater than the physical one.

I broke down as our friends shared stories from Mike's life. Grief surged in waves, crashing harder with every memory. A few drinks in, I crossed from mourning into oblivion. One moment I was holding back tears; the next, the room was empty, the screen dark, like Mike had vanished from my life all over again.

I poured another drink and rewatched the send-off, glassy-eyed. It was the kind of farewell he would've appreciated—one that echoed his own struggles. He, too, had wrestled with alcoholism and never truly broken free. If I was going to survive this, I knew I'd need to draw on the strength he showed in his final months.

"After drowning my sorrows, I had my last drink on December 30th," I said, wrapping up my account of the year that dragged me toward sobriety.

"That's incredibly sad and moving, John. Obviously a powerful motivator," Rada said gently. "Do you think you'll stay sober this time?"

"I'm not sure. Maybe I'll have the occasional glass of wine with dinner. I think I can handle that. But weed? That's gone for good. That habit's dead."

Saying it out loud felt strangely liberating. I'd made real progress—but I knew the road ahead was long. Alcohol had been so automatic in my life, the idea of quitting completely still felt foreign.

"You mentioned that you don't cry very often. Why do you think that is?" She asked softly, nudging a door I hadn't opened in a long time.

"I think it's because I went through an overwhelming loss when I was young. It built this emotional resilience—or maybe just a wall. The pain back then... it was like nothing else. It toughened me up."

"Do you mind me asking what that loss was?"

I inhaled slowly. "When I was eighteen, my three best friends died in a car crash."

Even now, nearly thirty years later, it still feels raw—like a scab that never quite healed.

"It was the weekend after my birthday. Six kids died. They were on their way home from the pub. The car crashed less than two miles from home. Hit a tree. Burst into flames. Trapped them all inside."

The days that followed were a maze of disbelief and devastation. I had just turned eighteen. I was still a child, and I was already learning what soul-crushing loss felt like.

"I still see the wreckage—it's burned into my retinas. I imagine them struggling, choking in the smoke, realising they were trapped. Just the week before, we were out celebrating. Then I got flu. Friday, Saturday —I stayed in. On Sunday, I still felt rough, but planned to meet The Lads at the pub. I stopped off at my mate Wiggy's first. He was watching a film. I stayed."

Rada's soft gaze urged me to go deeper.

"I've thought about that choice a thousand times. If I hadn't stopped. If I'd gone to the pub. Would I have taken a seat in the car? Would I have convinced them to take the bus? Would I have died? Would they have lived?"

The next morning, Dad stood over me.

"John? Wake up... Did you see The Lads last night?" Greg's mum was on the phone, worried.

I shrugged. "Nah, they went to the pub. I didn't bother."

That was the '90s—no mobiles, no updates. Once you were out, you were out. And you usually ended up out out.

More calls came. Concern turned to dread. Something felt wrong.

Then I saw the newspaper. Front page. Car Crash. Six young lives lost.

"Please, continue if you can," Rada said gently.

"Around lunchtime, I walked to the crash site. Twisted metal. Burned-out shell. Scorched concrete. I just stood there, telling myself it couldn't be them."

Then a hand touched my shoulder.

"It's them, John," Wiggy whispered.

And my world collapsed.

The weeks that followed were a blur. Nothing has ever compared to that kind of loss. I honestly don't know how I'd have coped without my mates. Our shared grief was the only thing holding us together. We clung to each other, desperate for answers. Why them? How could they be gone?

At night I'd lie in bed replaying the 'what ifs'. Futile questions. Pointless torture. But I couldn't stop.

We kept vigil at the crash site. Flowers, scarves, handwritten notes spread out along the tree and pavement. A Charlton scarf twisted around the bark like a tired flag. That tree became our anchor. A sacred space.

We rotated roles: one of us would break down while the others held steady, then we'd switch. Their absence left a void none of us knew how to fill.

"That's a big thing to carry at such a young age," Rada said softly.

"It was awful," I whispered. She waited. "It feels like life keeps taking people away from me."

Silence.

"I never really dealt with any of it. Just… got on with things."

"You survived."

That word again. Survived. I was starting to resent it.

"I kept going, yeah. But I buried the pain. Didn't process it. Just pushed it down."

"That's understandable."

"Most nights I'd dream about them. And for a few moments after waking, I'd forget. Just long enough to believe they were still alive."

She jotted something down.

"How did you cope?"

"Booze. We all got hammered. Constantly."

"Was that when it started?"

"Yeah, I think so. I'd dabbled before, but after that, it took on a life of its own."

"You numbed the pain."

"Exactly. I found the off switch."

"And did it work?"

"For a while. It's weird… all this stuff's been sitting in the background. I didn't realise it was still affecting me."

"Until now?"

I nodded.

"Yeah. Talking to you… I'm starting to connect the dots. Like I always knew, but didn't want to see it."

"That's trauma John. It buries itself. Until something shakes it loose."

The day of the funeral, we visited the parents. We didn't know what to say—no one did—but we showed up. It felt like the very least we could do.

We ended up at Gregg's house and walked to the church with his family.

Gregg had made a huge impact on me. I was fourteen, new at school, lingering by the football pitch, not knowing anyone. I leaned on the fence, hoping someone might invite me to play. When the ball flew toward me, I stuck out my foot and deflected it.

"What the fuck d'you think you're doing, fool?" someone shouted, charging toward me. "Tsssskkkkk."

He wasn't much bigger than me, but I wasn't about to get mugged off on my first day. I remembered Uncle Frank's advice: Act crazy, son. No one wants to fight a lunatic.

"YOU CAN FUCK OFF, MATE!" I shouted, shoving him mid-step. He stumbled.

I was suddenly surrounded.

Then—Gregg stepped in, blocking the gang.

"He's new. He doesn't know. Let me talk to him," he said, slinging an arm around me like we were old mates.

"You alright?" he smiled. "I'm Gregg. Nice to meet you. Listen, you can't do that sort of thing 'round here. Those boys are nutters."

I was stunned. Where I came from, kids would've welcomed a fight. But this—this was different. Gregg didn't know me but stepped in anyway. It was madness—or kindness. Something I wasn't used to.

He became my first real friend. Introduced me to his mates. Just like that, I was in.

New kid. New town. New life.

The Lads.

Even now, when certain songs play, I see Gregg's smile. He was a true music lover—it deepened our bond. A legacy I still carry.

I'll never forget the day of the funeral. Gregg's dad let us into his bedroom—untouched since the night he left for the pub. Me, Barry, Steve and Wiggy sat on his bed. On the sideboard was a note:

"Dad, I'm going to the pub to meet The Lads. I won't be late. I love you."

"I love you." That part stuck with me. He'd taken the time to remind his parents what they meant to him. Those three little words flood me with emotions I still can't explain. I've always struggled to say them myself.

We wiped away tears and hugged in that small room. Then Barry hit play on Gregg's stereo. Freddie Mercury's voice filled the space. *Wayne's World* had made *Bohemian Rhapsody* cool again, but this time it hit different:

Words about life just beginning…Lyrics. Like they were written for Gregg. For all of them.

Their voices, their quirks, their laughter—they still echo in my mind. Their legacy lives in every decision I make.

Sometimes I visit the cemetery. It's on a quiet hill above South London. The skyline faint in the distance. The graves, side by side, feel impossibly close—like even in death, they couldn't bear to be apart. I don't go as often as I should. It's not the graves that pull me back.

It's the tree.

Even now, thirty years on, the Charlton scarf is still there. A silent witness to our grief.

When I need clarity, I go there. And somehow, no matter the weather, I always seem to bump into Alan's dad. Standing quietly, touching that scarf he tied so long ago.

We don't talk much. We don't need to. The tree holds our memories. It's grown around our pain. A living monument to what we lost.

Dearest Dad,
Promise me you will always try to stand tall and hold your head up high.
Don't forget it's still human to cry.
For life isn't fair,
But Daddy, I will always be there.
(Poem by Alan's cousin)

Matilda Carlton
Amie Jones
Gregg Foulds
Alan Sedgwick
Nathan Griggs
Simon Moss
28th May 1995—RIP

A small plaque at the base of the tree is all that physically remains. But the love, the laughter, the friendship—those live on in every heart they touched.

Losing Mike felt like a cruel echo—the past reaching forward to remind me that grief, when ignored, never really sleeps. I had to reassess my values. I wasn't proud of myself. I was letting them all down.

Grief doesn't age. It doesn't fade. It lingers—clings to you like a shadow. You don't get over it. You learn to carry it. And though it never stops hurting, time makes it bearable. The weight lightens. But the sadness stays.

Where souls have touched, friendship will never be forgotten.

'Sometimes even to live is an act of courage.'
Seneca

Twelve
Knives Out

1990's
London

The early '90s in South East London were dangerous for a rebellious, naive teenager. We'd moved from the inner city—known for gang culture—to what seemed like a quieter, more "well-to-do" suburb. But the tree-lined streets and tidy semis of Eltham hid a darker truth.

The area simmered with racial tension and violence.

The British National Party had their HQ up the road in Welling, and the National Front's mark was sprayed across playgrounds and walls—angry graffiti that felt like a warning. Despite the middle-class veneer, this place was just as volatile—maybe more so—than where we'd come from.

A year after moving, danger showed its face.

It was the summer of '92, and I'd just begun to find my feet. Most days after school, we'd gather in the Park—a dozen boys and girls, all gearing up for our final exams. Typical teenagers in the pre-internet days: no TikTok, no doom-scrolling—just bikes, parks, and bottles of Diamond White. Half the time it didn't matter what we did. Just being together was enough.

That summer was long and hot, filled with laughter and the awkward tension of first crushes. The days stretched endlessly while Shakespeare's Sister told us to "Stay", and Charles and Eddie crooned one of the decade's best one-hit wonders.

Music saturated everything. It was the pulse of our youth. Britpop was on the rise. Girl power and boy bands were overtaking the gloss of the '80s. No Spotify, no downloads—just CDs, vinyl, and cassette racks at Our Price. Music felt tangible, like something you owned.

85

By the mid-'90s, it was full-blown battle of the bands—songs about cigarettes, alcohol, and charmless men. We sang them on repeat, doing terrible impressions, convinced we had the swagger. "Wonderwall" became our unofficial anthem.

One evening, we were in the Park as the sun dipped low. Energy fading. Then a group of blokes appeared across the open meadow— heading straight for us. Most of our lot didn't wait to find out what was happening. They scarpered—sharp enough to sense trouble. But me and Wiggy stayed. Stubborn? Stupid? Probably both. We hadn't done anything wrong, we told ourselves. Maybe they were just passing through.

My gut whispered: Run.

I ignored it.

They got closer—five of them, late teens or early twenties. The air shifted. They weren't here for a chat. The questions came fast and sharp:

"Where you from?"

"What school you go to?"

"You know so-and-so?"

It wasn't conversation. It was a hunt for an excuse.

Then one of them—massive—grabbed me by the neck. One hand tightening on my throat, the other flashing through the air in a wide, glinting arc.

Time stopped. Paralysed.

The knife hovered inches from my face.

Another guy from their group stepped in—firm, calm. He caught the arm mid-swing and gently coaxed it down. "They're not worth it," he said, like calming a wild animal. "Just some stupid kids."

I hovered, detached, barely breathing. Watching from somewhere outside myself. 'I don't want to die.'

Then, with a snarl of disgust, the big guy shoved me away like I was nothing. "Remember my name," he said.

I hit the ground hard. Heart racing. Hands trembling.

They walked off.

Wiggy helped me up. The others started to creep back. Then I spotted it—my St Christopher chain. A gift from Mum, the day I was born. Ripped from my neck in the scuffle. It lay in the grass, glinting, the clasp broken. I picked it up with shaking hands.

A keepsake. A warning. A symbol to remind me how close I'd come.

That night taught me something: Eltham was dangerous. I'd never seen a knife up close—let alone had one waved in my face. From then on, I vowed never to ignore that gut instinct again.

Fight. Flight. Freeze. That was the first time I truly felt it. I didn't run. I didn't fight. I froze.

Fifteen years old, facing a tooled-up twenty-something. My odds? Slim to none. Or as we said in Eltham—Bob Hope or no hope.

Freezing wasn't weakness. It was survival. My body had shut down to protect me—slowing my heart, numbing sensation, disconnecting. That out-of-body feeling? That wasn't panic. That was biology. An ancient code: play dead. Don't provoke. Adopt the fetal position!

That night, I lay in bed wired. Eyes wide. Replaying it all, over and over. What if he hadn't stopped him? What if that blade had found its mark?

My dad's words echoed: "You never know who you're messing with, John. Look at Uncle Frank—old, bald, fat. But you take the piss? He'll tear you to shreds."

He wasn't wrong. That night, I understood something essential: There's no shame in running.

Pride won't save your life. But your legs might.

Dad knew. He had seen both sides of knife crime.

His brother-in-law, Frank, once stood trial for slashing a local villain across the face with a Stanley blade. My dad had to sit in court and see the results of Frank's handiwork.

I was only ten when I first heard the story about Frank getting hit in the head with an axe—only to yank it out and chase his attackers down the street, bloodied and laughing, weapon in hand. "Hey hey boys, it's Jerzy! Let me drink your blood!"

Frank always reminded me of Alexei Sayle—except more "homicidal axe-wielding maniac" and less "deranged landlord."

That's how I coped with the madness—comedy and pop culture were my filter. *The Young Ones* turned horror into farce. It helped—kind of.

But for my dad, there was no punchline.

His only brother, Keith, was a victim. Christmas Eve, 1985. Keith was working as a bus driver when he heard commotion on the top deck. He went to investigate—and walked straight into it. One guy smashed a bottle across his face. The others stabbed him in the neck and stomach. If not for a Good Samaritan he would of bled out on the stairs.

Keith survived, but with life-altering injuries.

Oddly, I don't remember it at all. Maybe my parents shielded us.

Or maybe I buried it—like I always do.

I'd grown up with these stories—half cautionary tale, half folklore. But they never felt real. Not until I had my own close call.

The next day, the news spread: a young Asian boy had been stabbed to death outside the kebab shop by the Park. Wiggy knew him—not well, but the same school. Coincidence? Maybe. But it didn't feel like one.

They caught the killer quickly. A racially motivated attack. When I saw his face in the paper, I froze.

It was him.

The one who held that knife to my throat.

The one who told me to remember his name.

I used to convince myself he was just posturing. Trying to scare us. But maybe that was just easier to believe.

Thirty years later, I still don't know. How many others crossed his path before he finally snapped?

That moment haunts me. If that other guy hadn't intervened… would I have ended up like that boy?

That murder was just the beginning—a wave of racially motivated violence that culminated in the death of Stephen Lawrence. You've probably heard of him. But knowing the name isn't the same as remembering the truth.

Stephen was a Black teenager waiting at a bus stop with his best mate. A gang appeared. Shouting abuse.

The boys tried to run.

Stephen's friend escaped. He didn't.

They jumped him. Stabbed him repeatedly. He bled out on the street.

We knew people who knew Stephen. And people who knew the "alleged" attackers. The rumour mill never stopped. The killers weren't hiding. They were proud.

Even boastful.

A plaque now marks the spot on Well Hall Road where Stephen was murdered—just a mile from another memorial beneath a tree, where six kids lost their lives in very different circumstances.

Pain and memory embedded in concrete.

A brutal footnote on the map of our hometown.

We weren't boys anymore. Those years hardened us.

But we still had a choice: We could leave.

We could try to build a version of life not soaked in loss and fear.

For the ones who couldn't leave. For the ones who never got the chance.

We had to get out. We had to live.

'When you arise in the morning, think of what a precious privilege it is to be alive.'
Marcus Aurelius

Thirteen
Get Out

1998
London

As my apprenticeship neared its end, I stood at a crossroads. It wasn't just about work anymore—it was about meaning. What was the rest of my life supposed to look like? I wasn't a kid, and staying in Eltham, surrounded by the same tainted streets, felt dangerous. I loved my roots, but the town felt like quicksand. I was suffocating. The idea of leaving scared me, but staying felt worse.

If I didn't get out, I knew this place would swallow me whole.

The career I'd fallen into was starting to feel like a trap. I looked at the men I worked alongside—engineers stationed in London's basements —and saw my potential future staring back. Bitter, cynical, checked out. Funny, sure. Plenty of banter. But beneath the jokes was something hollow.

It hit hardest one Friday morning. We'd just polished off our bacon sarnies when the supervisor told us Old Eddie hadn't shown up. He was about fifty, quiet, set in his ways. Always on time. Same chair, same mug of tea, same newspaper. Like clockwork.

The night before, he'd thrown himself in front of a train.

Somehow, he survived.

The mess room went still. Everyone was shaken, but no one talked about it. A few whispered jokes about him losing his marbles, but any real conversation was avoided like the plague.

Mental health just wasn't on the agenda.

Then, one morning, Eddie was back—back in his chair, cuppa in hand, reading The Sun like nothing had happened.

"Morning, Eddie," someone said. That was it. Normal service resumed.

But I couldn't unsee it. He was there, but not really. I promised myself I wouldn't end up like that. No offence to him—I needed more than to wander through life like a zombie, just waiting for something to push me over the edge.

The only ones who bucked the trend on the maintenance circuit were the relief workers—usually young Aussies. They'd roll in on dual passports, earning cash while partying across Europe. It was like meeting a different species. These guys weren't just existing—they were living. Their energy was infectious. Their stories were fuelled by adventure and hangovers, not bitterness and boredom.

One temp, with long jet-black hair and a thick Aussie accent, loved to stir my imagination.

"You'd love it, Brommo," he said, flicking his hair from his face. "You and your mates wait in the street, thousands of people hyped up, then —boom!—you're legging it from these massive bulls. This one guy, right—got a horn straight up the arse. What a dickhead, but…"

The tales stuck. I hadn't known Pamplona even existed, let alone that people willingly ran from bulls. Injuries were common. Fatalities rare. Still, I couldn't help but picture the obituary: Died after taking a bull horn to the femoral artery.

Guys like the Aussie Lou Diamond Phillips were changing me. Each story chipped away at the walls I'd built around my small world.

Red pill or blue pill. Dead-end maintenance man or intrepid explorer?

My best mate Wiggy was all in from the start. The more we talked, the more it shifted from daydream to plan. This wasn't just travel—it was escape. The need to leave grew urgent, unspoken at first but undeniable.

Wiggy, usually the steady one, looked at me one night, equal parts excited and terrified.

"What if it all goes wrong?" he asked.

I didn't have an answer. I felt it too—the fear of stepping into the unknown. But staying put? That felt riskier. Eltham had become a lonely place.

The absence of The Lads was heavy.

So, we made a pact. We'd back each other, no matter what. We wouldn't let fear hold us back. We'd leave—even if we had no clue where we might end up.

Dan "Wiggy" Wiggins was sharp as they come. He had a city job—Forex trading or something money-related that was well above my head. Reading the Financial Times on the way to work while the rest of us buried our heads in the tabloids. He was well paid and well up for it—whatever *it* happened to be.

We'd been inseparable since '91. I'd just moved in—he lived across the street. We were both a bit lonely, but that summer we found each other—tennis in the road, football in the park, Atari marathons till we passed out. As we got older, the innocence gave way to mischief—alcohol-fuelled, hilarious, borderline insane shenanigans. Looking back, we were reckless, lucky, and full of life.

To make the Aussie dream real, we dialled it back. We swapped lager and late nights for Blockbuster video and tubs of Häagen-Dazs. Not exactly rock 'n' roll, but it worked. We were saving hard. Every pound brought us closer to the dream.

It was a golden year for Hollywood—*There's Something About Mary, Saving Private Ryan, The Big Lebowski*. We loved *Armageddon*. The action, the soundtrack. But for me, it was Steve Buscemi who stole the show.

I've always loved that guy. Goofy, awkward, unforgettable. Mr. Pink in *Reservoir Dogs*, refusing to tip the waitress in that era-defining scene. But what really hit me came later. After 9/11, he put his old firefighter uniform back on and joined the recovery crews at Ground Zero—

93

pulling double shifts, digging through rubble for survivors. No press. No fuss. Just duty.

That stuck with me. I've seen what disaster leaves behind—the silence, the loss, the faces you never forget. And then there are people like Buscemi. Quiet heroes who just show up.

That's the kind of person I wanted to be. Better. Braver. Real.

What a guy.

Hats off to Nucky Thompson—and to all the unsung heroes who show up when it matters most.

Now, back to the real turning point—the day we got our visas. It was one of those surreal moments burned into my memory. A good one, for once.

Wiggy and I stood outside the Australian Embassy on Aldwych at 7 a.m., jittery with anticipation. Commuters rushed by, off to offices and routines we were about to escape. We were choosing a different path —one filled with uncertainty, but also purpose, freedom, and fun.

The process was quick. We fit the age bracket, had enough cash, and were deemed to be of sound mind and good character.

Apparently.

"G'day boys." Stamp. "Good on yers."

Working holiday visas in hand, everything shifted. What started as a pipe dream was suddenly real.

Soon we were at Gatwick, backpacks strapped tight, waving goodbye to teary-eyed parents. We had no clue what was waiting on the other side of the world—only that it had to be better than what we were leaving behind.

'To travel is to live.'
Hans Christian Andersen

Fourteen
Fill The Void

1999
Australia

Once the idea of backpacking took hold, everyone wanted in —or more accurately, out. The Eltham exodus had begun. Australia had that magnetic pull: former penal colony turned paradise, with beaches so pristine the sand squeaked, a laid-back outdoor lifestyle, and a buzzing cosmopolitan scene—it was impossible not to fall in love with it.

We spent the first week hitting pubs and clubs, burning through our hard-earned cash as we adjusted to the backpacking lifestyle and the freedom it promised.

Then came my first lesson in Australian weather.

We stumbled across the Australian Open in Melbourne and scored $10 tickets to the outer courts—unreal! Kournikova, Henman—we watched in awe as they battled through the early rounds. I sat under thick cloud cover and, foolishly, skipped the Ambre Solaire. That night, I collapsed into my hostel bunk, completely unaware of what I'd exposed myself to.

I'd been cooked alive by UV rays under a sky missing its ozone layer.

Around 2 a.m., I woke up delirious. I staggered to the showers, still clueless about the damage. The moment the cold water hit my face, I screamed and dropped to the floor. Each droplet felt like broken glass. My skin was blistered and raw. When I caught my reflection in the mirror—swollen, red, bubbling—I vomited on the spot.

I crawled back to bed and spent days lurking in the shadows, crawling out only to sip precious water, just like Gollum. Even the smallest movement reignited the agony. This wasn't your average sunburn—

95

this was third-degree burns on a cloudy day.

"Stick a fork in me—I'm done."

Two weeks in and I'd already ticked off a major sporting event, severe sunstroke, and made new friends. Unforgettable.

George and Martin. A couple of Dutch lads from the hostel. We hit it off and agreed to road-trip the Great Ocean Road together—one of the world's great drives.

"Good news—you're driving!" George grinned, lobbing me the keys.

I nodded coolly. Inside? Panic. I'd never driven outside London, and now I was about to tackle Melbourne's chaotic streets, mystery road signs, and giant trams that came at you from all angles. I fumbled through a seven-point turn, scraped a hubcap, and prayed no one noticed. But once we escaped the city, anxiety gave way to exhilaration. The open road had a rhythm, and I fell into step. Waterfalls, coastlines, and some memorable moments.

One night, mid card game, we ran into a feisty hostel owner—and things went sideways. Without warning, he flew into a rage, grabbed the Dutch boys—one under each arm—and hauled them toward the fire exit like rag dolls. The bloke was built like a brick shithouse. Huge, hairy, terrifying. Like Hodor on steroids.

Instinct kicked in. Wiggy and I jumped on his back, trying to wrestle him off, but it was like bringing down The Mountain. He just kept moving, shaking us off like flies. In the end, he chucked us all out, one by one, tossing our backpacks onto the pile.

In the middle of nowhere and too drunk to drive, I drew the short straw. While the others squeezed into George's Ford Falcon, I crawled under an overturned boat on the beach and shivered myself to sleep. Not my finest moment—but definitely one for the scrapbook.

That trip lit a fire in me—for road trips, nature, escapades, and most of all, freedom. Until then, travel had meant sunbathing, a copy of yesterday's Sun and a full English. Luvly Jubly.

Australia shattered that myth. Here, I could roam without plans or purpose. I didn't just see a new country—I discovered a new way of being.

It inspired us to take the next step: buying our own Falcon. The car looked like it had survived a *Mad Max* shoot, but it was ours—a trusty camel to carry us wherever the road led. Me and Wigs left Melbourne in that beast, heading north to rendezvous with the Eltham boys.

We rolled into Sydney and quickly fell back into our mode operandi: beers and blurry nights out. That's when we met the infamous goon bag—a five-litre silver pouch of the cheapest wine imaginable. At $10, it was the backpacker's best friend and worst enemy. We passed it around like communion. Each gulp more vile than the last—but that wasn't the point. Getting smashed was.

And get smashed we did. Town after beautiful town.

Byron Bay was a postcard—surf dudes, sun, jazz in the air. Then came Nimbin, a trippy hippy relic where hash cakes were sold like souvenirs. Weird and wonderful. Somehow, it all made sense in this new world we were exploring.

The wildest moment came on a white-water rafting trip down Grade 5 rapids. "Expert class," apparently. Violent rapids, unavoidable waves, high fitness requirements, rescue unlikely… not for the faint-hearted—and definitely not for a bunch of well-lubricated Brits.

I didn't last five minutes before I was hurled from the raft. I hit the water hard, wind knocked clean out of me. I was helpless, bobbing down the river, bouncing off rocks and getting dragged under. Disoriented, winded, terrified—until I snagged on some overhanging brush. My ill-fitting life vest was the only thing keeping me afloat.

Wiggy and the boys hauled me back in, laughing their arses off.

All I could do was laugh too. That's how these trips went—hangovers, close calls, and lots of giggles.

By the time we hit Cairns, we were different people. The Ozzie lifestyle had absorbed us completely. Levi jeans and Chelsea boots gave way to board shorts and—of course—thongs. Wiggy, with his olive skin, looked practically Mediterranean. I, on the other hand, had finally mastered sun safety—after only two rounds of third-degree burns.

This was the life, and we were all in.

The road north had been fun, but something shifted. We'd stopped meeting new people. With so many of us, we unintentionally walled ourselves off. Whole dorms were overrun by our gang. New travellers would arrive, take one look, and check out. We were loud and completely unaware of how we came across.

It hit me one night—nine of us sprawled across bunks, plus one quiet lad in the corner. I finally clocked him getting dressed up.

"Big night, mate?" I asked.

"It's my birthday. I'm going to the pub," he said, smoothing down his ginger curls and drowning himself in Lynx.

"Not on your own?"

"Yeah. I'm travelling solo. I'm Gavin." I shook his outstretched hand.

"Nice to meet you, Gav. I'm John—and that lot's the boys. Get dressed, lads—we're taking Gav out for his birthday!"

His smile said it all.

That night reminded me why we were there—to connect. We'd built the same bubble we'd once tried to escape. Gavin changed that. He was a music man, just like me. When a song came on at the pub, he lit up. Back at the hostel, he played tracks from his favourite album. He spoke about Counting Crows like Gregg once spoke about Prince— with reverence.

There was something in those songs, a longing I didn't understand yet…but it felt like he was singing something I'd forgotten how to say.

The music from that time stitched a thread through my life—surfacing at key moments, woven in without me even realising. It reminded me of the power of strangers. You never know how a fleeting connection can leave a lasting mark.

The year flew by in a blur of adventure, mishaps, and moments worthy of their own book. That trip changed everything—how I saw the world, how I saw myself. It gave me confidence and perspective. We weren't the same boys who'd left Eltham. Even Dangerous Dave, who overstayed his visa and got deported, found a way back. He's still in Perth now, Ozzie to the bone, driving a ute and going walkabout in the Outback on weekends.

Maybe he was running from grief too. Or maybe, like me, he just couldn't let go of the freedom we found.

With the millennium fast approaching and funds running low, we packed up the ailing Falcon and hit the road back to Sydney—taking turns at the wheel, trying to sleep between gear changes and potholes.

The only real drama came when Barry took the wheel.

"Watch out for kangaroos, mate—they're everywhere," Steve warned as he slid into the backseat.

Not sixty seconds later, the car jolted violently.

"What was that!?" Barry yelled, wide-eyed.

A paw jammed in the flat tyre told us everything we needed to know.

"You twat," we groaned in unison.

With no plan B, we spent the night stranded in the Outback, sleeping in the car until daylight. But it was the only major hiccup. Twenty-eight hours later, drained but buzzing, we crested a hill—and there it was. The Harbour Bridge. That view lifted our spirits like nothing else.

But Sydney's nightlife would soon sink it's teeth into us. The first night out, the music thumped, but it wasn't just the beats—it was the energy.

Uplifting, electric, contagious. You didn't need drugs to feel it... but that didn't stop us.

"I'm gonna do half a pill. Want the other half?" Barry grinned.

"Alright then, give it here."

Yes. Man.

And just like that, it hit—a wave of euphoria unlike anything I'd ever felt.

The rush was good. Too good.

I told myself it was a one-off.

I knew it wasn't.

It would be a path I'd stumble blindly down for the next twenty years. They say weed's the gateway drug. I disagree—it's alcohol. Booze dulls judgment and defers reason. It had filled the void since we lost The Lads. It led to that first pill. From there, everything became fair game. I wasn't chasing drugs, but if something showed up, I'd say yes.

That became my default setting.

The highs were addictive. But the comedowns—anxiety, dread, emptiness. New emotions to me. The sinking feeling of watching sunrise with strangers whose names you never asked.

As 1999 wound down, Sydney's hedonism began to eclipse the freedom that had made the year so special.

Nine of us crammed into a grimy two-bed flat. It was a complete shit hole—mouldy, cramped, barely fit for squatters. We were living for the next night out. I'd tried to outrun the past—but somehow, it had followed me to the other side of the world.

Just before New Year's Eve, Bobby showed up. Classic Bobby—completely incognito. We returned from the cinema to find a stranger on the sofa. He gave a small nod. Dangerous Dave had let him in, and they'd sat in silence watching telly together.

"Who's this, Dave?" Wiggy asked.

"I dunno," he shrugged, swigging his longneck, completely oblivious.

I did a double take. "Bob? Bobby? Is that you?"

"Hello Maaaate!" he beamed, all 6'4" of him, pulling us into a massive hug.

He looked rough but radiant. Three months in Asia had transformed him. All skin and bone, but the reunion was pure joy—laugh-til-it-hurts stuff.

Bobby shared stories that stirred our imaginations. I wanted that too. Adventure. New friends. Something deeper.

There's a Polaroid from that day—Bobby in a stupid bucket hat and scruffy beard, the two of us grinning like idiots. One of my favourite photos. A moment frozen in time. I didn't know it then, but it marked the beginning of the comedown.

Millennium arrived in a blaze of lights and music. We sat on a hill watching fireworks over the harbour, then danced the night away on Bondi Beach. Legendary DJs. House music pulsing through the sand.

Two or three little fellas, maybe more. You'd take one, forget, take another. Somewhere in the blur, something shifted—euphoria gave way to escape. Hours melted. Everyone felt like your best friend. But somewhere inside, I knew I was losing myself.

What started as freedom was becoming a trap. The highs were incredible—but the lows? The lowest I'd ever known. And with each crash, it got harder to climb back out. Someone always had more pills. Sometimes, it was easier to keep going than to stop.

I told myself it was just a phase. But deep down, I knew better.

What we didn't see then was how much grief shaped us. The loss. The trauma. It was always with us. And Sydney didn't heal it—it magnified it.

But it also forged something lasting.

We didn't come out unscathed. But we came out together. To this day, we're still best mates. That's rare.

That's gold.

Fuck, I love my friends.

'The world is a book, and those who do not travel read only one page.'
Saint Augustine

Fifteen
Good Morning Vietnam

2000
South East Asia

Something had shifted. Bobby's arrival jolted us out of the dangerous routine we'd fallen into, reigniting the flicker of adventure. His tales of Southeast Asia—countries I could barely place on a map —were like a match to dry kindling: exotic cultures, ancient histories, landscapes beyond imagination, and strangers whose kindness left lasting impressions.

He'd met Mike almost immediately, and together they'd travelled, bonded, and forged a friendship that soon pulled me into its orbit.

So, the day before our flight home, Wiggy and I made a snap decision. We'd hop off the plane during refuelling in Singapore and see where the wind took us.

Australia had changed me. It stirred something deeper—a sense of living beyond the narrow borders I'd grown up with. I was chasing something now. Meaning, maybe. Experience. I wasn't sure. But I was hungry for it.

Wiggy, a year younger but miles ahead in worldliness, had been my anchor. Curious, clever, a history buff and borderline geek—we'd been inseparable since the summer of '91. Best friends. No— *Stepbrothers*.

"On the count of three, name your favourite dinosaur! Don't even think—just say it! Ready? VELOCIRAPTOR."

"What! Did we just become best friends!?"

But early on, I saw Wiggy had his own struggles. A few weeks into school, I found him looking terrified outside the gates.

"I've got to fight Trevor. He said he wished my dad had died, so I pushed him. Now he wants to meet in the woods. Everyone's coming."

"Alright then," I said. "Let's go."

Trevor was all talk, but Wiggy was rattled. I knew the feeling. Cato had trained me well.

As we reached the woods, a mob of kids stood clustered behind the school penis, AKA Trevor.

"What you hear for, John?" He sneered.

"To watch Wiggy bash the granny out of you, you mouthy little prick," I spat, my voice steady despite the knot in my gut. "And if any of you other wankers jump in, I'll tear through the lot of you."

All front. No trousers. Frank 101.

Trevor froze. Wiggy and I turned. Nearly out, he charged us from behind.

"He's coming," I said. "Turn and smash him. If you don't, he'll never leave you alone."

And Wiggy did. Dragged him down, landed a few solid punches. Good lad. From then on, we knew: whatever life threw at us, we had each other's backs.

So in 2000, I followed my brother into the unknown. And I was ready.

Without trying, we left behind the indulgence of Australia: pies, schooners, hangovers. Malaysia had a different energy. The strict drug laws kept me on edge—paranoia creeping in at night. I obsessively unpacked and repacked, checking for anything that might have slipped in. I'd heard the horror stories—travellers facing death sentences abroad.

I had no intention of being another unwitting mule.

Years later in Thailand, that fear nearly came true—me, Wiggy, and Barry, caught at an airport with a forgotten bag of weed. A customs check that somehow missed the stash. In another universe, we're still rotting in the Bangkok Hilton.

We started making healthier choices—maybe the heat, or just a desire to shed the love handles. We exercised. Ate better. The food helped: laksa, smoky satay, biryani, flaky roti. Each meal a cultural revelation. But the real awakening came at the Batu Caves during Thaipusam.

Thousands of pilgrims marched to the shrine. Some were pierced with limes and skewers—acts of penance. The energy was raw, hypnotic. So far removed from my world, yet it pulled me in. I'd walked away from religion after our God called The Lads' numbers too early.

And yet… something about this moved me.

Wiggy, ever the history nerd, turned each moment into a lesson—Eastern philosophy, the Khmer Rouge, war atrocities. Much went over my head. But not for long.

Cambodia loomed.

We reached the border crossing—a remote, desolate place that made you question your life choices. What was supposed to be a straightforward ride became a nightmare. Fourteen of us crammed into the back of a pickup, bags beneath us like cattle.

"This is a joke, right?" Wiggy muttered.

"Bobby said the journey was brutal."

"Fucking bollocks. We're fucked now."

The road was a bombed-out dirt track, full of potholes and craters. The suspension was gone. Each bump hurled us sideways. We clung to each other to avoid being launched overboard. At one checkpoint, a man with an AK-47 stood guard. Our driver handed over cash, exchanged words, and we were waved through.

"What the hell?" I muttered.

"Guerrillas," Wiggy whispered. "Told ya. The Khmer Rouge don't fuck about."

For a second, I thought he meant gorillas. I scanned the plains for apes before realising it was much worse.

Eleven agonising hours. 100 Kilometres. A journey I will never forget. By the time we reached Siem Reap, we were caked in grime and completely wrecked.

Our "room" was a sweatbox—two old mattresses, mosquito nets full of holes. Wiggy's snoring, buzzing insects, my brain replaying every sketchy moment. My heart still racing.

But by morning, the fear softened. Our hostel was filled with fellow travellers. We connected with two Japanese guys from the same hell-truck—Yohei and Tomra. We barely recognised each other under the dirt but made a pact.

We teamed up and hired motorcycle taxis. As the jungle rushed past, I realised how far we'd come. Trusting strangers to guide us through Cambodia. A leap of faith.

But the prize was worth it: Angkor Wat.

It was colossal. Otherworldly. The largest religious structure on Earth. Some temples were swallowed by jungle—others stood eternal. Ta Prohm would later be immortalised in Tomb Raider, but back then it was untouched by Hollywoods glamour.

The carvings. The steps. The sense of something bigger than yourself. It ignited something in me—a thirst for history. For wonder. Australia was a lads' holiday. Benidorm on steroids. This was something else. This was discovery.

The next stop for our new crew was Phnom Penh, Cambodia's capital, and the darker chapter of our journey. We'd been dreading the ride, still haunted by that bone-shaking truck trip.

It was worst. If that's even possible.

The road was mercifully smooth at first. But it didn't last. Soon, we were back on familiar terrain: potholes, ruts and machine gun-toting gangs.

Eventually, we pulled over at a rest stop in the middle of nowhere—a tiny rickety hut on stilts stood tall next to the restaurant. Tomra sprinted ahead, then reappeared gagging, shaking his head before vanishing behind a tree.

I should've taken the hint.

"How bad can it be?" I muttered, climbing the near-vertical steps.

At the top: a crude hole in the wooden floor. No toilet. Just a drop straight to the ground. I leaned forward, looked down—and recoiled. The earth beneath was alive. Maggots writhed in a gelatinous soup of piss and shit. The smell hit me like a sledgehammer. My bowels recoiled—then changed their mind and clamped tight. I stumbled back down, queasy and shaken.

Tomra had the right idea. But I wasn't about to wander off. The fields were quiet, but beneath the surface lay remnants of war—thousands of hidden land mines. Every amputee we passed—and there were a lot—was a chilling reminder not to stray from the beaten track.

Phnom Penh was bigger than Siem Reap, its streets lined with faded French architecture and quaint cafés. On the surface, it had charm. But underneath, it pulsed with grief. Where Siem Reap had temples to soften the edges, Phnom Penh was unflinching. Its identity was tied to the brutality of Pol Pot's regime. It felt wrong to call these places "tourist attractions." But bearing witness felt essential.

Between 1975 and 1979, nearly two million people were murdered—a quarter of the population.

Our first stop was Tuol Sleng, or S21—a high school turned torture prison. I'd read up on it, but nothing prepared me for the reality. The rooms were preserved as they were left—blood-stained floors, haunting photos of the victims. Men. Women. Children. Tourists walked in silence, afraid to disturb the ghosts.

107

It didn't feel like history. It felt present. Raw.

We had the incredible fortune of meeting Buo Meng, a survivor of S21. He smiled warmly sharing his story through an interpreter.

He had been captured with his wife—whom he never saw again. Their children were sent to another camp, where they eventually starved to death. Buo was tortured, but his skill as a painter saved him. He was forced to paint portraits of Pol Pot. His story—of surviving the regime's hell on Earth—was a quiet, staggering testament to human resilience.

That afternoon, we visited The Killing Fields. A place of unimaginable horror. Mass graves dotted the grounds. At the centre stood a tall stupa filled with skulls, stacked to the top. Each one stared out, lifeless. Silent. Children's voices rang out from a nearby school. Laughter cutting through the stillness. A chilling juxtaposition.

As horrific as Cambodia's past is, the country holds a serene beauty. The people celebrate their history—both the magnificence of the ancient temples in the north and the horrors of Pol Pot's era—with quiet resilience.

We played football with local kids on dusty streets lined with bullet-riddled buildings. Once, we were even invited to a wedding. It was surreal—laughing, dancing, surrounded by strangers who treated us like family. After everything we'd learned, I couldn't understand it. But maybe that's what made it so humbling.

Our time in Cambodia had to end. Reluctantly, we packed up and caught a bus to Ho Chi Minh City,—our first stop: the Vietnam War Remnants Museum. We wandered past tanks, helicopters, and rusting relics scattered around the courtyard. Inside, it was a barrage of images—raw, brutal, unforgettable. Photographs of jungles torn apart, villages destroyed, bodies burned.

One image seared itself into my brain: a young girl, running naked down a road, her skin melting from her body.

"Napalm," Wiggy said quietly.

I'd heard the word in *Apocalypse Now*—"I love the smell of napalm in the morning." But looking at that photo, it hit differently. This wasn't fiction. It wasn't film. This was real.

I couldn't look away. Photo after photo. Children. Civilians. Soldiers.

Lives obliterated.

As we climbed into a Huey parked outside, I tried to smile for the camera—but the weight of what we'd just seen clung to me. Paul Hardcastle's "N-n-n-nineteen!" pounded my eye sockets. Suddenly, the true intention of the song finally landed, and I was only a decade late to the party.

We were ready to move on. But Vietnam wasn't done with us yet. Just before our first overnight bus to Hanoi—a daunting 21-hour journey —we met a Dutch couple. After swapping the usual travel stories, the guy handed us two little baggies.

"Traveller's best friend," he said, passing over the pills.

"What are they?" Wiggy asked, suspicious.

"Valium," the woman smiled, slurring slightly. "Helpsh you relax and get shome shleep."

Curious, we accepted the gift. And let's be honest—it wasn't the first time we'd taken pills from strangers.

This time, I was in for a rude awakening.

An hour into the ride, we each took one. The bus was cramped, noisy, uncomfortable. When we stopped at a roadside café, I figured the first pill hadn't done much. So I took a second. Typical.

I grabbed a plate of noodles, a bottle of Tiger beer, and sat back. That's when everything changed.

The pills kicked in—hard.

My body turned to mush. My vision blurred. I stared at my food, trying to remember how to chew. The world slowed to a crawl. Wiggy vanished. So did my appetite. I drained my beer, just as the headlights flashed in my face.

A horn blared.

I was still sitting in front of the bus, drooling into my Pho, eyes barely open. Like that scene in *Dumb and Dumber*, where Lloyd zones out behind the wheel, dreaming of Aspen—except I wasn't in a shaggy dog van. I was semi-comatose in 'Nam.

"Pills are good. Pills are gooood."

I opened my eyes in Hanoi.

Eight hundred miles had passed in an instant. I was drooling on the shoulder of a stranger, out cold from the double dose of benzos.

Addictive, appealing, and available over the counter in Asia.

Hanoi was nothing like the south—refined, relaxed, almost untouched. While Ho Chi Minh City had the loud legacy of U.S. Marines, Hanoi felt softer. More cultured. But what really grabbed me was the music scene.

It was peak CD-burning season, and Hanoi was churning out $1 copies faster than I could grab them. I lost hours—days—hopping from stall to stall, my fifty-disc case filling rapidly. Back in Oz, I'd discovered new genres. Now I was finally adding them to my collection. I found *August and Everything After*—the album Ginger Gavin had raved about. One album led to another, and before I knew it, I'd filled a second case.

Another addiction, quietly taking hold.

Houston, we have a problem.

'I can pardon everybody's mistakes except my own.'
Cato

Sixteen
Dope

2000
Laos

Our meandering Asian odyssey led us to Laos. A country that instantly stole our hearts.

Getting there was, once again, an adventure. No one cared about bus capacity. Seats filled? Plastic stools. Those gone? Onto the roof. Some even preferred it up there. "Bagsy on top!" one shouted as he scrambled up, laughing like it was a theme park ride.

And in a way, it was—winding through green mountains, past untouched countryside, in a rickety bus overflowing with bodies and backpacks. This time, I skipped the pills. I'd learned my lesson. Instead, I lost myself in my new music, headphones in, until the batteries finally gave out.

We arrived in Vang Vieng with aching backs but clear heads. A sleepy travellers haven with a handful of cafés and guesthouses. But it had charm. Every bar had those triangular floor cushions, and without fail, each TV played endless episodes of *Friends*. You could roll in mid-morning, order a banana smoothie, and settle in to watch "The One Where...."

By lunch, food arrived. By afternoon, the beers flowed. It was a town built for pause—for weary adventurers recovering from the trials of the famed Golden Triangle.

One day, while exploring the caves around town, we bumped into familiar faces—the Valium-dealing Dutchies.

"We're going choobing, ladsh. You shhould come with!" the guy slurred, grinning.

Tubing. Big rubber rings. You float down the river, get pulled into bars by locals with fishing lines, and get drunk as you go. Sounded right up our street.

"Sure, why not?" said Wiggy, ever up for a spontaneous adventure. He already knew my answer.

We piled into a tuk-tuk, rubber rings hanging precariously off the sides as we rattled north toward the Nam Song River. The driver dropped us in a clearing, turned around, and vanished—leaving us at the water's edge under a sweltering sun, the river glistening like paradise.

The Dutch guy lit a joint and passed it around. I initially declined, content to soak up the view and snag my first beer. But then:

"Ahhh, c'mon matey. What better place for your firsht joint than floating down a river? You don't wanna missh thish!"

I caved. "Alright then—just a little lug," I said, trying to sound casual.

Yes. Man.

Big mistake. The weed hit me like a ton of bricks.

As everyone else floated off, laughing and waving, I lay back, limbs heavy, paranoia rising. I watched them drift away, too anxious to call out. The sun beat down. The river moved gently. My body didn't.

At some point, I passed out.

When I came to, I was grounded in a shallow ravine, surrounded by water buffalo sniffing my feet and nudging my rubber ring. I froze. 'Were they dangerous? Should I run?' My weed-addled brain offered no answers, so I slowly stood, dragged the tube behind me, and waded to shore.

Disoriented and unsure how far I'd floated—or if I'd floated at all—I stuck to the bank, hoping I wasn't miles from the village. The sun was sinking. Jungle sounds grew louder. Birds. Insects. Occasional Moos.

The paranoia hadn't faded.

I was scared shitless and hopelessly lost.

For over an hour, I trudged through rice paddies. No homes. No roads. Just me and my inner tube, alone in the thickening twilight. Praying I was heading in the right direction.

Then, just as full darkness fell, I spotted a dirt track—and at the end of it, a school.

Relief hit like a flood.

I knew that school. We'd played football with the kids there just days earlier. Somehow, against all odds, I'd made it back. I marched triumphantly down the road, clutching my rubber ring like a trophy.

Inside the guesthouse, Wiggy was fast asleep.

"Wake up, you wanker!" I shouted, hurling the tube at him.

"Urgh, what? Where've you been?" he groaned.

"Where've I been? I've been wandering through rice paddies in the dark with a rubber ring on my head! That's where I've been, you prick! Why didn't you wait for me?"

"We called out, mate. You didn't answer. Figured you'd catch up... So... how was your first puff?"

That broke the tension. We burst into laughter, the absurdity of it all sinking in.

We wasted a few more days in that tranquil town, soaking in the boundless hospitality of Laos. Our ragtag group of nomads bonded fast—like we'd known each other for years. One night, as we strolled home, a young boy ran up to us, tugging our arms.

"Opium? Opium?"

"What's he talking about?" I asked Wiggy, my default source of wisdom.

"Opium," he shrugged, half-laughing. "You smoke it. Comes from poppies or something."

It seemed absurd—a child, out at night, hustling drugs. But with our pissed-up pilots steering the ship, we followed the kid through the backstreets to his family home.

His father welcomed us, guiding us into a room that felt like a harem—sarongs hung across the windows, incense thick in the air, mattresses and bright cushions covering the floor. A long, thin pipe was passed around. The man prepared a dose and showed us how to draw it in.

"Relax," he smiled. "Lay back. Suck."

I had no idea what I was doing. I sucked too hard. Too fast. I didn't really get it—maybe I hadn't taken it down properly.

At some point, the man pointed to each of us. "10,000 Riel, 10,000 Riel, 10,000 Riel... and 20,000 Riel for you."

He pointed at me, laughing. "You sucky sucky too much! No stop!" He mimed my wild inhaling, nearly falling over with laughter. Too drowsy to argue, I paid and stumbled out.

"You crack me up, Brommers," Wiggy said. "You always go OTT, don't you?"

"Not on purpose, mate! I didn't know I was doing anything different... Am I gonna be alright?"

"How would I know?" he grinned. "I've never done heroin before."

"What! Heroin?"

"Yeah, same family, innit? Didn't you know?" he said, on the wind-up.

A chill crept down my spine. Heroin.

I'd seen what it could do. One of my cousins died from an overdose. Alone. Choked on his own vomit. His mum found him, too late, sprawled on the bedroom floor.

Years later, another cousin got hooked. Always stealing, always chasing. His whole life revolving around the next fix. It still does. Frankie Jr. was a legend when we were kids. Summers at Nan's caravan. Football. Swimming. Arcade games. I never suspected what he was going through. We'd come back from the arcade to find he'd rolled the van—stealing whatever he could get his hands on, even things that only held sentimental value.

I didn't understand it back then. I just thought he was a tea leaf. But now… I see it. He was a smack-head. Addiction doesn't leave room for anything else. It consumes you. Steals you from the inside out. He was fucked—trapped from a scandalously young age.

Frankie's life was so mental it ended up on film. *Nil by Mouth*—one of the grittiest depictions of addiction and life on a South London estate I've ever seen.

Watching it opened my eyes to the horrors buried in my own world.

That night, lying on a thin mattress in a Laotian hostel, I thought about Frankie. About Uncle Frank. About the disease that takes and takes and takes. And I thought about how lucky I was. Sometimes, the environment you grow up in grabs you before you know you have a choice.

I had escaped. Right?

Then sleep took me. A deep, comforting embrace.

The images came fast—movie scenes bleeding into memories. Faces, flashbacks, hallucinations. A spinning kaleidoscope of what-ifs.

I woke a day later, groggy but grateful.

I'd crossed a line. And I knew I wouldn't cross it again.

Whatever you called it—dope, smack, H—I'd stared down the same demon that had devoured my cousins.

Kind of.

That was close enough for me.

I'm sorry. As I write this, I can feel myself stalling. Telling these stories —who I was before the tsunami—feels important. Like these tales somehow make it easier to say what I really came here to say.

But they don't. Not really.

Avoidance is a hallmark of PTSD—I know that now. I've spent years dancing around the thing at the centre of my existence. Skirting the edges. Basking in nostalgia. Distracting myself with jokes and memories and travel tales.

And this—this is my homework. I've been putting it off for too long. I'm building the courage, I promise. But it's harder than I thought. Harder than I ever imagined.

What happened on that day still grips me, even now—twenty years later.

But it's coming. I promise you—it's coming.

Stick with me—it all connects, I swear.

'No man is free who cannot control himself.'
Pythagoras

Seventeen
24 Hour Party People

2000
Thailand

The three months we'd spent in Asia had been transformative. We'd discovered passions for history, music, art, and, most importantly, food. Our bodies had snapped back into shape, shedding the weight we'd gained in Australia. The drinking had eased off, and aside from a few dicey moments, we'd stayed relatively compos mentis. It felt like we were back on the straight and narrow.

That was, until the Thai islands came into our lives.

Koh Tao, at first, was exactly what we needed. An idyllic island known for snorkelling and diving. It felt like we'd stumbled into paradise. The beach huts were simple—rustic even—arranged in a loose semi-circle right by the ocean. Close enough to nature that you could hear the waves lapping against the shore.

It was perfect in its minimalism.

Days drifted by, reduced to the simplest pleasures—fruit shakes, green curries, watching the sea, listening to the music I'd collected. Life was quiet. Calm. For the first time in a long while, it felt good. Really good.

Then the Eltham boys arrived—and all hell broke loose.

Naturally, they turned up on mopeds. Rookie mistake. Koh Tao's roads weren't roads so much as dried riverbeds—divots and potholes carved by tropical rain and hardened by sun. One wrong move and you'd be thrown off like Eval Knievel.

Steve was the first casualty. He showed up on day one sporting a graze that ran from his ankle to his arse—red, raw, and painful just to look at. He wasn't alone. The island was full of travellers wrapped in gauze and bandages, all victims of the same miscalculation—thinking they could tame Koh Tao's terrain on two wheels.

Against our better judgment, we jumped on the back of Barry and Steve's bikes and rode out to a remote cove for some snorkelling.

The coral reefs were stunning—tiny fish darting between rocks, rays gliding in the shallows. The water was clear and impossibly turquoise, a mirror of sky and sea. I floated in it for ages, suspended in warmth and stillness.

The ocean around Thailand always felt gentle. Maybe memory's playing tricks, but back then the sea felt like a warm, flat blanket. Still. Safe. Embracing.

That evening, we stopped off at The AC Bar. A thatched hut perched on the sand, perfect for watching the sun slip behind the sea with a cold beer in hand. The vibe was pure island—Bob Marley, Jack Johnson, sand underfoot, sea breeze in your hair.

But this place was… unique.

Scattered around the bar were massive glass jars, like something from Dr. Jekyll's lab, filled with dead snakes coiled in murky liquid. The owner would tap a jar, declare it "ready," and pour a shot like it was no big deal.

Jet fuel. Harsh, fiery—a gut punch in liquid form.

Naturally, we couldn't resist.

The night spiralled immediately. Snake shots. Thai whisky. Singhas. We knocked them back like there was no tomorrow. The result felt more hallucinatory than drunk.

One minute we were laughing at Steve, inexplicably launching his Reebok Classics into the ocean. The next, I was dragging Wiggy off a dog he'd put in a playful headlock. Ironically, it was the same hold he used on the school penis all those years ago, and despite myself, I cracked up at the absurdity.

Then… blackout.

I came to lying flat on my back in a 7/11. Leg dangling inside an open freezer, wedged between tubs of ice cream and frozen peas. My calf was swollen, red, and burnt raw. Pain screamed through me as I moved. 'What the fuck had happened?' I blinked against the harsh fluorescents, the cold buzzing hum of the store warping my sense of reality. I didn't recognise the place. I didn't even know the island had a 7/11.

The Slurpee machine in the corner confirmed I wasn't dreaming. This was real alright. I dragged my leg out of the freezer and limped toward the exit, half-expecting someone to shout. But the shop assistant didn't bat an eyelid—like this kind of thing happened all the time.

Outside, the daylight made things worse. My head throbbed. My mouth tasted like snake piss and regret. I stumbled onto the beach and collapsed in the sand. I couldn't move for what felt like an hour—leg throbbing, brain mushed with Thai whisky and panic.

The sun burned higher. I fought the urge to vomit. Eventually, I peeled myself off the sand and started walking, hoping I'd recognise something. Anything. A bar, a restaurant, a path.

Hours later, I finally stumbled across a familiar restaurant. Another hour after that, I limped back to our hut.

"What the fuck happened to us?" I asked, shaking Wiggy awake from his booze-soaked coma.

"Eh? Oh fuck, that hurts. Where am I?"

He looked as rough as I felt—cut on his nose, dried blood around his mouth, bruises and scrapes all over. His Thai fisherman pants were in tatters. As he stood, I realised the main tear had left him fully exposed.

"For Christ's sake, will you cover yourself?" I tossed him a sarong and turned away, doing my best Chet-from-*Weird Science* impression.

"What happened? Do you remember anything?"

"Only Steve launching his trainers into the sea."

That's when the memories started trickling back. We'd taken Barry's moped. Now the injuries were starting to make sense.

Cuts. Burns.

We found it half-buried in a bush along the dirt track.

The brilliant idea? Nick Barry's bike so he'd have to walk home. Give me a backy. Drunk, laughing, out of our minds. Like evil geniuses.

We hadn't even made it ten feet before we crashed straight into a tree. The bike pinned my leg beneath it, searing my calf on the exhaust like a medium-rare steak. Dazed and confused, we wandered off in opposite directions. He somehow made it home. I found somewhere to cool my leg off.

It took days for the leg to heal. But the chaos? That was just beginning.

Here I go again.

The states we got ourselves into were nothing short of reckless—flirting with danger more times than I care to admit. Each one a blend of stupidity and total disregard for our own safety.

Looking back, it frustrates me—even shames me—how carelessly we treated life. But that's what drink does, doesn't it? It strips away the part of you that's meant to say: Hang on a minute… this is a terrible idea. Beer goggles. Liquid courage. Whatever you call it, once you're pissed, the world shifts. Consequences blur. Risks feel irrelevant. You just don't give a fuck.

And it wasn't always the chaos we caused—it was the danger we didn't know was there.

Koh Tao seemed like a safe haven. A sleepy island paradise where backpackers lived carefree, letting loose in a rule-free bubble. That's what we thought, anyway. But paradise often hides its cracks. In 2014, two backpackers were murdered—shattering the illusion. We hadn't known any of its history. Turns out, for decades, it had been a penal colony, cut off from mainland Thailand, left to self-govern. Justice here wasn't a courtroom—it was handled quietly, locally. Murders, disappearances, hushed-up investigations. Tales that never made it into tourist brochures.

We were playing with fire. Dicing with danger in a world we didn't fully understand—where one wrong move could've cost us everything. I mean… whose dog even was that? "You killed John Wick's dog… oh…"

Koh Phangan raised the stakes. The infamous Full Moon Party.

Bars lined the waterfront. Every inch of sand pulsed with bodies—dancing, tripping, stumbling, or just trying to stay upright. Pills, weed, mushrooms—whatever you wanted, it was there. Thai whisky was the key, served in a plastic bucket mixed with amphetamine-laced energy drinks.

A chemical cocktail for maximum mayhem.

Wiggy thrived in this world. His sharp humour and effortless charm made him a magnet for strangers. He could walk into a bar, drop a few lines, and have the whole place in stitches. We were constantly surrounded by new faces, fresh stories, shared madness. We wove our way through the crowd—laughing, dancing, drinking, indulging.

Then someone offered me a bump. Casual. Like passing a beer.

No big deal.

And before my brain could catch up, I'd already swallowed it. I assumed it was coke, another first for me—too naive to know I was meant to snort it.

The music thumped. The world pulsed. For a moment, everything felt good.

Then it didn't.

My body slowed, like I was wading through treacle. My mind detached from my limbs. Something was wrong. I couldn't control my body.

Then, like a slow-motion pratfall, I toppled backwards off the stage—Johnny Weissmuller-style—landing flat in the sand five feet below.

I lay there like a sand angel, staring at the stars. The music pulsed in the distance like a lullaby.

The sky spun softly. I could've stayed there forever.

"Hello darkness…"

When I came to, I was no longer on the beach but lying on a Thai cushion inside a bar. Around me: Wiggy, Barry, Steve, and a half-dozen strangers who all seemed to know me.

One leaned in and grinned. "You should've told me you'd never had Special K before, fella."

I blinked. "Special K? Like the cereal?"

He laughed.

"Nah. Ketamine. Horse tranquilliser."

It sounds absurd, doesn't it? Who finds a drug meant to take down a horse and thinks, Yeah—perfect for parties? I hadn't meant to do it. I didn't even know what it was. But it was my fault. I necked it without thinking.

Yes man.

The after-effects lasted ages. I made it back to the hut and collapsed into a sleep so deep it felt like death. Warm, weightless, absolute.

When I finally resurfaced and returned to the beach bar, I saw Wiggy, staring at me like I'd lost the plot.

"What are you doing here, John?"

122

"I'm meeting the guys from last night," I mumbled, still groggy.

He raised an eyebrow. "What you talking 'bout Willis?"

"I said I'd meet them for a farewell drink…"

"Mate. That was two days ago. They're long gone."

As we walked back to the hut, the weight of it all hit me. Whisky. Snake oil. Uppers. Downers. Sidewinders. Reddies, Blueies, Greenies, Auntie fuckin' Jeanies.

Nothing was off-limits anymore.

Eighteen months on the road—filled with adventure, friendships, freedom—and yet, the moments that had started as fun were beginning to rot from the inside.

I used to think I had a line I wouldn't cross. But that line had vanished somewhere between the islands. I always considered myself sensible. A man with limits. Morals.

But now… I wasn't sure who I was anymore.

The months blurred—island to island, party to party—until the darkness swallowed everything. Every morning, I'd wake to paradise—sunshine, white sand, calm blue sea—and feel like it was mocking me.

The void inside was louder than the party.

Wiggy and I were both breaking. Neither of us said it aloud, but we were pushing each other to keep going when all we really wanted was to stop.

The highs were shorter. The crashes were longer.

Wiggy was making plans with Steve to travel to Indonesia—Komodo dragons, something we'd dreamed of seeing since Singapore. But I was drifting. Detached.

Then came the Black Moon Party on Samui. We brushed up against another pill. Another stranger. This time it was Ya-ba. Thai meth.

We didn't know until after we swallowed it.

It doesn't get much worse than that.

Eighty-six hours later. No sleep. The sun rose over another picture-perfect scene, friends all around me... but I couldn't feel anything but dread. A horrifying clarity gripped me:

I'm done. Not just with travel. With life.

A year earlier, I was a casual—maybe overzealous—binge drinker. Now I was necking random drugs from complete strangers. What started as curiosity in Sydney had spiralled into something ugly in idyllic Thailand.

I grabbed my passport, walked to a travel agent, and booked a flight home.

Enough is enough.

'All of humanity's problems stem from man's inability to sit quietly in a room alone.'
Blaise Pascal

Eighteen
Home Alone

2000 - 2003
London

I knew straight away I'd made a monumental mistake. As the cocktail of party favours finally drained from my system, I found myself alone on a long-haul flight, hurtling back toward the life I'd been so desperate to escape. I was leaving behind my friends, my freedom, and the promise of more adventure.

I'd thrown it away on a whim—driven by a darkness I couldn't explain.

Honestly, I was lucky to make it home at all. I arrived at the airport in fisherman pants and a Bruce Lee T-shirt. I hadn't worn shoes since my last pair of flip-flops disappeared outside a restaurant—standard practice in Thailand.

No big deal, until I rocked up to security barefoot.

The official took one look at my feet and shook his head. "No shoes, no entry." Brilliant.

As if that wasn't bad enough, there was an exit tax I hadn't factored in. So there I was—shoeless, penniless, and stuck in a foreign airport. Long before Tom Hanks made it look fashionable. Then, out of nowhere, the woman behind me stepped forward. She offered me a spare pair of sandals and paid my exit fee. She had no reason to help me. No motive. Just kindness. I was floored. I could've cried on the spot.

"You're good to go now," she smiled. "Just... pay it forward." And with that, she waved me toward home.

Except, home wasn't home anymore.

My family were pleased to see me, of course. But I wasn't the same boy who'd left. The changes weren't visible—not on the outside. But inside, everything had shifted.

London felt sterile. Predictable. Mundane. Suddenly, I was back to greasy takeaways, and the highlight of my day was watching telly. Mum never missed her soaps, following the characters' lives like they were real people. It was surreal. Not long ago, I'd stood on Ramsay Street with Wiggy, hamming up the opening credits. I'd been to Summer Bay—now hearing the *Home and Away* theme tune would trigger flashbacks.

All my real friends were still out there, making new memories without me. And I was here—adrift, bitter, and full of regret.

'What have I done?' I kept asking. 'What the fuck were you thinking, John?'

Loneliness hit deep. They had always been my constant. But now, with all of them still on the road, I felt the void in every quiet moment. I didn't know it yet, but I was spiralling into my first real bout of depression.

The worst part? I couldn't stop thinking about Wiggy and Steve. Off chasing Komodo dragons. If only I'd stayed. If I'd fought through the comedown, pushed past the darkness. But I didn't. Now I was alone. Depressed.

Sometimes the weight of regret sent me spiralling into old memories —some heartbreaking, some hilarious. Like that day in Sydney with Steve...

We were labouring—ten-hour days digging footings on a building site. Brutal work. Pickaxes. Blistering heat. Our only salvation? Smoko. Crash in the shade, kick off your boots, and listen to Triple J count down the best songs of the '80s.

I was half-dozing one afternoon, Michael McDonald crooning about dancing to a different beat, when something tickled my toe. I flicked it away. It came back. I cracked one eye open… and froze.

A giant green lizard—the size of a small dog—was licking my big toe.

"Sstteeeeeeeve! What the fuck is that?! Help!"

I leapt onto my chair, crouching like Mammy Two Shoes from *Tom and Jerry.*

"Holy shit! I don't fucking know, mate—get rid of it!" Now we were both on chairs, towering over this reptile like two panicked toddlers.

"You get rid of it! I'm not touching it!"

The lizard gave us one last look, scoffed Steve's half-eaten sandwich, and waddled off into the neighbour's garden.

Turned out it was a Blue Tongue lizard—harmless, really. But not when it wakes you up mid-smoko with a lick to the foot. Steve couldn't stop laughing all afternoon.

Even though the work was hell, that moment made it memorable.

I laughed too, thinking back on it. Those days felt distant now—like they belonged to someone else. The lightness I once carried had been replaced by something heavier. A darkness no joke could shake.

I was holed up in my old bedroom, shut off from the world behind a closed door. I barely left the house. Days blurred together—grey skies, cheap wine, old movies, and numb repetition.

Most days I drank early and heavily.

Mum hovered constantly, fussing over me—meals, tea, clean clothes. But I could see it in her face: this wasn't the son she'd sent off.

And she wasn't about to let me slide any further.

"If you're not getting a job," she snapped one day, "I'll send you to work with Frank."

"What am I gonna do with Uncle Frank? I thought he was a bouncer."

"He does other stuff. I'm calling him. Get off yer arse."

And that was that. Mum called her brother, and next thing I knew, I was reporting for duty.

"Hello, John," he said, squeezing into the passenger seat. "What'ya waiting for. Drive."

"Drive where?"

"Don't ask stupid questions. Just drive."

Nice to see you too, Frank. I should've known—this wasn't going to be a run-of-the-mill job. Frank didn't do normal.

Frank was collecting debts.

"You wait here. Keep the engine running. If anyone comes after me— run them over," he barked, slamming the door behind him.

I sat there gripping the wheel, heart racing. 'How the hell did I end up here?' Thankfully, there was no need to redecorate the bonnet that night. I drove around for a few hours, kept the car warm, and made a monkey for my troubles.

Good money. Easy work. But not my world.

That one night with Frank was enough to jolt me awake. It reminded me who I was. What I wasn't cut out for. Looking back, I think that was Mum's plan all along. Maybe Frank's too. They double-teamed me. And it worked.

Salvation came in the form of my old work mate Joey. A quick call and we were back working together. It felt like just what I needed— structure, a purpose, and someone to laugh with again.

And it worked. Life steadied. I had a mate to lean on. A reason to get out of bed again.

Then one day in our office, my Nokia 3310 buzzed in my pocket. It was my sister Louise.

"Have you got a telly where you are?"

"Yeah, why? What's up?"

"Turn it on. A plane's just flown into a building in New York."

"Joey—quick, turn the telly on!"

The screen came alive. There it was—one of the Twin Towers, smoke pouring from the top.

Then the second plane hit.

It was like watching a disaster movie—only it was real. We stared in silence as the second tower collapsed, dust and chaos flooding the streets.

People running, screaming, covered in ash.

September 11, 2001. The world shifted that day.

We were convinced London would be next. We were surrounded by landmarks—potential targets in every direction. The fear was immediate. We packed up and bolted for the suburbs, calling our families as we ran for the train. We'd just watched people die live on TV. Some had jumped—hundreds of feet—because it was somehow less terrifying than fire.

That image burned into me. It became the terrifying symbol of that day.

For me, something cracked. London had always felt safe. Familiar. Mine. But now, every street corner held a shadow. Every crowded tube felt like a risk. The atmosphere shifted—like the city itself was holding its breath.

Eventually, things returned to normal. But the fear never fully left. It just moved underground, humming beneath the surface.

By 2002, the boys were back in town. We fell into old routines, like nothing had changed. Soon, we found ourselves orbiting a new group of local girls. Wiggy, as always, got in there first. Then one by one, they all dropped like flies.

Not me. Not at first. None of the girls caught my eye. But after months of group hangs and watching everyone pair off, I started to feel it—that ache. That quiet, gnawing sense of being the odd one out. Invisible. Like even if I was the last guy on earth, no one would pick me.

Then one night, a few drinks in, Wiggy nudged me toward Tina. Gave me that look—the classic: "Why not?" So we hooked up. It was casual at first. The odd date night. Nothing serious. I didn't fancy her, not really, but it was fun. Easy. And I liked not being alone.

But just as quickly as it started, it ended. Tina dumped me—no warning, no reason. Even though it wasn't serious, it stung—more than I wanted to admit. 'What's wrong with me? Why doesn't anyone want me?'

Maybe I was a wrong 'un?

A few months later, Tina called out of the blue and asked to meet. I didn't think much of it, but over dessert, she dropped the bomb—she wanted to get back together.

I stared at her, stunned. Inside, my mind screamed: 'No. Do not go back. No. Never go back.'

I excused myself and headed to the bogs. Splashed cold water on my face. Stared in the mirror. She'd dumped me without a word. Now she wanted another go?

No spark. Not then. Not now.

But then that old voice crept in: 'Better than being alone, loser.'

I went back upstairs, still undecided. I didn't feel what I should. So I avoided the truth.

"I'll think about it," I told her.

A few days later, we fell back into the old rhythm. Same dynamic. Same nothing. But the companionship numbed the ache. And for a while, that was enough.

But London felt heavy. The dangers, the rejection, the sense that life had stalled—it was all too much. So me and Barry made a snap decision.

We were leaving. Again.

What started as casual pub banter became a full-on escape plan. Flights booked. Countdown on.

I should've ended things with Tina immediately. But I didn't.

That same voice that decided to "think about it" agreed on "long-distance."

Weak. Afraid.

So we made plans of our own. She would save and join me later in Thailand.

As my trip with Barry would end, we would start our own.

Seemed smart. And it would keep me on the road even longer.

Away from London.

It was a massive mistake—one we wouldn't fully understand until it was far too late.

One that would change both our lives forever.

'You have power over your mind—not outside events. Realise this, and you will find strength.'
Marcus Aurelius

Nineteen
Weird Science

29th July 2021
London

The afternoon sun scorched the city, its heat bouncing off the square mile like a blast furnace. The sky was a sheet of unbroken blue, the heat thick and oppressive. London felt like an oven—its familiar streets warped into a shimmering mirage.

I wrapped up work a little early and decided to walk to Rada's office. Even at 4 p.m., the weather was punishing.

Sweat pooled beneath my cheap polyester suit jacket. But I didn't mind. Walking was my refuge. My reset. A time for quiet introspection and escape.

The further I walked, the more alive I felt. Each step offered discovery —odd bits of history tucked into alleyways, street art clinging to brick walls like secret messages. My way of reclaiming space in a city that often felt too small and predictable.

Eventually I reached the northern bank of the Thames near Limehouse. The sun dipped lower, casting a golden shimmer over the water. The riverside quieted my nerves. Even in London's chaos, peace could be found—if you knew where to look.

But today wasn't about the walk.

Anxiety simmered just beneath the surface, bubbling stronger with every step. The early sessions with Rada had been gentle— pleasantries, background, small talk. We'd been circling the trauma like prey. Today, I knew we'd start digging. Peeling layers. Exposing wounds.

And I wasn't ready.

I slowed my pace, desperate for distractions—snapping photos, lingering over a crooked old house squashed between new glass towers. The contrast reminded me of myself: fragments of the past trying to coexist with newer, shinier parts that didn't quite fit.

My steps grew heavier. The weight of what was coming pressed me physically into the pavement.

But I had my armour now.

In the months leading up to this, I'd devoured information, clung to the words of people like Ant Middleton—who talked about fear like it was a bubble you could contain until it was time to act.

The old me—Version 3.0—would've spiralled. I'd have found a hundred excuses to cancel, crawling back to the safety of weed and wine.

Fragmented. Fragile. Bent out of shape and terrified I'd never be whole again. But this was Version 5.0—battle-tested, slightly upgraded, no longer running. Jackie Chan's words echoed in my head: "Don't think. Just do."

He wasn't talking about therapy. He meant leaping off buildings and crashing through windows. But for me, this felt just as dangerous. If he could face that kind of risk, I could walk into an office and talk.

Still, as I rounded the final corner, the urge to disappear surged again. I could vanish into the crowd, take a different street, bury the memories deeper. My subconscious knew it—I slowed with every step, dragging my feet, delaying the inevitable. My hands clenched. The heat pressed in.

This was it.

Don't think. Just do.

Jackie Chan had always been one of my heroes. Hong Kong's finest. An innovator. A one-man stunt team who blurred the line between comedy and action. My cousin Sam introduced me to him in 1986, when he came to stay for the weekend with his ninja suit and a pack of throwing stars.

We spent hours in the garden hurling stars at the fence before Sam dragged me to the local video shop for the latest Hong Kong release: *Armour of God.*

We raced home and slammed it into the top-loader VHS. From the opening scene, I was hooked. Jackie's mix of humour, kung fu, parkour, and batshit stunts blew my young mind. Jackie wasn't just brave—he was unrelenting.

There's a stunt in Armour of God—a jump from a wall to a tree, then a swing to another ledge. He nailed it first time. But being Jackie, he went again. On the second try, he slipped, crashed through the branches, and slammed his head on a rock. Part of his skull shattered. Doctors had to implant a plastic plate to protect his brain. He nearly died. And he still came back.

That "never say die" attitude stuck with me—though it took years to understand. During my misspent youth, I imitated him—flinging myself out of trees and off buildings. As an adult, I tried to channel his mindset to push through my mental frailties.

By the time I reached Rada's office, the ninety-minute walk—and all the mental gymnastics—had taken their toll. My legs ached, and my head was foggy.

I ducked into the toilet to splash cold water on my face. The icy shock snapped me back into focus. Here we go.

Don't think…

Sweat clung to my back as I peeled off my jacket and dropped my bag beside the familiar couch. That fear bubble I'd built up all week was about to burst. I could feel the pressure rising. I sank into the cushions, which welcomed me like an old mate—already shaped to my body. A near perfect arse groove. Homer Simpson style.

"Would you like some water?" Rada asked, handing me a bottle.

"Yeah, please." I grinned, trying to hide my nerves, and gulped half of it in one go.

"Don't tell me you walked here?"

"Of course! It's a beautiful day. I love walking, remember? Came from the City, walked along the Thames."

I launched into my usual spiel—walking as mindfulness, walking as discovery. It was a sleight of hand. A distraction. My way of buying time.

But deep down, I knew why I was here. Everything—relevant or not, remembered or buried—had led to this moment. Today, I'd have to open up in a way I never had before. Not even to myself.

Just do…

Something was different this time. I could see myself more clearly. Version 5.0 wasn't perfect, but he was self-aware-ish, reflective. Capable of holding himself accountable. Johnny 5's alive.

But I wasn't fixed. I wasn't done. I was just getting started.

This would be okay. I'd be okay.

Rada watched me settle in, her voice calm and steady. "So, you know what we'll be doing today, right? Are you ready to start, John?"

POP!

"I think so…" I said, but the fear hit harder than expected. I shrank into the cushions, arms crossed like a makeshift shield. Defence mode. Hold. Hold the door. Hold door. Hodor…

Rada outlined the technique we'd be using. EMDR. Eye Movement Desensitisation and Reprocessing.

It sounded like something out of Stranger Things—part science experiment, part witchcraft. Apparently, EMDR uses eye movements to help reprocess traumatic memories, rewiring the brain to think about them differently. Trauma gets stuck in an isolated memory network, sealed off like a bomb shelter. It overwhelms the brain's coping systems.

For years, mine had been locked away.

So maybe this weird science wasn't as crazy as it sounded.

Because of COVID protocols, we couldn't do the eye movement part —too close for comfort. Instead, Rada would guide me through a tapping method. I had to cross my arms and tap each shoulder alternately while recalling a specific memory. The rhythm was meant to mimic the same neurological response.

It all sounded ridiculous. And felt more so.

"Before we begin, we need to establish a safe place," Rada said. "Somewhere you can go mentally if the memories become overwhelming. Can you think of one?"

My mind leapt. It had to be vivid—something I could picture clearly. This should've been easy, but the silence squeezed me. Why was this so hard?

I scanned recent memories, but something held me back. No—keep that part clean. So I rewound.

"My childhood bedroom," I blurted, eyes shut, breath shallowing as the image took shape.

"Good. Look around. Tell me what you see."

"Blue wallpaper with flecks of yellow," I said slowly. "A small cabinet with my TV. A shelf above it with all my wrestling tapes. My bed's under the window. I can see the street outside. Our blue Mini Metro's parked in front of the hedge."

With each word, the picture sharpened. My photographic memory locked in. I felt the carpet under my feet—dark blue, familiar, grounding.

136

"That's great. Now take your time. What can you hear?"

That one was harder. The visuals came quick. Sounds took longer. "Trains," I said after a pause. "There's a track just over the road. I can hear them going past."

"You're doing very well, John. Now—can you think of a smell that reminds you of this place?"

It hit me instantly. "Roast dinner," I said, smiling. Mum's Sunday roast. The smell filled the house, wrapping the memory in warmth. I could almost taste it.

"You can open your eyes now," Rada said gently. "This is your safe space. If the memories become too much, return here—the sights, the sounds, the smells. Let them ground you."

I nodded.

"Now we'll go through the memory in pieces," she continued. "I'll stop you if it gets overwhelming, and we'll use EMDR to interrupt the negative loops and help reframe how you think about it."

Deep breaths. Don't think…

"Are you ready?"

No.

Every cell in my body screamed I wasn't. I was never ready to go back —to unlock the memories I'd padlocked, chained, and sunk into the darkest part of my mind. Down with Davy Jones' locker.

I closed my eyes. Breathe. Just breathe. Each inhale carried weight. Each exhale, release. I focused on the rhythm, trying to calm the rising panic.

Stay with the breath. Shut everything else out.

Time stretched.

Then—cracks. First in the lock. Then in me.

Not just the tsunami. The whole year that led to it began rising like floodwater. Images flickered—slow motion at first, then spinning into reverse. A mental rewind of 2004.

The surreal buddy movie trip. The noise, the fun, the laughs.

Then December. The month everything changed.

The reel spun up.

Christmas time. The final days.

Before the world unravelled.

Just do…

'Traveling – it leaves you speechless, then turns you into a storyteller.'
Ibn Battuta

Twenty
The Beach

Christmas 2004
Koh Phi Phi

Christmas arrived faster than expected, marking twelve months since Barry and I jumped on that flight—first stop: Bangkok. Thailand, with its chaotic streets and tropical beaches, had become our second home. There was something magical about it: the heat, the humidity, the sounds and smells. Every visit felt like a warm, sticky embrace—comforting and wild all at once.

From the moment we hopped in a tuk-tuk, I knew we'd made the right call—leaving behind my job, my home, and, controversially, my girlfriend. It was drastic, sure, but sometimes, to save yourself, you have to walk away from what everyone else expects.

The journey was immense. We criss-crossed Asia, passed through Africa, and then tackled North America. By the time we hit South America, we'd clocked twenty plus countries. I felt like Uncle Travelling Matt from the Fraggles—racking up strange tales and sending mental postcards home.

This time, we'd upgraded—actual hotels instead of hostels, flights over 24-hour bus rides. Not luxury, but it made a difference. It seems sacrilegious to skim over such an important time, full of incidents, close calls, and unforgettable moments. The memories from that year are hazy, but I can feel them surfacing. Still, I need to keep moving forward.

If you're still with me, thank you.

We came full circle in early December. But we weren't alone—Joey had flown out for a two-week holiday, bringing along a mate we'd never met. They'd heard all our stories and wanted a taste for themselves.

And who better to show them around than us—two seasoned 'experts'? Shame we nearly blew our credentials on day one.

Me and Bazza were supposed to meet them at Bangkok airport. The plan was simple: meet, grab a cab into the city, acclimatise for a few days, then head down to Phi Phi. Easy enough. Except we'd forgotten one crucial detail—confirming any actual plans.

"What time are we meeting them?" I asked, casually assuming Barry had it sorted.

He shrugged. "I figured we'd check what flights are coming in from London and go from there."

I stared at him. "Do you know how many flights come in from London? Please tell me you have a flight number?"

Barry shook his head. "Nah."

I wanted to scream—but I'd done nothing to help either, so I couldn't exactly take the moral high ground. Still, we were now at Don Mueang Airport, one of two airports in Bangkok, with no clue where they were, and no way of contacting them.

"Let's recap," I said, leaning into the sarcasm. "No airport, no airline, no time, no number, and one of them is a total stranger?"

Barry nodded. "Correct."

I wanted to implode.

"I'll send Joey an email," I muttered. "If he's already landed, maybe he'll check it and meet us at that bar on Khao San Road."

Barry, ever the optimist, scanned the crowd. "Let's just look around. Looks like a flight just came in."

I burst out laughing. "You want to play Where's Wally with thousands of passengers? We don't even know what his pal looks like!"

"Joey called him 'The Moroccan Sunrise.' That's probably him," Barry offered, pointing across the concourse.

A shock of blazing orange hair bobbed above the crowd. Easily a foot taller than anyone else. 'No fucking way.' Standing beside him—Joey.

Of course.

Lucky Barry had struck again. He shot me a smug grin as we walked over. Disaster averted.

Darren—aka The Moroccan Sunrise—was 6'5" with traffic-cone hair and the subtlety of a flare. The four of us couldn't stop laughing at the absurdity of our airport "plan." Barry's "just look around" strategy had actually worked.

As we boarded the boat to Phi Phi, the captain sized us up, then pointed at Joey. 'You sit here,' he said, motioning to the port side. The rest of us were ushered to the opposite end—human ballast. The 'Boat Tipper' was born.

But the real comedy gold came on day one on the island. We'd decided to get Thai massages. Me, Barry, and Darren were already laid out on mats in this big open-plan room, half-asleep, surrounded by about fifteen other people being poked and prodded into bliss.

Joey, however, was taking his sweet time.

Then he emerged—from behind the curtain—completely stark bollock naked. Holding his clothes wrapped up inside the loose Thai fisherman trousers they'd given us to change into.

While the rest of us had followed the simple instructions—change into the trousers and store your clothes—Joey had misread the brief and bundled everything into the trousers instead.

The room erupted in laughter.

Joey froze, red as a beetroot, trying to hide his manhood with the trouser bag as a horrified mama-san rushed over, giggling as she whisked him back behind the curtain.

It was like a live sketch show. I could almost hear Uncle Travelling Matt narrating: "Dear Gobo, today one of the silly creatures failed to understand trousers." You had to be there—but it set the tone for the trip: gut-splitting laughter—the kind that leaves your face aching and your abs sore.

We were in that rare sweet spot of travel: nothing to prove, nowhere to be, and everything to enjoy.

Some of the best days of my life.

But soon, their holiday ended—and just as they left, Tina arrived. I left Barry on Phi Phi and travelled to Phuket to meet her.

But the moment I stepped off the boat, everything went wrong.

The car I'd arranged didn't show. No taxis. No buses. Panic set in. Eventually, I flagged down a tuk-tuk—a rickety, three-wheeled snail crawling along the highway at 40mph while I silently screamed into the wind.

By the time I reached Phuket Airport, it was nearly empty. Tina's flight had landed and she was nowhere to be seen.

I'd failed—completely. One job: meet my girlfriend after a year apart. And I'd blown it. I ran through the terminal, scanning the arrivals board, searching desperately. Yes, the flight had landed. All passengers and bags had cleared.

My stomach dropped.

Alone, the panic rose with every step, my footsteps echoing off the cold terminal walls, taunting me... You're a cock. You're a cock. You're a cock!

No plan. No phone. Had I learned nothing from the Moroccan Sunrise fiasco?

I was just about to make the dreaded call to her dad—trying to imagine how to explain that I'd managed to lose his daughter within an hour of her landing—then I saw her.

She walked toward me across the deserted baggage hall. Relief flooded me—until I saw her face.

She wasn't just angry. She was furious. "Where have you been?" she asked, voice calm, eyes blazing.

I froze. "I'm so sorry," I stammered. "I couldn't get a cab. Then the tuk-tuk... I've been trying everything to reach you."

Didn't matter. I'd missed her flight, missed our moment.

No Hollywood reunion. No dramatic kiss at the arrivals gate. Just failure. Total, gut-wrenching failure.

That first night was silent. Tense.

The next day, we made the journey back to Phi Phi—but the frostiness lingered. Even my Boat Tipper story couldn't crack a smile. And I didn't blame her. How could I?

The first week was a mess. I didn't know how to be her boyfriend and Barry's travel buddy at the same time. I tried to please everyone and ended up pleasing no one.

We'd grown apart. Substantially.

It wasn't going to be as simple as picking up where we'd left off. We were strangers now, sharing a tiny hut, dodging conflict, walking on eggshells. I didn't think she liked me much.

I didn't like me much either.

Time passed, and slowly the frost thawed. Day by day, she slid into island life—lazy mornings, hammocks, pad Thai, and laughter echoing across white sand. The magic of Phi Phi worked its spell. The island had a rhythm all of its own. Days drifted by in the haze of sea air and cheap beer. Nights lit up with fire shows, beach bars, and the legendary buckets.

Ah, the buckets.

We lucked out thanks to Nok, a good friend who owned a bar and helped us land a hut in Gypsy Village. A horseshoe of bamboo huts circling a grassy patch, hammocks swaying from every porch. A proper little community.

Christmas Day kicked off early. We gathered outside our hut with beers in hand, blasting Christmas tunes and singing like idiots. It wasn't traditional, but it was perfect.

We shared Christmas lunch with our makeshift travel family: me, Tina, Barry, Nok, and a couple of familiar Danish faces—Lisbeth and Camilla—who we'd met on Phi Phi a year ago.

That was the thing about this island. It pulled you back. People came and went, but Phi Phi had a way of making everyone feel like they belonged. No cars. No chaos. Just paradise, served up with a chilled Chang and a smile.

That night, we made our way into town—first stop, of course, the Rolling Stoned Bar. I must've dragged everyone there a hundred times. The Thai cover band was electric—Guns N' Roses and Metallica. And the guitarist? An absolute beast. He didn't imitate solos. He owned them.

They knew me well by now. I'd stumble in, plastered, and they'd grin and play "Mr. Jones" by Counting Crows—my unofficial anthem. I'm pretty sure they hated it, but they played it anyway. That night, they called Tina and Lisbeth onstage for the chorus. The whole bar swayed as they belted it out, arms in the air, singing like it meant something.

It did mean something. One of those perfect travel moments— unrepeatable, fleeting, golden.

And then...

T-minus five hours.

We didn't know it yet, but the earth was shifting beneath us. Somewhere far away, a fault line cracked. A surge of pressure began

144

its journey across the Indian Ocean. Toward us.

But in that moment, we were drunk, sun-kissed, happy. No one saw it coming.

Back at the hut, the night melted into stillness. A faint breeze. The tail end of "Last Christmas" looping on someone's speaker.

The day was done.

A young guy walked past, wide-eyed and fresh off the plane—his first time in Thailand. We invited him for a beer. Talked for hours.

At 4 a.m., we said goodnight. I collapsed on the bed, exhausted. Content. The kind of peace that wraps around you before sleep…

My mind slowed. The room dimmed. Those weeks before Boxing Day played like a movie on fast-forward—laughter, firelight, faces, the heat.

Too sharp. Too vivid.

My hands trembled. My throat closed. The words were there, burning, clawing up—but still stuck.

How do you tell a story like this? How do you rip open the worst moment of your life?

Then finally, it came.

Just the beginning.

"It's Boxing Day morning," I whispered. "I'm asleep in the hut. Tina… she's out in the hammock. We partied hard on Christmas Day."

'I am the master of my fate: I am the captain of my soul.'
William Ernest Henley

Twenty One
Double Impact

Boxing Day 2004
Koh Phi Phi

"John... John!... JOHN! Wake up!" Tina's voice sliced through the pain in my head, her hands shaking me back to life.

"Arghh... what's up?" My voice was thick with sleep and a monumental hangover. My limbs refused to cooperate as I forced my eyes open. My head throbbed with each pulse.

"I've been robbed," she snapped.

"What?" I sat bolt upright. The movement made my stomach lurch. "How the hell did that happen?"

"I fell asleep in the hammock... I just woke up. My bag's gone."

'For fuck's sake,' I thought. I swallowed the words. This wasn't how I planned to start Boxing Day. We'd gone hard last night. I wanted to laze in the hammock, nursing Cokes and letting the island heat melt away the residual pain. Now this.

"Are you sure it's not in the room?" I asked—stalling more than anything. I slid my flip-flops on, yanked a T-shirt over my head. My body was moving on a delay.

"No, it's not," she barked.

The irritation bubbled in both of us, but I bit my tongue.

These three weeks had been draining. I wasn't sure we'd last till New Year at this rate.

At least our passports and cards were safe—locked in our rucksacks.

146

Still, we'd have to report it. Maybe insurance would cover the losses.

We trudged down the sandy path to Barry's hut. He was still in his hammock, one leg dangling, a stray kitten on his chest like a drunk pirate.

When we told him, he groaned and sat up.

Lisbeth emerged from her hut, already dressed and bright-eyed despite last night's carnage. "I can't believe it! What did they take?" she asked, her Danish accent cutting through the haze.

"Just my bag, some money, and a camera," Tina muttered.

"We have to go to the police," Lisbeth said instantly. She was a cop back in Copenhagen and always took charge when things went south. "Bring your passports."

That was Lisbeth—always helpful, even when it wasn't convenient.

The rest of the Danes were still out cold, so she grabbed her things and followed us down toward Tonsai Bay. The sun was climbing, shadows stretching across the sand. The salty air mixed with last night's smoke and booze.

Something about it felt... off.

The island was too quiet. Too still. No buzz of longtails. No laughter from early risers. Like the island was holding its breath.

T-minus 28 minutes.

The "police station" was barely a kiosk—just a small window at the back of a dusty Muay Thai gym. The officer behind the glass looked half-asleep and fully unimpressed.

Tina explained what had happened. The guy barely blinked. His disinterest grated. I was hanging and getting more pissed off by the second. I stepped away before I said something I'd regret.

"He can't do anything from here," Lisbeth said. "We'd need to go to Krabi or Phuket for a real report."

"Not happening," I said. "There won't be any ferries—it's a holiday. And even if there were, is it worth the cost for what we lost?"

Lisbeth frowned, thinking. "There's an internet café near the pier. Let's check the boat schedules. I want to email my family anyway."

"Cool. I've got our insurance info in my Hotmail. Maybe we're covered."

The café was nestled between dive shops a stone's throw from the ocean. A row of PCs humming quietly inside. It was empty—most of the island still asleep or easing into breakfast.

We logged into separate computers. I pulled up our insurance documents—yep, we'd need a police report to file a claim. Brilliant. That meant Krabi or Phuket was unavoidable.

I sighed, printed the policy, and handed our passports to the guy at the counter for copying. Then I began typing an email:

Merry Xmas guys,
Hope you all had a great day. We spent the day…

And then I heard it.

Screaming.

At first distant, muffled—then louder. Frantic.

I froze. Outside, people were sprinting past the café, faces twisted in panic.

"What the bloody hell is going on?" I muttered, standing slowly.

The crack-crack-crack of something echoed through the street. Gunfire? It sounded like it—sharp, relentless. My brain leapt to the worst. 'A terrorist attack? Gunmen on a boat?' It was absurd—but in that split second, it made sense.

Fear rewrote logic.

The café owner pushed past us toward the front door, holding our passports, fresh from the copier. He glanced outside—and something in his face changed.

Terror. Pure, unmistakable terror.

Then he ran.

No words. No warning. Just gone.

Barry's voice shook. "Do we run or hide?"

My thoughts were in the quantum realm. Then it clicked. "If they're running, we run!" I shouted. "Go, go, GO!"

We bolted. Barry and Lisbeth leapt down the steps first, turning left with the crowd. Me and Tina followed. Heart pounding. Legs burning. Adrenaline surging.

We took another sharp left—cutting through a narrow alley.

And that's when the water hit.

At first, just a shimmer around my feet. Then up to my ankles. Fast. Too fast.

It wasn't a towering wall like in the movies. It was worse. A quiet invasion. A creeping surge—steady and unstoppable, like the ocean was reclaiming the land.

I glanced down. The water was swirling now, tugging at my legs.

Barry and Lisbeth were ahead. Barry gripped her hand, forging through the current.

I turned. "Tina, come on!"

But she wasn't there.

My blood went cold. I stopped. Heart hammering.

'Where the hell was she?' I'd fled so quickly I'd forgotten to grab her —the guilt hitting harder than the water.

I spun around. The crowd pressed past me in a tide of panic, but no Tina. I shoved my way back, fighting through the throng.

I reached the corner. Then I saw her. Still on the steps of the café. Frozen. Staring ahead. Blank. Pale. Trapped.

"Tina!" I screamed.

Nothing. She didn't move.

The water was up to my calves now, rising fast.

"Tina, MOVE!"

No response. Like she couldn't hear me. Like she wasn't there.

I charged back, kicked off my flip-flops so I could run, and grabbed her by the arm.

Her skin was ice—but solid. Thank God.

I yanked her into the flood.

We had to run.

But every step was war. The current pulled at us. Tina stumbled, half-dragged beside me, her Birkenstocks sticking with every step.

I stopped. Looked her in the eyes. "Kick them off! Kick your shoes off! You don't need them!"

I mimed it.

She blinked. A flicker of awareness.

Then she got it.

She kicked them off. A dead weight swallowed by the water.

We surged forward, barefoot, pushing through the tide. My grip locked on hers. We ran—not thinking, just reacting.

Then: crash. Bang. Wallop.

The waves met.

Loh Dalum Beach had been hit too—on the opposite side of the island. Now, the two waves collided in the middle.

A vortex.

No warning. No build-up. Just a wall of violence.

The water surged to chest height in seconds, slamming into us like a train. We were yanked off our feet and pulled under like rag-dolls.

No time to think. No breath to catch.

The world flipped. I couldn't tell which way was up. My chest burned. I fought for air but inhaled only seawater—choking, coughing, throat on fire.

But I didn't let go.

The wave pinned us against something hard—a fence. Pain shot through my back. We were trapped, the ocean pressing her down on top of me.

My mind screamed surface! But there was no surface—only the violent weight of the ocean.

I planted my feet. Found leverage. Pushed.

Lifted her.

Her waist in my grip, I gasped as our heads broke free of the water.

We were alive. Barely.

The torrent raged, battering our bodies. It wasn't a wave anymore—it was a river. A monstrous, roiling current squeezing through the alley.

Beside us, a Thai family had been swept into the same trap. A father. A mother. Three small children.

They clung to him. His arms wrapped around them all. His lips moved in silent prayer.

I will never forget that.

The water kept rising. I made a snap decision—I didn't want to drown pinned to a fence.

I could pull us out into the flow.

Somehow, I braced and lifted us up and away from the fence. I reached out a hand toward him. Our eyes locked.

Please, I begged silently.

But his look said everything. He'd made peace. He shook his head slowly. Pressed his hands together in a wai.

I kept reaching. He didn't take it.

And then the current jerked us away.

We were ripped from the fence, torn from that family, back under the water's crushing force. The image burned into my mind—those kids, clinging to their dad, waiting.

We were dragged under again—harder.

The alley had become a violent flume. The wave slammed us against walls, yanked us sideways, down, around. Bodies thrashed—some above, some below. Faces twisted in terror.

We'd been pulled into the centre of it all.

On the international scale of difficulty, this was off the charts. Grade X—beyond dangerous. Impossible to survive.

I could hear nothing but crashing wood and the crack of splintering fences.

The world was a maelstrom of agony. The water trying to tear everything apart.

I couldn't tell where Tina ended and I began. Every instinct told me to hold on. She was everything. I wrapped both arms around her and braced.

The water spun us, lifted us, dumped us. We hit the ground hard, bones jarring. But the jolt shifted our direction.

I kicked. Searching for the surface.

We rose. Broke through—gasping. Choking. Gulping air that burned. Still together.

The fence was nearly submerged. Chaos everywhere. Screams. Currents. Debris.

The Thai family—gone.

Vanished.

I'd see his face in dreams for years. That wai.

No time to process. The water pulled us again. Under. We flipped. Twisted. Sucked sideways. I held on. With everything I had.

That was all I could do. Grip Tina like my life—her life—depended on it.

Because it did.

And then—everything shifted.

'Do what you can, with what you have, where you are.'
Theodore Roosevelt

Twenty Two
No Escape

29th July 2021
London

"John, can you think of your safe place and start tapping, please?"

Her voice reeled me in. My face was damp, eyes raw from squeezing them shut. I accepted the tissue Rada offered and dabbed at my cheeks—the cool paper grounding me more than I'd expected.

"I'm sorry," I muttered, surprised. "I didn't even know I was crying." The tears had crept out silently, salt catching at the corner of my mouth—hauntingly like the taste I'd just relived.

"That's okay," Rada said gently. "It's expected, John. We're accessing a powerful memory."

I closed my eyes again and focused on my breathing—shallow and ragged at first, then gradually deeper, steadier. I needed out of the swirling images. I forced my mind back to my bedroom—the muted clatter of a passing train, Hulk Hogan staring from the cover of *WrestleMania VI*. It almost worked.

Almost.

But the nightmare broke through again. My mind's clapperboard slammed shut—Cut! I begged silently.

But the reel kept spinning: Act 1, Scene 4; Take 32—the dying family.

The man clutching his children as the water swallowed them, eyes fixed straight ahead, lips moving in prayer. I could feel myself sinking back into that moment, fully immersed, like I'd strapped on an Oculus visor and been dropped back onto that island.

154

Cut. Enough!

It was Mum's roast potatoes that saved me—the warmth of that smell pushing back the cold, briny taste clinging to my tongue.

The tapping resumed. Rada's voice was a gentle anchor. "How are you feeling? What emotions are coming up?"

I struggled to answer. The weight in my chest wasn't just one thing—it was a tidal wave of guilt, rage, helplessness. Things I'd done. Things I hadn't. Things no one could undo. Rada had promised we'd tackle it in pieces. I was grateful. I couldn't face it all at once.

I felt hollowed out, my face drained of colour, water bottle trembling in my grip. I didn't want to speak. I just sipped, shivering, avoiding her eyes.

"What are you feeling right now?"

It seemed simple—but it wasn't. My mind was a demolition site. How do you point at one shard when they're all buried together?

Back then, everything happened so fast. My lizard brain had run the show, survival on autopilot while my conscious mind scrambled to keep up. But now—in this slow-motion reliving—the truth cut deeper than I expected.

Anger.

It was raw, simmering just beneath the skin.

"I'm... I'm angry," I said, voice barely steady. It felt wrong, shameful, but I couldn't swallow it.

Rada didn't flinch. "What's making you angry?"

"Everything," I blurted. "Everything about that morning. I'm angry I couldn't help that family. Angry he just... prayed instead of saving his kids. They were so small, so terrified, and he just held them there. They didn't stand a chance."

155

The image crashed back in, high-definition hell: Take 33, freeze frame —the father, the kids clinging to him, the water swallowing them. I'm gasping for air, twisting in the chaos, praying he'd followed. But he hadn't. He stayed. Locked in prayer while the ocean devoured them.

And I lived. 'Useless bastard, John. You let them die.'

Tap, tap, tap—the rhythm cut through the agony.

"How could you have helped them?" Rada asked softly.

"He could've taken my hand," I hissed. "We made it. They might've made it too."

"But you don't know they didn't survive, do you?"

Her question stunned me.

"No," I admitted. "Not for certain."

It had always felt final—they were gone. But she was right. I didn't see them drown. I saw a snapshot. A terrible, still frame.

"I'm sad," I whispered after a long pause. "Really sad. Whether they all died or not... they were gone in an instant."

Anger and grief tangled like barbed wire. Tears came again—quiet, unstoppable. All these years, I'd blamed myself for not saving them. But the real wound? Watching them die and carrying that silent horror alone.

Rada broke the silence gently. "Let's go back a bit—to when you had to go back for Tina."

The memory hit instantly. I nodded. "Yeah... she didn't run. Everyone else bolted, but she froze. I didn't even clock it at first—I just yelled for everyone to move and legged it."

"But you realised quickly. And you chose to go back for her."

156

"Yeah." The word scraped out like gravel. "One of the hardest things I've ever done. Barry and Lisbeth were ahead, running, and I had to stop. Turn around. Push back into danger, screaming people all trying to escape... something. I didn't even know what it was. But leaving her wasn't an option. She was my responsibility."

The tapping resumed. Steady. Grounding.

"I'm angry again," I confessed. "Angry at myself for not grabbing her hand before I ran. Pissed off that she didn't run like the rest of us— she just stood there. I had to fight back through that stampede. It was the scariest thing I've ever done. I didn't even register the water yet— just people fleeing like hell had opened up behind them."

My breath hitched. The memory sharpened—Tina's blank face, frozen on the steps of the internet café, the water lapping at her feet. I screamed her name. She wouldn't move. Wouldn't even look at me.

The noise! God, the noise. Screams, crashes, things smashing, cracking. It wasn't just chaos. It was an assault on the senses.

When I finally reached her, she was rigid, stiff as a board. I grabbed her, yanked her off the step. I was still running from an unknown threat. For all I knew, Godzilla was smashing boats in the harbour and about to round the corner.

But Tina wasn't focused on any of that—just clinging to her stupid silver Birkenstocks.

"I hated those things," I said, half-laughing, half-growling. "It's so ridiculous, but I still hate them. Because I had to keep stopping, dragging her along, shouting for her to kick them off. Inside, I was raging. I wanted to scream, WAKE UP! RUN! But she was in shock— I know that now. Back then, it just felt like she was slowing us down to save her shoes. And something was coming."

The room fell quiet, the echo of my confession filling the space. I felt raw, scraped open.

"We wouldn't have even been there if she hadn't fallen asleep and had her bag stolen," I muttered. "We'd have been back in Gypsy Village, probably safe."

Rada's voice cut through the spiral. "And do you think you'd have been safer there?"

I paused. Logic and regret knotted together. "I don't know. Maybe. Maybe not. It was wide open space. Everyone we knew there ended up okay. But who knows—maybe we would've died there. Maybe the thief saved our lives."

The thought settled over me like cold water.

You are exactly where you're supposed to be.

Rada instructed me to tap again. "Do you feel anything besides anger now?"

"I'll never wear Birkenstocks, that's for sure," I said, trying to break the tension. "Yeah. Guilt. Shame. Embarrassment for being so angry at her... at the shoes. She was terrified. She needed me. Outside I was calm, but inside I was a volcano."

"You shouldn't feel ashamed," Rada said firmly. "Your anger kept you alive. It kept her alive. It was your fuel, John."

Her words rewired something. For the first time, I wondered—maybe my rage wasn't the enemy. Maybe it was my sidekick. My propellant. My symbiote. My survival switch.

Maybe. Definitely maybe.

We wrapped up the session—the tapping, the breathing, the gentle nudges to reframe what my brain insisted on replaying. But when it was over, I felt hollowed out. Rinsed. Like my skin barely contained everything I'd just dragged into the light.

Rada handed me another water. I drank it in one go. Too fast. It hit my empty stomach like a stone, but I didn't care. She scolded me for coming in on an empty tank. Trauma work burns calories, she said. I promised it wouldn't happen again—next time I'd come fuelled-up. Ready for battle.

We said our goodbyes. I stepped out into the warm dusk and felt the hard edge of reality press against my raw nerves. The heat was fading, but inside I was still boiling. My mind looped: anger, grief, a flicker of something lighter—then back to rage.

The thought of a packed tube train made my skin crawl. I needed air, not a crush of strangers.

So I walked. South, toward the Thames.

My legs felt wobbly, but moving felt safer than standing still. I shoved my AirPods in and hit play on my 2004 playlist—Counting Crows, old memories, my life before the wave. Adam Duritz's voice flicked a switch in my head, and suddenly I wasn't in London—I was in South Africa, Kruger Park, Barry laughing like an idiot while a monkey stole his trainers.

I could hear Steve singing "Holiday in Spain" under a sky of BBQ smoke and starlight.

For a moment, the flood receded. Just me, my music, and a good memory. My steps felt lighter. My chest looser.

I reached the north bank of the Thames and stood still, taking photos of the Royal Naval College glowing in the evening light. My ritual— snap the moment, tie it to a fact, anchor myself in the now. It helped. Mostly.

I headed for the foot tunnel. Terrible idea. A cast-iron relic running under the river, surrounded by the very thing I'd just spent an hour revisiting. But I was on autopilot. Feet already descending.

I distracted myself with strange stories I'd read about the tunnel's construction. *Twilight Zone*-like tales. Time loops. Sci-fi nonsense.

I fantasised, my over-stimulated mind turning the tunnel into a gateway to an alternate reality. A place where the tsunami never happened.

Where I wasn't broken.

Where Thor fought Dark Elves on the Naval College lawn and the Bifrost could beam me to safety.

What If.

My head spun with it, even as my steps echoed off the damp tiles.

Then—whoosh. A cyclist shot past me from behind, so close he sucked the air right out of my lungs. My AirPods had blocked his approach. Fear detonated. Rage followed.

"Wanker!" My voice ricocheted down the tunnel. "You fucking cunt! You could've killed me!"

My pulse spiked. I wanted to chase him down. Drag him off the bike. Smash his stupid face into the tiles.

Fight. Survive. React.

My knees buckled. I slid down the tunnel wall, gasping.

In my head, I heard it—the water. Splashes behind me, echoing down the spiral stairs. It was coming. Coming for me again. My ankles tingled with phantom cold.

Run.

I scrambled up, trainers slipping on the concrete. Bolted up the stairs two at a time, lungs burning, the phantom wave pounding at my heels. I burst into sunlight, shaking on the south bank.

No water. No Asgardian gods. Just London. Just me.

My reality.

My chest heaved. My brain caught up. No flood. No wave. No roaring current swallowing the tunnel. Just echoes in my skull.

I whispered it to myself, breathless but certain—you are exactly where you're supposed to be.

Not drowning. Not today.

No more running. I will be free of this nightmare.

'Let everything happen to you: beauty and terror. Just keep going. No feeling is final.'
Rainer Maria Rilke

Twenty Three
The Day After Tomorrow

31st July 2021
London.

The strain on Meg was immense. When therapy peeled me raw, she became the last line of defence against the zombie version of me—irritable, vacant, empathy on pause. But she never flinched. Even when I snapped or sulked, her patience held firm, eyes flicking to me in quiet concern but never judging.

She made sure I ate, made sure I rested, quietly sidestepping the tripwires that might tip me over.

But even Meg couldn't protect me from the nightmares. They came back with a vengeance—vivid, suffocating, louder than ever.

Nights spent pinned under water, streets swallowing me whole, breath stolen again and again. I'd wake gasping for air that wasn't there, heart hammering like the wave was still crashing over me.

Sleep didn't revive me—it drained me further.

Some mornings, just getting dressed felt like a battle. But there she'd be, asking gently how I'd slept, though she already knew. She'd heard the thrashing, the muffled cries through clenched teeth. I wanted to tell her the truth—that I felt like I was drowning all over again—but the words stuck. So I muttered the same line everyone says, even when they're teetering on the edge:

"I'm fine."

The dreams faded with daylight but left their poison behind—anger, dread, a thin film of static over everything. Therapy had stirred the sediment. Now, every damn thing felt like a trigger. A word, a sound, a random image on TV—any one of them could yank me back under.

I'd been told to face them. No more dodging. Feel it. Name it. Survive it.

Easier said than done.

Some triggers I could brace for—the obvious ones. Like the day I stumbled onto a documentary about the Fukushima disaster. Just days after my toughest session yet, there it was: a wave swallowing a Japanese town, raw and merciless.

Not my wave. Same same, but different.

A normal person would've switched over. Not me. No. I leaned in, like it was homework. Watched the water devour streets, houses, lives— strangers halfway across the world reliving my nightmare in a different dialect.

Their stories mirrored mine—sleepless nights, the rage, the survivors' guilt. Every word hit like a hundred-hand slap, but I kept watching. For once, I didn't feel alone.

Their pain was my pain. Their rage, my rage.

Meg found me there, locked in a trance.

"Why are you watching this?" she asked, gentle but worried.

I shrugged. "It's exposure therapy, right? I can't run from it forever."

She didn't scold. She never does. Just gave me that look that says, I see you. I wish I could carry this for you.

The Fukushima doc cracked open another box in my head: March 2011. Tina had just walked out. My career was wobbling. I'd stumbled into work, bleary-eyed, telling myself I could fake my way through one client meeting.

The office was brand new—steel and glass. I sat on a spotless sofa in the lobby, flicking through glossy magazines I couldn't read. Then the massive TV on the wall caught my eye.

Breaking news: 9.1 quake off Japan's coast. A wave rolling out to obliterate everything in its path.

I stood inches from the screen, transfixed. 'Not my tsunami,' I thought. 'I wonder what magnitude mine was?'

I don't remember how I left that building. Just that my bag was on my shoulder and suddenly I was on the train home, numb. The next three days were a blur—me, glued to the news, chain-smoking spliffs, watching that wave flatten towns and threaten Chernobyl 2.0. I didn't flinch. I drank it in—punishment or proof that what I'd survived was real. Maybe both.

Funny thing—I'd never watched Boxing Day footage. I didn't need to. I carried every frame in my skull, sharper than any broadcast could capture. But Fukushima from above? Seeing the scale from the sky instead of inside it's throat—that hit different.

Meg sat beside me, watching in silence. The images rolled on—ocean swallowing streets, people pointing at rubble where families used to live. I could feel her eyes on me, checking for cracks.

"Maybe stop flicking, John," she said softly. "It's like you're looking for it."

She wasn't wrong. Maybe part of me was—for proof that other people were still stuck too, still awake at 3 a.m., still gasping for air. Listening to Japanese survivors talk about nightmares, anger, numbness—it was like hearing a translated version of my own head. I told Meg as much. For once, I didn't bottle it.

"You okay now?" she asked when the credits rolled.

"Yeah. Just weird to see it from above. I always had the fish-eye view—inside the belly of the beast."

I switched the channel to Sky Sports. No more tsunamis tonight. Just transfer rumours and pundits arguing about who'd bottled the season.

PTSD is a complex mistress—it hides in plain sight. Some triggers announce themselves like sirens; others come disguised in jokes on daytime TV.

Obvious ones I could handle. Give me a tsunami documentary? Fine —I'd brace, summon a John McClane grounding monologue: "Fly in the ointment, monkey in the wrench, pain in the ass." I'd grit my teeth and let it wash over me. Brave boy. Well done.

But the stealth ones? They were assassins. One casual word and I was back underwater, lungs burning.

When did tsunami become fair game for metaphors? Greg Wallace raving about a "tsunami of flavour"—fuck off, mate. It's just a passion fruit panna cotta.

And just like that, I was drowning again. Surrounded by bodies. Brilliant.

It hit like a Hadoken—sudden, sharp. Memory bomb dressed up as banter.

I never told anyone how much I hated it. But Meg clocked it.

"You okay, love? They really can't stop saying it, can they?"

"I thought I'd be safe with *MasterChef*," I groaned.

She laughed, but it didn't escape her that my fists were clenched.

I had to toughen up. Build my shield. The world wouldn't censor itself for me. And it shouldn't have to. This was my fight. My monster. And the triggers weren't just words—they were smells, sounds, water, floods, Thai food, music, art, clothes… anything could drag me back.

You win!

Triggers were everywhere. Maybe they always had been. But after peeling the Band-Aid off in 2018, my mind started looping the greatest hits.

I used to be a movie fiend—action, horror, you name it. VHS shelves buckling under the weight. DVDs stacked like Lego towers.

Now? I couldn't sit through half of it. *Harry Potter and the philosopher's stone* ends with him nearly drowning? Brilliant. Just what I need before bed. Gore? Forget it. One squelch of fake blood and I'm back in the real thing—except there, the screams didn't cut to credits. The wounded didn't get up for another take.

Therapy had started to rob me of my simple pleasures. So instead of doom-scrolling Netflix for hidden landmines, Meg and I started taking London on—one wander at a time.

Weekends became rehab. No weed, no blanket fort. Just me, her, and the complicated city I'd never truly explored sober.

It wasn't easy. Some days I wanted to hide. Draw the curtains. Let the old patterns win. But then Bruce Lee's voice would whisper up:

Don't think. Feel...

So I felt it all—the fear, the grit, the resentment. Step by shaky step.

...Don't look at the finger, or you'll miss all the heavenly glory. Thanks, Bruce.

We picked the Natural History Museum. I hadn't been since I was a kid, when dinosaurs and blue whales were all it took to blow your mind. Now, older and haunted, I wanted to see it again—proof I was still here. Still curious. Not just a ghost of Christmas Past.

We kicked off with artisan coffee and warm croissants—small things, grounding me. Then into the cathedral to nature—grand arches, Victorian stone, and the mighty skeleton of Hope, floating like an ancient guardian above us. We drifted through exhibits—Meg lingered, asking questions, squeezing my hand when she sensed me drifting.

Outside, we looped the gardens. Bees and butterflies doing their thing. Meg crouched in the flowers, snapping photos, alive in her element. I wandered—drawn to shadows, brickwork, the unnoticed details.

And then I saw it.

A brutal slab of stone. Big enough to stop you in your tracks.

I read the inscription—and my pulse flatlined.

In Memory of all those who died in the Indian Ocean tsunami, 26 December 2004.

I froze. The museum's hum disappeared. It was just me, the stone, and the roar of waves that weren't there.

Names carved deep—lives lost while I got to keep mine.

It should have been mine too.

I don't know how long I stood there. My lungs tight. Eyes burning. Every name a spinning bird kick to the soul.

K.O.

I could have joined them. Another name for strangers to whisper.

Meg's arm slid around my waist, anchoring me. She didn't speak. She didn't need to.

"I didn't know this was here," I whispered.

"Me neither," she said softly.

Together, we read. Together, we grieved. Together, we gave thanks for the impossible fact that I wasn't etched into the stone.

We left in silence, my feet moving but my mind still shackled to that granite slab. Like Homer the Great in that old *Simpsons* episode. I dragged the stone of shame behind me, its weight impeding every move.

Even on the tube home, squashed between tourists and commuters, the question clanged in my skull: 'Why me? Why did I get to walk

167

away, while their names were frozen in granite forever?'

I'd asked it a thousand times. But standing there, it hit differently.

No therapy, no EMDR, no tapping could erase that question.

By the time we got home, my exhaustion weighed ten tonnes heavier. Guilt, fragile gratitude, and survivor's shame—all tangled up. I sat on the bed, scrolling through photos I'd taken that day: jewels, arches, Hope hanging above the crowd… and finally, the stone.

The memory I hadn't asked for—but knew I needed.

I posted it. Broke from my usual travel trivia and London quirks to share something raw:

No matter how far I run, the past finds me.

But I'm still here. Still fighting. Still grateful.

A moment of honesty, tucked between the curated snapshots.

Then I set my phone down and went to find Meg.

My constant. My Stone of Triumph. My proof I'd survived for a reason.

My reminder that there's still a life worth living—even on the days the wave comes knocking.

'Neurosis is always a substitute for legitimate suffering.'
Carl Jung

Twenty Four
Panic Room

6th August 2021
London

The walk to therapy wasn't just unpleasant—it was a slow, punishing drag. Every step felt heavier, like I was trudging into the open jaws of my past. Dread coiled tighter with each pace. I ducked into side streets, pretending to admire graffiti that blurred into meaningless swirls.

I wasn't looking—I was stalling.

My mind was a minefield: memories and nightmares jostling for control. They weren't content to be ignored anymore—they hammered at my skull, demanding release.

Each step felt like one closer to opening the floodgates I'd spent years barricading.

I knew exactly what waited in that office. I'd have to relive it. Again. The next piece—the one I hated most.

Maybe I could turn back. The thought flitted through me like a lifeline. Run. Hide. Crawl under a duvet and numb out with mindless TV. But not this time. I couldn't pussy out. I forced myself forward.

The darkness wouldn't win today.

When I finally reached Rada's office, she greeted me with her usual calm, but her eyes scanned me—I was leaking tension like a cracked dam.

"Are you okay?" she asked, eyes sharp and searching.

I swallowed hard, trying to put on the mask I wore for everyone else.

169

"Yeah, I'm fine," I muttered—the lie sticking in my throat.

Fine: Adjective—1) All right; well, healthy. Not sick or injured. 'I feel fine today'.

Rada tilted her head, unconvinced. "Come on now. Tell me the truth."

I sighed. "Well... I'm not exactly looking forward to this session," I admitted, voice cracking. I fumbled for something softer than fear. "It's making me... nervous." Not quite right. It was deeper than nerves.

"That's perfectly fine," Rada said gently. "Try not to worry. Sit down. Take a breath. Tell me what you and Meg did this weekend—something nice?"

Fine: Adverb—2) All right; very well. 'Everything's going to work out fine'.

The diversion worked. I latched onto the safer ground and launched into a blow-by-blow of the weekend. Every restaurant Meg had dragged me to, every moment she'd made me laugh. She knew I was barely holding it together after the nightmares and panic attacks, so she'd built the weekend around keeping me afloat.

I told Rada how we stood in front of the tsunami memorial, reading each name carved into cold stone. I hadn't flinched.

Rada listened, her expression soft but focused. "You didn't avoid it. You faced it, even though it hurt. That's progress. Good job, John."

I nodded. The praise sat awkwardly on my shoulders. "Thanks... the good outweighed the bad this time. And when I did start to lose it, Meg was there. She's... she's amazing."

"She sounds special. You two must love your time together."

A small smile slipped out. "Yeah... more than anything." This time, the words came easy. "I'm far from perfect, but she's my reason. We love the same things. And when I'm not floundering, we're out there

170

living—gigs, movies, food, exploring. Life's just better with her."

Rada gave me a few more seconds in that light space. But I felt the shadow creeping back. The real reason I was here. She wouldn't let me dodge it forever.

I swallowed, breathing deep, fighting the dread crawling up my spine. I shut my eyes, tried to steady my breath.

This was the part I hated: the drop into the abyss.

The family.

The last scene we'd touched. Burned into my mind. My hand reaching out, theirs refusing it. That helpless moment, just before the wave wrenched Tina and me away. Still see their faces, frozen, as the torrent swallowed us.

The water didn't just pull—it hurled us. It spun me under, spat me out, dragged me back. No direction. No thought. Just one command: Breathe. Fight. Breathe. Fight. Steal a gasp before the ocean claims it back.

The water wasn't just water—it was a foaming, roaring wolf. I felt it all: wreckage, shattered trees, bits of buildings… and bodies.

Tangled shapes slammed into me—limp or fighting, I couldn't tell. A giant washing machine from hell.

I was half-conscious, but I couldn't black out. If I did, I was done. Tina's hand in mine was the only thing anchoring me to life. I couldn't save that family—but I could save her. My grip became a clamp. My mind locked onto her survival, not mine.

We rode the raging sea side by side. The current tried to rip us apart.

My body screamed, but I refused to let go.

Then we were hurled out into a wider street. Still savage, but less murderous. Shops lined both sides, brick buildings. Solid. A funnel.

171

I broke the surface, gasping, arms cinched around Tina's waist. Doorway tops peeked above the flood. The world was gone.

Tina drifted limp—until her arms shot out, clinging to a doorway. She anchored herself. I kept sliding. The current yanked at us, and I clamped around her ankles, locking on like a human G-clamp.

She held on. I held her.

The water thundered. My lungs begged for air. I clawed up her body inch by inch. Just before blackout—I broke the surface.

Then everything shifted.

The door exploded inward. Water found its exit and formed a whirlpool. Tina was closer. Her grip couldn't hold. I had to let go—or drown her.

She vanished into the shop's mouth, feet first.

Instinct overrode fear: I fought the pull trying to rip me away, then lunged forward, I found the vortex, the right moment, and was sucked straight into the shop after her.

I surfaced inside a different world. Outside had been a maelstrom. In here, an eerie hush. The water rose steadily, but slower. Chairs, desks, debris bobbed around us. Floating toward the back wall.

People drifted too—pressed to the ceiling. Moaning softly. Not screaming. The sound of people who'd already surrendered.

Tina doggy-paddled toward the back. I lunged, grabbed her leg. She spun, wide-eyed—but awake. We clung to each other, hands pressed to the ceiling.

"There's no way out that way!" I shouted. "No windows. No exits."

Her eyes flickered with fight.

Move. Don't think. Just Do.

"Trust me. I'll be back. Don't move."

Before she could argue, I dived. Sliced into the dark. Aimed for the break of light.

I smashed through junk, pulled myself through the tiny opening, emerged into open water. Broke the surface. Gasped.

No time. Back down. Kicked off the wall. Muscles screaming. Get Tina out. Now.

Then—she was there. Swimming toward me. A ghost in the gloom.

We collided, clutched hands, pivoted. Together we kicked for the door. Broke through. Burst into the air outside—gasping, clinging, alive.

The air stank of salt and carnage. But it was air.

We clung to the roof's edge, too dazed to speak.

Not fine.

Just breathing.

"It's calmer," I panted. My mind scrambled: chaos outside, eerie stillness inside, now this limbo—half-drowned, half-alive.

"Up," I rasped. "Grab the roof. Climb."

I ducked under, held my breath, braced, and boosted her up.

Then more survivors surfaced—pale, gasping. No time for questions. Just lift. Grab. Hoist.

Again and again I dived, kicked, shoved them upward. Tina pulled from above. I pushed from below. My body begged for mercy.

One more. One more.

The last woman was heavy—forcing me under. I fought. Arms like jelly. I was slipping.

Then—hands grabbed her shoulders. The others pulled her up.

Together, we saved her.

I clung to the edge, lungs ripping at the air.

"I'm so tired," I croaked.

I couldn't pull myself up. Then hands. More pulling. I flopped onto the tiles, staring at the sky. Salt crusted my lips. Around me: survivors, silence, stunned faces.

Somehow, we were still here.

Around us, buildings stood like tombstones.

What the fuck. One minute I was checking emails. The next, lying on a roof, surrounded by an ocean that had no right being there. The sound of waves lapping the tiles was almost peaceful. But the reality clung to me like salt on skin.

The island was gutted. Only these buildings stood—like ribs in a watery skeleton. Funnelled to safety.

A dozen of us perched on that roof. Tina sat with her back against the slope, soaked and shivering. Others cried. Some just stared. I dragged myself beside her. My breath still ragged. My mind spinning.

The ocean stretched out where streets and shops should've been.

I turned to the local man beside me and blurted, "Has this happened before?"

'Stupid idiot!' Like tsunamis visited every Sunday. Shame flushed my face.

Later, I'd learn the full horror. The island was hit from both sides. Waves colliding. A landmass just over nine square kilometres, barely a metre above sea level. It was a miracle anything remained.

By sheer luck, we'd washed into a street with some of the only brick buildings on the island. The wolf couldn't blow hard enough.

We watched the massage shop across the way—our measuring stick. The water receded. Its sign reappeared:

Head Massage – 100B
Foot Massage – 80B
Full Body Massage – 200B

Relief fluttered in my chest. Maybe it was over.

Then the water rose again—faster this time. The letters vanished. One by one.

Fear cracked through us like lightning. We yelled. Prayed. Cursed.

And then—it stopped. Hovered, menacing, just below the eaves.

Back in Rada's office, my voice cracked. "I want to stop. Can I stop now? Please."

She nodded, gentle. "Of course. Take a breath. You did so well."

I gulped air thick with ghosts. In the flood, I was all reflex. All survival. But on this soft couch, panic finally caught up.

I shook. Exhausted. Hollow.

The regression had taken me deeper than I'd expected. Deeper than I wanted. I could still smell the air. Feel the panic. Taste the fear.

Rada's voice reached me. "Tell me about being trapped in the shop. How that felt?"

"I handled it," I said, brushing past the terror. "It was fast. No time to think."

"No fear? No panic?"

"No. I was fine."

Fine.

I'd been trained by a misspent youth. I trusted water. In that moment, I was calm.

"Really?" she pressed. "No fear of drowning? Think, John. You must have been terrified."

I shook my head. "I was fine. Calculated. I knew I had to get to the front. No other way out. I didn't feel like I was going to drown."

Fine: Adjective – True meaning 3) Not OK. Sick or injured but afraid to admit it.

Clearly not fine. Not on this couch. Not back then.

"I wasn't afraid," I whispered. "I was in control. I knew what to do. I was calm."

Rada wasn't convinced. "John, I need you to really think back. You couldn't breathe."

"I am," I said, closing my eyes. I could see the walls, the water inching up, furniture floating toward the ceiling. It all appeared in sequence, each element assembling itself like the scene from *The Matrix*, when Neo enters the training simulation. The Construct—stark white, empty, then populated with furniture, code.

The tomb.

"I'm there".

"Tell me."

"I'm calm. I'm in control."

Not my tomb.

She pressed harder. "No. When you were under the water—couldn't breathe. What did you feel?"

"It's okay," I said. "I saw the light. I knew where to go. I didn't feel fear."

She exhaled. "Okay. I need you to breathe deeply. Think hard. You were nearly drowning. It must have been terrifying. Focus on that moment. When you couldn't breathe."

I paused. "No... I don't think so. I'm not scared. Wait..."

The words caught. A different memory surfaced. Something buried.

The room disappeared, and suddenly, the water pushed me under. It flowed out of the panic room, pushing me with it.

Into another pool. In another time.

I couldn't breathe. Panic seized me.

I was drowning.

I sat bolt upright, heart racing.

"I can't breathe. I'm dying."

'The trials you face will introduce you to your strengths.'
Epictetus

Twenty Five
The Waterboy

Summer 1987
Portugal

Our family holiday when I was ten felt like a big adventure. The Algarve—sun, sea, cheap booze for the grown-ups, and ice cream for the kids—was the perfect escape for bored Brits.

We weren't alone: my mum's cousin and her family were coming too, which meant her son Jake—my ready-made best mate—was along for the ride. We were born just weeks apart, raised like brothers, and at that age where mischief and curiosity ran the show.

My mum didn't care for sightseeing or local delicacies. She was a professional sun worshipper. Factor 8 was laughable—coconut oil was her weapon of choice. Zero protection, maximum tannage. By the end of every holiday, her skin glowed bronze like no one else's.

My dad was her opposite: pale, hidden under the biggest parasol he could find. Ironically, a few years later, he found a mole on his shin—melanoma. Caught early: a few skin grafts, all clear.

My mum, who practically deep-fried herself under the sun, stayed lucky—at least with that cancer. The others would find her in time.

The heat was brutal. I'm no Michael Fish, but it was easily 35°C daily. By week's end, my shoulders were sizzled. Mum made me swim in a T-shirt, but it was too late—my first bout of third-degree burns, leaving battle scars in the form of freckles that stuck around long after the tan faded.

Our routine was classic Brit abroad: up at dawn to bag the best sunbeds, evenings in the clubhouse, repeat for a fortnight. My parents with their vodka and cokes, singing along to *Black Lace*, while me and Jake roamed the apartment complex.

178

Back when leaving your kids unattended in Portugal wasn't frowned upon.

That's when we met Mark—with freckles, a wide grin, and northern wit sharp enough to cut glass. We clicked instantly and he joined our band of intrepid explorers.

Next day, in my soggy T-shirt, we followed Mark to a nearby hotel pool he'd found.

It was massive compared to ours, with no lifeguards—*Baywatch* had yet to make it a cool, or necessary, profession. Two pools side by side: one shallow, one deep, separated by a wall with a laptop-sized hole to balance the water. Our dare? Swim through the hole, pop out in the deep end, touch the bottom, surface. Easy.

Water was my element. Dad taught me everything. From the age of four, every weekend without fail, he'd take me to the pool at Elephant and Castle. I learned the basics there and tackled the iconic wave machine every 20 minutes.

By the time primary school came, my confidence was unstoppable. Tuesdays meant Crystal Palace—Olympic length, super deep, and crowned with towering dive boards. I earned my stripes fast—certificates nailed, soon diving for bricks in my pyjamas, feeling untouchable.

Outside school, I lived for endless days at Brockwell Park Lido with Nick. Rain or shine: underwater races and breath-holding contests.

The Lido was South London at its best: music thumping from battered Casio stereos—Soul II Soul from one corner, Suzanne Vega's "Tom's Diner" drifting from another... "da da dur dur da da dur dur da..."

It was the soundtrack to one of the best summers I ever had.

So in Portugal, my confidence was sky-high. Water was my stage. So when Mark said, "Let's do the hole again, no mask this time," I didn't flinch.

Round one: smooth. Mark through. Jake through. My turn—easy.

Round two: Mark through, Jake through, my turn—and I got stuck.

Maybe the T-shirt snagged. Maybe I twisted wrong. But suddenly, I wasn't moving. My arms were pinned to my side, my head poking into the deep pool, but my body jammed.

Panic.

I thrashed—no give. Opened my eyes—chlorine stung—saw Jake, treading water, oblivious. My last air fled in bubbles as I screamed a muffled cry. Just as black spots danced in my eyes, hands grabbed my legs.

Mark shoved me free. I shot through, broke the surface gasping, lungs on fire. Mark bobbed up beside me, grinning through the scuba mask like he hadn't just saved my life.

Mitch Buchannon would've been proud.

I didn't say much after that. Embarrassed, rattled—but I hid it. I curled up under a towel next to my mum, pretending to nap while my heart thumped out a new fear. I never told my parents. Too close to drowning, too young to grasp what almost happened.

By the time we flew home, the memory had sunk beneath the sunburn. A real trauma—tucked away for later.

Twenty Six
Die Another Day

6th August 2021
London

"How old were you when this happened?" Rada asked.

"About ten. Late '80s. I can't remember the exact year, but I remember the music in the clubhouse—Chaka Khan, La Bamba, Whitney Houston. Funny how clear it is now. I'd buried it for so long."

I knew exactly what Rada was probing for: that raw panic—the moment death taps your shoulder and you know you're powerless. It was vivid. Back then, I'd been terrified, completely helpless.

But it wasn't the same in the Panic Room.

"The feeling wasn't there in the room," I said. "I never panicked or thought I'd drown. It's hard to explain—I was calm. It wasn't conscious—it just… happened." I hesitated.

It always felt arrogant to talk about this part. Like I was bragging about staying cool while everyone else lost their shit. But it wasn't that at all.

Some deep part of my brain just took over—steady, focused, automatic.

"I hate saying it out loud. It sounds like I'm an arsehole, 'Look how amazing I was.' You know what I mean?"

Rada leaned in, brow furrowed. "You think it sounds like bragging? John, you're not bragging. You're funny, you know that? You never accept praise for your courage. That wasn't some separate part of your brain—that was you. Your instinct. Your ability. You're really…

181

how do you say… humble."

I cringed at humble. I hated it. I wasn't brave. I just did what I had to —there was no choice. Writing this now feels as awkward as saying it then.

How do you write someone calling you humble without sounding like a dick? But maybe that's part of telling the truth—owning the uncomfortable bits too.

It wasn't pride or modesty. Just a fact: a kid who felt invincible in the water nearly drowned, and years later that same kid used those instincts to survive something far worse.

Was it muscle memory? A reflex? Maybe. But it was still me.

Rada watched me, nodding slowly. "You blame yourself for not saving that family, but you ran back into danger to save Tina. That was courage, John. You don't see it that way—for you, it was duty. But it was still brave."

Her words hit hard. I hated it—hated my part in all of it. Hated that Tina was there at all. Hated that I'd left her on the steps. Hated that when the wave hit, my first instinct had been to run.

Everything after that—saving her, fighting to survive—wasn't heroics. It was just… what had to be done. Anything less was unthinkable.

"I get it," I muttered. "But the guilt's different. I understand the anger now—it fired me up. But the guilt… fuck… it hurts."

"Tell me how you could have done more," she pushed.

"I don't know. I just… feel like I could've."

She shook her head, kind but firm. "You ran back into a tsunami. You tried to save a family. You escaped a flooding room, helped people climb to safety…" She laughed softly, handing me a tissue as tears welled up.

"Really, John. You've done more than enough already."

I wiped my eyes, feeling the truth in her words but not ready to wear it.

"Thank you. I'll try to feel proud. But the guilt—there was so much loss. What's there to celebrate?"

She paused, choosing her words. "It's not unusual for victims of major disasters to feel what we call 'survivor's guilt.'"

'Survivors. Victims. Victim?'

The word slammed into me, drowning out everything else. 'Victim? Me?'

No. The victims were the ones who died, or lost everything. Me? I walked away. No injuries, no lasting scars. How could I be a victim?

"...so John, this was a good session today," she said, her voice faint as my mind raced. "We uncovered some deeper layers, and I look forward to next week. Rest now—you'll feel this later."

"Yeah. I've got the day off. Last time wiped me out."

I left, but victim stuck to me like mastic. Real victims wore it in their eyes—the pain, the ruin. A victim was weak, someone who couldn't fight back. Uncle Frank had beaten that out of me long ago, right after I'd been on the receiving end of a grown-up's dry slap.

What did it mean for me now? Was I blind to my own scars?

The Tube doors opened. I wasn't even sure how I'd got there. Escalator up, AirPods in, world out.

I'm not a victim, I told myself. I'm here because of work stress. That's all. Sure, I survived a nightmare... but that was ages ago.

I looked it up: A victim is a person who has suffered harm, injury, or loss... including natural disasters. Fuck.

There it was. In black and white. Not so easy to argue with.

Maybe I was a victim. Or a victim of circumstance. Maybe.

That near-drowning memory had cracked something open—a domino effect, pushing me to question it all. Those fun childhood days —how fun were they really? The estate years felt legendary then: danger woven into daily life. For us, danger was normal.

I found a seat at the back of the bus, AirPods still in, shutting out the engine's hum but not the questions. Hunched in my corner, I let my mind drift—revisiting the glory days with new eyes. 'Was I normal? Or had I always been blind to risk?'

I'd thought surviving a tsunami was normal. Maybe I wasn't the best judge.

Aside from being the local water-boys, Nick and I were nuisances. Not full-blown troublemakers—but far from angels. Climbing was our favourite thing: buildings, walls, rooftops—if it could be scaled, we were on it. No amount of anti-climb paint or barbed wire stopped us. The estates, schools, parks, and shops were one giant urban playground.

Long before parkour was even a real word, we were competing. Testing our limits.

The woods behind the estate were perfect for a couple of reckless kids. Tall trees begged to be climbed. Jackie Chan's tree trick—we tried it constantly. You had to find the right tree—bendy but strong. I misjudged once: wrong tree, wrong angle. It cracked, sent me crashing through branches into a pile of rubble, half the tree on top of me. All I got was a bruised arse and a good laugh.

No broken bones, no plastic insert for my skull. Lucky.

A railway track ran alongside the woods. A chain-link fence was all that separated us from the main line trains. Easy to climb, crawl under, or snip open. And we did—walking the tracks for miles, sometimes all the way to Crystal Palace.

Kids in London loved playing on the tracks. Teachers showed us every deterrent they could find—movies with kids on the line, their shoelaces stuck, ketchup for blood, limbs scattered—but like any kids, we thought we knew better.

One day, we pushed it too far. It started with a dare: run to the other side and back before a train came. We vaulted tracks like Ed Moses, laughing, hearts thumping.

We escalated: placing stones on the tracks to watch them flatten into shiny discs. Pennies doubled in size.

Then Nick upped the stakes: "Put one on the middle rail."

"Alright," I said, clueless that the middle rail was live.

I thought the challenge was distance, not death. I grabbed a rock, sprinted, cleared the first track, knelt down—instant heat seared my hand. I bolted back, adrenaline spiking. Only later did I clock it: the rock melted on contact, branding a deep black hole in my middle finger.

If I'd been holding a conductor, like a coin, I'd have fried on the spot.

Jesus—closer than I remembered. And recounting this tale has just reminded me. A few years later, my old next-door neighbour died on those tracks. I'd already moved to Eltham, but the story reached me quickly.

Same age, same spot, same silly games.

Damn.

The estate itself was a death trap masquerading as a playground. Every couple of years, they'd rig up scaffolding to clean the flats. No barriers, no alarms—an open invitation for wannabe ninjas. We climbed them, hopping rooftop to rooftop. Whatever one of us did, the other copied.

We felt invincible.

At the peak of the ninja movie craze, we made our own gang. No costumes, just balaclavas and black clothes. We must've looked more like burglars than shinobi. I'd sneak out my bedroom window at night, shimmy down the drainpipe, meet the others under the streetlights. We split into teams, hide-and-seek style, but the real thrill was the chase.

Once I hit the scaffold, no one could catch me.

My boldest stunt: jumping from the top floor, six stories up, grabbing the pulley rope used for hauling bricks, swinging two or three stories down, landing back on the scaffolding, ducking just in time to miss the metal poles jutting out. Exhilarating doesn't cover it.

Looking back, I wonder how we didn't die. Running, jumping, diving off buildings—we flirted with disaster daily.

It all seems mad now, but that was our world. By ten, I was streetwise, fast, agile, fearless—or so I thought.

Beyond the badly thought-out stunts, I learned a very particular set of skills on that estate, skills acquired over a very long career... Skills that may seem useless on the surface, but one day, one day in the distant future, they would be all too essential.

Excuse the Liam Neeson moment—couldn't resist. But weirdly, that dangerous childhood did prep me for what came later.

Who knows how many times death had an easy chance but let me off? Fall from a rooftop, zapped by a rail, hit by a train. Drowned. In some parallel universe, a thousand versions of me didn't make it.

But here I am—the last John standing. In this strange branch of the multiverse, hoping he makes it to the end.

The Prime.

'Be kind, for everyone you meet is fighting a great battle.'
Ian Maclaren

Twenty Seven
Don't look Up

12th August 2021
London

I was starting to get used to the process. Every session began the same way: arrive, bag of nerves, terrified of what I was about to dig up. Pleasantries, shoes off, slump on the couch—then sink back into the past.

Rada would guide me, inch by inch, back to another slice of that hellish day. I'd exhale, eyes shut, head down, until I was staring at my younger self's lap. Bare feet—dirty, but uncut.

"I'm sitting on the roof, and I can't sit still," I said, the memory pressing down like a weight. "I'm out of breath, fidgeting. Watching the water on the shop across the street. Trying to think—but I can't. What the fuck just happened?"

The water had drained like someone had yanked out a giant plug. One moment, we were clinging to the roof thinking this was it—the next, it receded like it had never been there. Down and up, over and over. I was sure the next surge would take us all out. The uncertainty was torture.

Don't look up, John. Don't look up.

"John, what's going on?" Rada's voice anchored me.

I didn't answer. If I didn't look up, maybe I could stay frozen here—safe in denial. Just feet and flip-flop tan lines. Don't look up. Don't see it.

"John? What are you thinking?" she pressed.

"I… I don't know. Confused. Tired," I mumbled. "We're still alive!"

"Where is Tina?"

"Next to me. She's fine… I checked. Not hurt. Just… normal. Like nothing happened."

"And the water?"

"It's going down. The massage shop's nearly clear…"

The words snagged in my throat as emotion clawed up my chest.

I was staring at the shop, trying to believe it was over. Then I saw him —a man emerged, drenched, trousers shredded, bare-chested, cradling something. A small, lifeless shape.

A baby.

The cloud in my head vanished, replaced by a cold, brutal clarity. Not an accident. Not a pipe burst. This was real tragedy.

Sonic boom to the heart.

The man collapsed, wailing. That sound cracked the last pieces of denial. I turned away, but the image burned itself in anyway.

"Open your eyes, John. Take a moment," Rada coaxed.

I was sobbing. Proper, gut-wrenching sobs. I hadn't even felt the tears whilst in my trance.

"This is powerful. Let's process it," Rada said softly. "We'll do some EMDR, okay?"

"Yeah…" I croaked, dragging a sleeve across my face.

I started tapping my chest, trying to untangle the storm inside. Sadness for that father. Fear for what he'd endured. Guilt that I was still here, just watching.

The baby's tiny, limp body—that oversized nappy, sodden and loose.

It wasn't fair. Babies aren't supposed to die like that. But they did. And I'd carry that sight forever.

No one else needed that burden—not Tina. She hadn't seen it, or maybe she'd checked out. Either way, I kept it locked up. I didn't want it. It's one I wish I could ditch. Leave on the cutting room floor.

I shifted on the couch, but Rada's voice couldn't drown it out. Nothing she said could change what I'd seen. No therapy could erase that baby from my mind.

"Ground yourself, John," she soothed. "You're here. You're safe. Feel the fabric."

I gripped the armrest, made fists with my toes, breathed deep. It helped—barely.

"You stayed with Tina," she said gently. "You made sure she was safe. That's something to be proud of."

I nodded. Logically, maybe. But words were just words. They didn't stop the loop: the baby, the father's screams, the truth that nothing I did could change it. Talking didn't fix that.

"When you're ready, let's go back in."

Back on the roof, Tina's voice cut through the fog. She was talking about New Zealand—our next stop after this so-called holiday of a lifetime. Her words snapped me back just as the grief threatened to drown me. She was planning our future while I was mentally digging graves for our friends.

'New Zealand?' I thought. 'I'm not going to New Zealand. I'm going home.'

"It depends who's dead, doesn't it?" I snapped.

Cruel joke. Wrong moment. But when death's in the room, sometimes the only words left are the wrong ones.

She didn't react. She was gone—lost in some other place, oblivious to where my head was at.

Barry. Lisbeth. Dead, probably. The baby proved death wasn't picky.

Not again. Please not more friends. Not Bazza. Please lads, shine down on Bazza… Lucky Barry, come on.

"I feel anger again," I muttered. "I know it's misplaced. I get that now. But then? I was livid she was talking about flights while I was terrified our friends were dead."

Rada's eyes softened. "What else?"

"Guilt," I said, voice raw. "She wouldn't have been there if it weren't for me. I shouldn't have been angry. It wasn't her fault."

I knew she was right—logic said so. But guilt ignores logic. Hate creeps in where reason fails. I hated myself for it.

I was exhausted—clinging to a rooftop in my mind, weak, drained, hollowed out.

So I slammed the door on it all. No more feelings. Not yet. We were still in the shit. Tina was hanging by a thread—I couldn't unravel too. The baby, the dead, the talk for New Zealand—it all blurred as I braced for what was next.

I had friends to find. It wasn't over.

Don't think.

Just do.

'You can plan for a hundred years. But you don't know what will happen the next moment.'
Neem Karoli Baba

Twenty Eight
Ordinary People

12th August 2021
London

This session was spiralling fast. Dark images crashing in like waves. The weight of it pressed on my chest, suffocating every other thought. We'd barely started and I was already in full flight mode—every cell begging to bolt, barefoot if I had to, down the street and away from Rada's questions.

Over the weeks, I'd braced myself to relive Boxing Day, but today wasn't about that. Today we cracked open a sealed door. I'd always known it was there—whenever babies came up in conversation, a warning light blinked: don't forget me. And I'd slam it shut again.

Easier that way. But here it was, wide open, waiting to pull me under.

Beyond the obvious trauma, therapy was digging up layers I hadn't known were there. Two weeks ago, I didn't even think I had scars from the tsunami. Now I was peeling back more than one nightmare, unearthing childhood wounds I'd ignored for decades.

It felt like coming here for one problem and discovering an entire back catalogue of unresolved shit.

Enlightening. Terrifying.

I remember so much. It all plays out in HD. But can I trust it? Forty-six years—that's over sixteen thousand days. And yet, only snippets survive.

Our brains record fragments, distorted each time we replay them. The rest is lost—or protected, walled off so it can't hurt us.

What I do remember is sharp. Painfully so. That's just how my head works.

Lucky me.

"Are you happy to continue?" Rada asked, pulling me back.

Not really. My mind was stuck in a loop. But I couldn't walk out. Might as well get on with it.

"You were telling me about the roof. What happened next? Focus on that."

Easier said than done. The man and the baby were still front and centre. It took everything I had to steady my breathing and drag myself back up there.

In my mind's VR headset, I scanned the rooftop. People huddled close, fear crackling in the air, the stench creeping in. The heat was brutal. My feet burned on the tiles. I shifted, trying to ease the scorch.

"Bloody hot, isn't it?" I muttered, mostly to myself. Sweat stung my eyes, salt from the seawater burned my skin.

"Yeah, boiling. Here, try this." A woman next to me poured water on the roof. For a moment, the tiles cooled under my calves.

It was absurd—in the middle of a nightmare, we were making small talk about the weather.

But the heat wasn't the real problem. We couldn't stay here. If the water came back, we'd be washed away.

I scanned the street looking for options—Tina was chatting with the woman, other survivors clustered together. I shuffled away, mind racing.

We needed off this roof. Now.

Behind us, the hotel. A plan formed. Heart pounding, I edged along the roof peak, measuring the jump. No time to overthink. I slid down the back slope, feet bracing, then leapt to the hotel's first-floor balcony with the ease of someone who'd spent too many childhood afternoons defying gravity.

Solid landing. Vaulted over.

Easy—I'd done riskier jumps a hundred times.

Inside, empty. The water hadn't reached this high. Tables abandoned mid-breakfast. I moved fast—through the room, into the corridor, down the staircase.

Below, debris littered the street but it was passable. Survivors were heading to the Reggae Bar—higher ground. Good enough for me. But my jump? No chance everyone could do it.

I scanned for an alternative—spotted a scaffold plank, sturdy enough. Grabbed it and bolted back upstairs.

"Tina!" I yelled. She turned, more alert now. I laid the plank across the gap. A man—the lady's husband?—edged closer, grabbing the end and anchoring it. I tested it. Solid.

"It's safe. Come on, one at a time!" I called.

I crossed first to show it was fine. Just a couple feet, but a slip could be deadly. The group gathered, eyes darting between the roof and the hotel.

My voice left no room for debate.

"You can stay here if you want, but the hotel's safer. And the Reggae Bar's higher ground. People are gathering there. We move now, before the water comes back."

That did it. Fear broke their paralysis. The husband braced on the balcony while I stayed halfway up the slope, guiding each person down to the plank. No ledge—one wrong step and it was a straight drop.

I gripped hands tight, didn't let go until each pair of feet was planted safely on the other side. The sun roasted my soles raw but I ignored it.

One by one, they crossed—six, maybe eight people. When the last crossed, I herded them inside. Some moved to the top floor—sensible. But I couldn't sit still. Barry and Lisbeth were out there somewhere.

"We should go to the Reggae Bar. People are gathering there."

"We'll come too," said the couple Tina had befriended. Their accents made them Kiwis.

"Right. Let's move."

We stepped out into the street—or what used to be a street. Now it was a foul swamp: oil, petrol, sewage, broken timber, and random debris mashed into a stinking slick. No time to dwell on it. If the sea came back, ground level was a death trap.

I grabbed Tina's hand, and we pushed on, wading through the sludge, over fallen trees, weaving around smashed buildings.

The Reggae Bar was just ahead—three storeys tall, still standing. It loomed like a lighthouse in a sea of ruin. Nearby, the Rolling Stoned Bar was a heap of splintered memories—only hours ago we'd danced there, carefree. Now it was gone.

Inside the Reggae Bar, the ground floor was gutted—walls ripped away. We climbed to the second floor, past the battered Muay Thai ring, its "FREE WHISKEY!" sign hanging absurdly intact.

The higher we went, the louder the hum of voices. Survivors. Dozens of them. Faces pale, clothes ragged, eyes vacant. Ordinary people, spit out by the ocean and clinging to whatever scraps of hope were left.

I scanned the crowd. Barry? Lisbeth? Nok? Nowhere. I swallowed the rising dread and focused on keeping Tina close.

We found a spot and collapsed, lungs burning, legs jelly. All around us, people sat in shock—some sobbing quietly, others staring at nothing.

Minutes blurred—fifteen? Thirty? Who knew. Voices cut through the murmur: "Mummy! Where are you?"…"Blake! Daddy's here! Please son where are you?"

Each call punched through my chest. Raw desperation filled every corner.

I needed to move. Sitting still made it worse. I got up and walked the floor, eyes raking every face. Nothing. The bar had become a nerve centre, scraps of info traded in hushed voices.

A kid tugged my arm: "Have you seen my mum?"

I knelt down, forced a steady tone. "I'm sorry sweetheart. She'll come. Promise."

Lies, maybe. What else could I say? I hated it. So many wandering ghosts. My friends. Out there somewhere? Trapped under some fallen building, bleeding out, desperate for help. I couldn't stand it.

Without a word to Tina, I pushed back into the street.

The scene was apocalyptic. The silence hit me—an eerie hush broken only by distant shouts. Each step sank me deeper into filth.

Then I saw them: a few guys struggling with a body outside a shop. The bass player from the band locked eyes with me. No words. Just pain. He waved me off—they had it.

I turned away, throat tight. Later, I'd learn it was his brother, pulled from the rubble of their tattoo shop.

I reached the beach—or what was left of it. A graveyard of sludge and broken dreams. The ocean had vanished again, sucked far out, exposing black mud and garbage. I stood there, numb, feet sinking.

What am I doing? Barry would head to the Reggae Bar. I was being an idiot, risking more.

And Tina—I'd promised her I wouldn't wander off. I spun back, wading through the same filth, each step heavy with dread and shame.

195

Tina's face lit up when she saw me. "Where've you been?"

"I'm sorry," I whispered. "I had to look. Nothing out there. It's all gone."

She didn't scold me—just squeezed my hand. Promise: I wouldn't leave again.

We sat with the Kiwi couple, an unspoken bond in the middle of ruin. More survivors trickled in. Hope flickered—maybe Barry would walk through the door any second.

But panic kept sparking too. Rumours of another wave flew like arrows:

"It's coming! It's coming!"

Each time, hysteria boiled up, then fizzled out.

The fifth false alarm broke me—I snapped, screamed at the ceiling. A primal release. It helped. For a moment.

The bar morphed into a makeshift hospital. The injured lined the floor. A woman—clearly a nurse or doctor—barked orders, patching wounds with whatever she could find.

Then someone shoved a man in front of me—blood streaming from a cut on his scalp.

"Sort this!"

I froze. My mind blanked. St. John's Ambulance training? Gone. Basic first aid? Gone. Just blood, and my useless hands.

"Help me?" I begged a passing woman who looked like she knew what she was doing.

She tossed me a water bottle. "Clean it, cover it."

Obvious. Embarrassment burned my face. I rinsed the cut, pressed paper towels to it.

"Hold this tight," I told the man. Small victory. Focus returned.

"What else can I do?" I asked the medic, desperate to stay useful.

"Come on. Clean wounds. Talk to them. Keep them calm."

I found a man in the corner, pale as a ghost, staring at nothing. His leg was torn open between the knee and ankle. It was bad. Flesh severed to the bone. Blood seeping from the wound, barely hanging on.

My earlier hesitation was gone. I found a box of nappies—perfect makeshift bandages. Wrapped them with gaffer tape. It wasn't pretty, but it would stop the infection from setting in.

"Where were you when it hit?"

"Diving," he murmured, voice distant. "Deep. Got thrown into coral."

Small talk. Anything to keep him conscious.

Suddenly the medic's voice rose: "I need painkillers! Anything!"

A scruffy, half-naked lad shuffled up, holding a baggie of blue pills.

"Valium!" he declared proudly.

"How strong?"

"The good 'uns!" he grinned, thick Cockney accent cutting through the gloom.

"10s?"

"Yeah, the pukka ones!"

It was darkly hilarious—Christmas party stash turned into triage supplies. It was like a scene from *Trainspotting*, if Begbie had been lost in a war zone.

"Can you check other buildings?" the medic asked me. "Pills, medical supplies, anything you can find."

I nodded. Helping people kept my head straight.

I darted out again—searching crumbling shops, climbing over doors, rummaging through drawers. No meds. But in a dive shop, I spotted an oxygen tank drifting in filthy water. I hauled it back like a treasure.

Back at the bar, I rigged the tank, strapped the mask on the diver. His breaths rasped under the hiss of oxygen. I sat with him a moment, watching his chest rise and fall, wondering: 'Is this enough?'

When I rejoined Tina and the Kiwis, the Valium kid gave us a moment of grim relief. We let it come. It didn't fix anything, but for a few seconds, we could breathe.

I leaned against the wall, head back, exhaustion pressing down. Maybe, just maybe, we'd made it through the worst.

But beneath the silence, the fear pulsed like a heartbeat. Another wave? Another horror?

It wasn't over. Not by a long shot.

For now, we sat in the quiet.

Waiting to die.

'The soul becomes dyed with the colour of its thoughts.'
Marcus Aurelius

Twenty Nine
Stand By Me

14th August 2021
London

I carried the weight of Thursday's session for days. This time, I wasn't watching from a safe distance—I was right back there, inside it. Every conversation, every terrified glance, every smell flooded my mind, dragging me deeper into that nightmare.

It consumed everything. I couldn't think straight. Even the simplest tasks felt impossible. I couldn't talk to anyone. Everything felt wrong. Every word I said was sharp. Every reaction overblown. In short: I was a prick.

I needed out. I needed peace.

Peace—that elusive thing. How do you find it when the noise of modern life never quits? Texts, emails, calls piling on more demands. I was drowning in it. I had to shut it down.

Bye bye Buzby. I was done talking.

First, I silenced my phone. No notifications, no pings. Then I went further: I left every WhatsApp group without a word. No explanations, no goodbyes—just gone. It felt incredible. For good measure, I dumped the phone on the bedroom floor. Out of sight. Out of mind. Mostly.

But it tugged at me anyway—that little devil whispering: Just check. Something might be happening.

Not this time. I refused. I needed space—my mind was chaos and I had to clear it or drown in my own thoughts. If I kept scrolling, I'd just feed the anxiety, doom-scrolling through memories, stacking worry on top of worry until the weekend vanished into the digital black hole.

199

I was already on a mental tightrope—one slip and I'd fall hard.

I needed to mute the world and focus on fixing myself.

Part of me was doing the work: therapy, staying clean, moving forward. But another part of me was a mess—obsessive, restless, one step from a meltdown.

Quitting the chat groups wasn't just about peace and quiet—it was about freedom. I'd turned into a slave to every ding. Keeping up with banter, the digs, the constant chatter—it was killing me. Negativity outweighed any comfort I got from pretending I was part of it all.

Some days I'd look at my phone and see a hundred unread messages —from one group. One app. I'd clear it, only to feel the itch to dive back in five minutes later. It was endless. It sucked the energy out of me, and I hadn't even realised how much until I cut the cord.

I'd been tethered to a slot machine I couldn't stop pulling.

An addict, without knowing it.

It's a crazy world. For all its so-called connectivity, I'd never felt lonelier. Everywhere I looked, people were glued to screens—even when they were together.

What happened to the glory days? Begging for sleepovers just to squeeze out a few more hours together. Being together was the main event—not an afterthought.

Late-night video games, squashed around an old TV, tangled controller cords at our feet, fighting over Paperboy, Sonic, or Mario. And now? We play online, alone in dark rooms, swearing at strangers on headsets. The connection's gone.

I miss it—the camaraderie, the thrill of loading a ZX Spectrum, waiting twenty minutes only to get Failure to Compute. "Semtex Error"—whatever the hell that meant.

Lonely. Bam. There it was. I hadn't clocked it properly until now, but that emptiness was the same ache I'd dragged home from Thailand that first time. Back then, my friends were a continent away. Now they were local—but hidden behind a digital curtain.

I'd drifted, not by one big decision, but by a thousand tiny ones. Small life edits that quietly locked me into isolation. Maybe I was built for it —my default setting when my head went south was to bolt the doors and vanish inside myself.

Sure, I had loads of mates. But I wasn't close to any of them anymore.

Except Meg.

Meg was my anchor—my best friend. She knew how to keep me steady when I couldn't steady myself. Long walks, rummaging through markets, lazy sofa days lost in binge-worthy TV. She always knew what I needed before I did. This weekend was no different.

We caught the train to my old neck of the woods. My estate, school, and hangouts.

A walk down memory lane. The happy alleyways.

Stopping at hipster coffee spots for overpriced lattes and flaky croissants. We wandered side streets splashed with bold street art— gentrification mid-step.

The walk through Crystal Palace Park was a trip. There was the swimming pool, where I honed my survival skills. We passed the giant plastic dinosaurs by the lake—childhood landmarks for every local kid. Back then, I barely noticed them. This time, I lingered, snapping photos, reading plaques I'd never bothered with.

They'd stood there since 1854, the original 'Dinosaur Court': the world's first life-sized prehistoric sculptures. Now a Grade I-listed wonder. Beasts hiding in plain sight my whole life.

Strange how something that monumental can vanish from your memory—until the right person reminds you to look up.

Everywhere I looked now was a trigger for long-forgotten incidents.

No near-death experiences this time, but as I surveyed the skate park and the Roman ruins, I could count at least three serious concussions.

Good days, despite the repeated head trauma.

Those memories danced in my head, fencing with the darker thoughts therapy had dredged up—an unplanned riposte that lifted my spirits.

Good vs. bad, the eternal match. And I was smack in the middle.

By the time we reached the heart of the park, it felt like I'd slayed the demons from Thursday's session.

"What an excellent day for an exorcism." Wandering old haunts, poking at childhood memory gaps.

Maybe all those knocks to the head explain my Swiss-cheese memory more than age does. Or maybe it's the PTSD. Or maybe something else entirely—the so-called Homer Simpson Effect: remembering one thing wipes out other, similar memories.

Neuroscientists back it up—retrieving a memory can make related ones inaccessible. It's unsettling when you think about it. By middle age, you've probably overwritten half your life just by replaying your greatest hits.

Life imitating *The Simpsons*. Homer was right: "Remember when I took that home-wine making course and forgot how to drive?"

Marge blamed the booze—but maybe the brain does just push out the old for the new.

Makes you think.

Anyway—back to this memory before I erase it.

On the train ride home, though, old habits crept back. I slipped straight into Instagram—looking up facts about the park . Lost in my phone.

And then it hit me harder than ever: for all the ways Insta had helped me explore, document, and distract myself, it was stealing my now.

It was pulling me away from the only person who always put me first. Meg.

I looked over at her—content, oblivious to the fact I was half here, half lost in my feed.

The guilt hit like a slap. This endless need to scroll, update, stay 'connected'—it was stealing the only thing that mattered: real connection.

With her.

Right there on that train, I deleted the app.

This summer, I'd focus on the present. On real love, real people, real life.

No more virtual insanity.

'We suffer more often in imagination than in reality.'
Seneca

Thirty
They Live

Boxing Day 2004
Koh Phi Phi

The wait was unbearable. Where were they? What had happened? Possibilities crowded my mind, each more horrifying than the last. Dead, dead, dead. The word pounded inside my skull like relentless tinnitus—a buzzing I couldn't silence. It wore me down, trying to crush any last bit of hope.

I fought it, clinging to the belief that Barry—the whole gang—had made it. If we were alive, they could be too. They had to be.

Barry, of all people, was too charmed. Lady Luck always had his back, like he carried a hidden amulet no disaster could touch. 'Barry's fine,' I repeated like a mantra. He has to be.

I clasped my hands, mimicking the father I'd seen earlier—not praying to gods, but to The Lads. "Please look after Barry. Keep him safe. Please."

We were the lucky ones in that makeshift rescue centre—but no one felt lucky. Not then. Fear, dread, grief. It clung to every blank stare, every wounded body, every quiet sob.

Some injuries were obvious; others buried so deep they'd never fully heal. I hadn't so much as a scratch, which somehow made it worse—like I was a ghost drifting through someone else's horror.

I don't belong here.

The minutes crawled by, each one an amplifier for my guilt. 'What if they're still out there? Hurt? Dying?'

I sat there chewing my lip, staring at the door, begging the universe for a sign. 'Poseidon, Neptune, Aegir—whoever's listening, get him through this. I swear I'll be good if you do.'

Every time someone stumbled in, I held my breath—hope flaring, then dying when it wasn't him. Faces fell. Silent sobs. Each new arrival ramped up the guilt. 'What the fuck am I doing here? I should be out there. What if he needs me?'

My fists clenched so tight my nails dug bloody half-moons into my palms. 'Barry. Where the fuck are you?'

I was seconds from bolting when Tina's hand closed on my arm. Her voice—soft but iron:

"No. Don't leave me. You can't go back out there."

I didn't answer. Just nodded, eyes burning. Inside, I was unravelling. Schrödinger's cat—alive or dead. "What's in the fucking box, man?!"

Then—movement. A shape at the staircase. I blinked, certain I was hallucinating.

Barry!

His mop of hair. His grin. Alive.

Alive!

Relief hit so hard my legs buckled. I didn't care how ridiculous I looked—I just stumbled forward.

"John!"

We slammed together in a hug. For the first time since the wave hit, I could breathe again.

"You're alive," I rasped, half to him, half to the universe. Praise Odin.

Thanks, Lads. He's alive.

When we finally pulled apart, we just stared at each other, speechless.

Words weren't needed—the relief, the gratitude, the love—it was all there, unspoken, in our eyes.

Barry shook his head, half-laughing through shock. "I can't believe you're alive!"

I swallowed the lump in my throat. "What about the others?"

"They're okay," he said, grinning wide. "Everyone's heading up to the viewpoint. Come on—Lisbeth, Camilla, Michael… even Nok. All safe."

All of them? The words sank in slowly. Disbelief mingled with a fragile, fierce hope. Against all odds—we'd all survived.

Relief washed through me, but the guilt stayed. Pure, stupid luck—that's all it was.

The dread of another wave still hovered in every glance toward the sea. We'd lingered too long in that wrecked bar, drained to the bone. But now, with Barry back, it felt like a dam had burst. We had purpose. We were moving—not just waiting to die anymore.

Barry turned, gesturing to the quiet figure hovering behind him.

"This is Tyler," he said. "He helped me look for you—and he's searching for his mate, James."

Tyler stepped forward, hope and fear written all over him. He shook my hand fast, words tumbling out:

"Have you seen him? James—my best friend."

A knot twisted in my stomach. Tyler's desperation slammed into the fragile bubble of joy we'd just found. His hope was raw, painful to look at. I knew that feeling too well—the soul-crushing limbo of not knowing.

He'd wandered the wasteland with Barry for near on six hours. It didn't feel right to celebrate when he was still praying for his miracle.

We set off again, pushing through the debris. Tyler walked beside us, scanning every broken shopfront, every shell of a bungalow, calling James's name.

With each shake of the head, Tyler's hope dimmed a fraction, and I felt it too—leaking out of me like a slow puncture.

I prayed quietly, bargaining with The Lads. 'One more time, please. Let him find James. He doesn't deserve this.'

But the plea felt hollow this time.

The emotional whiplash was brutal. Relief for Barry and the others— heartbreak for Tyler. It felt wrong to feel this happy when so many were still lost.

Every new survivor we passed offered a nod, a whisper of comfort, but none had seen James. I hated it—the unfairness of it all. I wanted to fix it. I couldn't.

Tyler's shoulders sagged more with every step.

He glanced up the path, voice cracking: "Maybe he's at the viewpoint. Maybe he's waiting there."

Please let him be right.

"I still can't believe it," I murmured to Barry as we hugged again, both of us clinging to the absurd, beautiful truth:

We're alive.

"Fucking hell, Bazza—you're here."

We fell into single file, threading through the wreckage toward higher ground. Each step felt heavy, like the island's misery had seeped into my bones. We retraced our steps past the broken shopfronts, the Reggae Bar shrinking behind us.

Viewpoint. Funny how many times Lisbeth had begged me to hike up there, and I'd always laughed it off. Now it was all I wanted: altitude, safety, distance from the sea.

Familiar landmarks blurred past, ghosts of paradise. The tattoo shop stood wide open, silent as a grave. Its regulars were long gone—one carried out wrapped in makeshift cloth.

I had turned back at this point. Barry hadn't given up. Good old Bazza.

The beach was a wasteland—the ocean sucked so far out it looked like a mudflat, littered with unrecognisable shapes. No one lingered; none of us wanted to stare at what had tried to kill us.

Barefoot, half-dressed, we trudged through filth and debris. Each breath scraped my chest as the incline bit into exhausted muscles. But we climbed anyway, glancing back now and then, half-expecting the sea to roar back for more.

We weren't alone. More survivors joined our slow procession, moving as one battered tribe. A nod here, a half-smile there—proof that even stripped bare, people still found ways to encourage each other.

Step by step, we rose out of the nightmare. Higher ground. Sanctuary. Maybe.

When the slope levelled off, I spotted them—perched near the viewpoint's edge, staring at the ruin below. My chest tightened.

"Nok! Lisbeth! Camilla! Michael!"

My voice cracked but carried enough. Lisbeth turned. For a heartbeat, she froze. Then sprinted at me. We collided in a crush of tears and relief—one more miracle in a day that shouldn't have had any left.

We pulled away just far enough to breathe. No words. None needed. Just grateful sobs and shaky smiles.

We drifted under a cluster of trees, collapsing onto the dirt, letting the thin shade wrap around our huddled group. For a moment, the horror felt far below, muffled by distance. Fragile safety—but safety all the same.

Rumours buzzed like flies: a huge earthquake near Indonesia or Malaysia, no one knew for sure. Didn't matter. What mattered was simple: it had birthed the monster that swallowed our island. A tsunami.

We now knew its name.

"The water came up, dropped, then came back," I said quietly, half to myself, half to anyone listening. "Must've been two waves."

"What if there's another one?" Lisbeth's voice trembled.

Barry squeezed her hand. "We're safe here. This is the highest point—nothing can touch us now. We wait it out, then we get rescued."

He sounded sure enough. I clung to it. One truth: we were alive, together, for now. And sometimes, for survivors, for now is everything.

My hangover had vanished the moment I bolted upright at that PC terminal—adrenaline erasing every trace. Now, with Barry beside me, exhaustion had replaced the buzz and the headache returned with a vengeance.

We were all running on fumes.

The viewpoint became a rough, open-air camp. People shared what scraps they had: a bottle of water here, half a chocolate bar there, a few clumps of sticky rice.

It wasn't much, but no one hoarded.

I'd read about disaster altruism—how crises pull strangers together. But seeing it in real life was humbling. One battered tribe, pooling everything, asking nothing in return.

Barry and I scavenged the woods for branches and leaves, trying to build something—anything—to lift us off the dirt.

Bear Grylls would've laughed at our sorry excuse for a bed. Years later, when my mind hit rock bottom, I'd binge his survival shows obsessively, memorising tricks for doomsdays that would never come. I wasn't sure when I'd need to know how to use urine, plastic, and a hole in the sand to make drinkable water, but I was unconsciously preparing—arming myself for whatever life might throw at me next.

Proper Preparation Prevents Piss Poor Performance. Dib Dib Dib. Dub Dub Dub.

Somehow, we lashed together a rough frame and lined it with coconut fronds. It wasn't much, but it kept the bugs off and the damp out.

"Quick, guys—come on!" Lisbeth's voice cut through the silence. "Someone's got a phone. We can text home—just once!"

A stranger. A battered Nokia, a half-dead battery, rigged together from salvage. One text per group, to save the precious charge.

"Who knows a number?" Barry asked.

"Only Joey's," I said. "He'll call my mum, she'll spread the word."

"I know my dad's," Tina said confidently.

It made more sense, so I didn't argue. She typed fast, hit send. The phone vanished again, switched off to save every ounce of power.

That was our link to the outside world. A single message in a bottle.

None of us slept that night. We lay shoulder to shoulder on our makeshift beds, staring up at stars that felt too bright, too normal, above a world that wasn't anymore.

Every rustle, every shout in the dark made my heart hammer. The weight of what we'd survived—and what might still come—pressed down on us all.

The longer I lay there, the more my bones ached. Phantom pains that never quite left me, even now. My body still remembers that night, punishing me for it with restless sleep, seven thousand nights later.

Somewhere before dawn, Barry nudged me. "C'mon. I can't just sit here. Let's see what's happening down there."

I didn't know what we thought we'd find. I wish we hadn't gone.

There was one more thing the island wanted to show us.

'It's not what happens to you, but how you react to it that really matters.'
Epictetus

Thirty One
Red Dawn

27th December 2004
Koh Phi Phi

Neither of us said much as we slipped away from the group and into the dawn. There was no plan—maybe water, maybe food, maybe a way off the island. Or maybe we just needed to move, to do something. Sleep hadn't come for either of us. The air was still, heavy with dread, and the silence between us said everything words couldn't.

We were both afraid, but men don't talk about that. We just walked.

We headed toward the hillside bungalows overhanging the bay, far from the cheap backpacker huts we'd called home. It felt wrong to be up here now, among stone walls and manicured gardens, when everything below lay in ruin. Luxury felt like an insult.

Then, out of the shadows, a figure burst toward us—a young man, breathless, eyes wide.

"Please! You have to help! We can't move her alone. She's losing blood —please!"

Classic Bazza—no hesitation, just go.

We followed the kid through a narrow path winding up to the clifftop bungalows. But the groans spilling from the open door reminded me: the nightmare was still unfolding.

Inside, a woman lay twisted in soaked sheets, thrashing and moaning. Dark hair plastered to her forehead, skin ghostly white. Three young men hovered uselessly, eyes flicking from her to us like we might know what to do.

"She's anaemic," one stammered. "She's lost so much blood... we can't move her."

No one had a plan. No time for questions. No time for fear. Her cries carved through the room, cutting clean through my numbness. All that mattered was getting her out.

"We need a stretcher," someone said—voice steady despite the panic. Was it my voice? I'm not sure anymore.

Nobody knew what they were doing, but somehow we made it work. Bits of wood, a broken table leg, torn sheets—it looked flimsy as hell, but it was all we had.

Time was killing her.

Lifting her was the worst part. Her screams tore through the bungalow and out into the jungle. But we couldn't stop. Once she was strapped down, four of us grabbed the corners—our arms trembling before we'd even taken a step. Two more went ahead, clearing the trail, barking warnings when the path turned steep or slippery.

Each footfall was a fight. The ground under our bare feet shifted constantly, sharp rocks biting into soles softened by saltwater and sand. My shoulders burned after just a few minutes. I had to tag out, shame gnawing at me as someone stronger stepped in. I shook out my arms, sucked in a breath, then grabbed my corner again.

Thirty seconds. Twenty yards. Swap again. It went on like that—a slow, punishing relay down a mountain that felt endless.

We barely spoke. Eyes on the ground, teeth clenched. Her moans the only reminder we couldn't stop. There was no time to feel sorry for ourselves—every rotation felt like both failure and necessity.

My brain spat insults at me: 'Useless. Weak. They're carrying you.'

'Shut up and lift.'

But my body didn't care. It kept moving. It had to.

Now we had a real mission: get her down, alive, and hand her over to someone—anyone—who knew what the hell they were doing.

By the time the jungle gave way to sand, my arms and legs felt like someone had poured acid into the muscle fibres. I could see Barry's face twisted with the same pain. None of us were built for this, but we did it anyway. If this had been a military selection, I'd have flunked out at the first checkpoint.

Reaching the beach should have been a relief. It wasn't.

Worse than rock, worse than anything—sand turned out to be the real killer. Every step sucked us down, every inch forward an uphill fight. The helicopter ahead was our only focus: a bright red promise on a black day.

I could hear the insults in my head, my own voice mixed with R. Lee Ermey barking—"What's your major malfunction, Private Bromfield?"—and Arnie screaming—"Get to the chopper!"

It was ridiculous—but it worked. I kept moving. Didn't look at her blood-soaked sheets.

Didn't think. Just did.

Closer to the shoreline, the sand firmed up, packed by the sea's retreat. Our pace picked up, bare feet slapping wet ground. Barry urged me on, his hand on my shoulder when I stumbled. I kept my eyes on the helicopter, tuning out the glittering puddles reflecting the cruel morning sun.

But then—shapes.

Small, wrong shapes, scattered near the tide line.

The closer we got, the clearer they became. The sunlight bounced off them like a spotlight, showing every awful curve, every limp… limb.

My throat closed. My heartbeat tripled. I croaked it out, barely audible:

"Oh no… oh no… Barry, it's—" But the words stuck.

Bodies.

Tangled and still in the blood-red dawn.

Scattered like broken dolls along paradise's edge.

'I am out with lanterns, looking for myself.'
Emily Dickinson

Thirty Two
Dawn of the Dead

27th December 2004
Koh Phi Phi

It was clear now. Close enough to trip over. A stranger lying perfectly still—too still.

A body.

The closer we got, the more the awful truth sharpened: he was dead. Flat on his back, naked, limbs frozen mid-reach like he'd tried to grab hold of life and it had ripped away. His mouth was wide, locked in a silent scream at the blood-red dawn. His skin had turned that sickly blue only an icy death brings.

I froze.

The world narrowed to just him—the grotesque pose, the twisted fear etched on his face. My feet stuck in the sand. The stretcher's weight gone from my arms, but my chest squeezed tighter than ever. A sob punched through before I could stop it. Tears came hot and sudden. My legs wobbled. For a second, I wanted to just drop right there beside him.

"Don't look!" Barry's voice cut through, harsh but needed. He stepped in front of me, blocking the corpse from view.

"John—look at me. Shut it down. Focus. We're nearly there."

How could I shut this down? How could I unsee it? But he was right. If I fell apart now, we all failed. I forced the sobs back down my throat.

Left foot. Right foot. Left foot. Right foot. Slam a door shut in my head. Lock it away.

The image of the dead man stayed with me—a grotesque painting lodged in my thoughts, like Munch's Scream, but twisted on the sand, staring into oblivion.

Don't think. Don't feel.

The helicopter snapped into focus—bright red against a sky gone wrong. Its blades whipped sand in our eyes. I locked onto the sound: whomp, whomp, whomp, syncing with my heart. Thump, thump, thump.

The woman moaned on the stretcher. My arms burned, but I didn't dare stop now.

Thirty hours with no food. No water. No hangover anymore—just raw, intense exhaustion.

At the rotor wash, a paramedic ran toward us. No fuss. No chit-chat. He checked her pulse mid-stride.

"Priority—get her on board, now!"

The stretcher lifted from my hands. I staggered back, arms dangling useless at my sides.

"You've probably saved her life gentlemen," he said—but I didn't feel like a saviour.

I felt pathetic. My muscles had given out every few minutes. My brain had short-circuited at the sight of one dead man. Hero? Don't make me laugh.

I was glad it was over. And I hated myself for that.

We stepped away from the chopper, stumbling clear of the noise and spinning sand. It was done—the woman was in good hands now. But my brain wouldn't shut up: 'You didn't save her. You barely held your corner. Useless.'

Barry caught my eye. He knew. We both knew I'd struggled the whole way—tagging out every few minutes, barely holding it together when it counted. But he said nothing. That was Barry. No judgement. Just a nod that said: We did what we could.

Ahead, the beach buzzed with life. More survivors dragging themselves out of hiding, word spreading fast:

Boats are coming.

A way out. The only thing we wanted now—to get off this graveyard.

I forced myself not to look back at the man in the sand. That nightmare image begged for attention, whispering at the edges of my vision. But I shut it down.

Left foot, right foot. Don't think.

Halfway up the path, we passed a survivor—a man coordinating the rescue. Calm voice, strong eyes. He was everywhere at once: directing people, checking on the injured, lifting debris like it weighed nothing.

A proper leader. A proper man.

"Hey—can you come back?" he called when he spotted us. "We need strong lads like you. There's more people needing help."

I wanted to say yes. God, I wanted to be that guy—the hero who goes back for one more round. But my shoulders drooped before I could answer.

Barry spoke for us:

"We've got to get the girls. They'll be worried."

It was true.

But it felt like a lie.

"We'll come back," I said over my shoulder—knowing I wouldn't.

My chest burned with shame. Gutless wonder.

Even that voice in my head sounded tired now.

We trudged upward, the beach and bodies shrinking behind us, the morning sun glaring down with no mercy. A tiny part of me hoped I'd never see that stretch of sand again.

By the time we reached the summit, the sun was brutal overhead, stripping away any last illusion that this was still paradise. Survivors milled around in tired clusters—faces that should've been relaxing on a beach now hollowed out, clinging to scraps of news.

Barry called out that boats were coming. A ripple of relief ran through the group.

Escape. Finally.

Then someone produced the Nokia—that battered little brick of hope. A hush fell as it was passed around. People cried reading replies from home.

Tiny messages that meant the world: Are you okay? We love you. Come home safe.

Tina edged closer, her eyes locked on the phone. When it landed in her hands, she scrolled fast—then stopped. Her shoulders stiffened.

"What is it?" I asked, my gut already knowing.

She turned the screen toward me.

Message Not Sent.

I blinked.

"What?"

"I don't know what happened," she said.

"There's only ten digits," Barry said, squinting at the number. "You missed one."

Tina's lips trembled. "I'm sorry. I didn't realise. I just... I didn't think..."

The anger punched me first—a hot flare in my throat.

If I'd sent it, Joey would have called my mum by now. They'd know we were alive.

Instead, they were sitting at home, watching the news, picturing our bodies on that beach.

But I looked at Tina—her pale face, the way she'd folded into herself since the wave. She wasn't all there.

How could I blame her for that?

"It's not your fault," I lied.

Or maybe I told the truth. Hard to tell anymore.

She nodded, tears brimming.

I just turned away.

All I could think was:

We failed. Again.

We just had to wait now. Wait to leave the island—and hope the worst parts didn't follow us home.

'Life is warfare and a journey far from home.'
Marcus Aurelius

Thirty Three
A Quiet Place

19th August 2021
London

"I can't do this anymore. Please, can we stop?"

I wasn't just asking for a pause—I was begging for escape. Each retelling left me more depleted, my memories splintering under the weight. Today was especially brutal—one dark corner after another. I was trembling and felt like I might break apart.

Rada nodded, her tone soft, almost maternal. "Of course, John. We can stop here for today. Let's just take a moment to come back."

I couldn't look at her. Shame weighed on me—not about Thailand, but about how fragile I still was. How weak it made me feel, decades later, and how I still struggled to say it out loud.

"Close your eyes," Rada guided. "Take a deep breath. Picture your bedroom—the trains humming in the distance, the smell of dinner from the kitchen."

I clutched the fabric of the couch, grounding myself.

"You're safe now."

I breathed in, shoulders dropping a fraction. "Thanks… I'm back."

She gave me space, then asked softly, "What are you feeling right now?"

"I could've done more," I murmured, voice hoarse.

She tilted her head. "What do you mean? John, from what you've told

221

me—you did so much. You carried that woman. You helped save her."

I knew she was right. Logically. But logic and guilt rarely agree.

"I don't know... maybe. Maybe I was too slow. Maybe we didn't reach the helicopter fast enough. No matter what I did... it just wasn't enough."

"There's always more that could be done. But you did what you could. That matters."

I said nothing. Because deep down, I didn't buy it. I kept seeing the man on the beach, the one leading the rescue. He needed strong people like me. I'd promised to go back. And instead, I'd left. I'd walked away. How could I ever make peace with that?

"I should have stayed," I whispered. "There were still people out there. Lost, hurt."

Rada's eyes softened, but there was a sharpness too—the truth behind the kindness. "What does Barry think?"

I shrugged. "I don't know. We've never talked about it."

She dropped her pen, stunned. "What?"

"We've never spoken about it," I repeated, like it was normal. "Not properly."

Her disbelief stung. "You nearly died together—and you've never talked about it? He was there with you, John!"

I half-laughed, embarrassed. "Yeah, but... you know. We see each other all the time: golf, birthdays, dinners. When it comes up, it's just, 'Lucky we made it.' That's it."

She rubbed her forehead. "John. You and Barry survived something massive. You thought he was dead. You need to talk about it."

I shrugged again. "He did tell me his side—sort of. Lisbeth wrote about it in a book years ago. He sent me a translated copy. That's how

I found out what really happened to them."

Rada looked at me like she didn't know whether to laugh or cry. "And you never spoke to him about it directly?"

"No," I admitted. "I read it once and... that was it. He was the hero. He saved Lisbeth. Dragged her onto a fridge and rode the wave on that. He even got invited to her wedding as a guest of honour. I just... left it alone."

Rada sighed. "It's not just Barry, though, is it? You didn't talk to Tina either, did you?"

I shifted my eyes away. "No... not even her."

She dropped her pen completely now, her frustration clear. "Why, John? How can you go through hell with someone and never speak about it?"

"I don't know," I snapped, then my voice softened. "She was in shock all the way home. She barely spoke. I waited for her to bring it up. She never did. So I didn't either."

"And she never thanked you? For going back?"

I snorted bitterly. "No. I ran back into that wave for her, dragged her out of the shop—and she never said a word. Never asked. Never thanked me. It pissed me off a bit, yeah."

"But you understand that anger now, don't you?"

"Yeah. I get it now. But back then, I shut down. I didn't want to talk about it at all."

I hesitated. "Meg's the only one who knows the full story. All of it. I told her last year, over an anniversary dinner. I broke down a few times, but I didn't hold back. By the time the starters came, I'd emptied the vault."

Rada fell silent, letting my words settle. Then she asked, softly but firmly, "What about your family? Have you ever talked to them about

223

it?"

"No," I said, shaking my head. "They were just glad I was alive. We didn't need to talk about it."

Classic stiff upper lip—the unspoken British creed: Get on with it. Don't dwell.

But her words lingered, slicing through my justifications. They went through their own trauma too.

I'd never really thought about it. I'd vanished into a natural disaster, and for two days, they'd assumed the worst.

"My mum had to call a hotline," I said quietly, the reality hitting me mid-sentence. "She gave them a description of my tattoo in case... in case they found my body."

It landed like a stone in my chest. All these years, and I'd never truly pictured what that must have been like for her.

Rada nodded, her voice gentle but unyielding. "You need to talk to them, John. Promise me."

"Okay," I said, meaning it—and not meaning it—at the same time.

She leaned forward, eyes locking with mine. "And Barry. You need to talk to Barry too."

I nodded again, dread crawling under my skin. Of course she was right. That didn't make it easier.

"I always blamed myself for the text," I confessed, the words tumbling out before I could stop them. "I should've just texted Joey. I knew his number off by heart. If I'd done that, they would've known we were alive. Instead, they spent days thinking we were dead. It was avoidable."

Rada cut in gently, "Maybe. Maybe not. Looking back doesn't change it, John. They did live through that loss. It probably shaped them, just like it shaped you."

I felt a ripple of shame. I'd never really grasped how selfish I'd been. Always stuck on my guilt, but never theirs.

"I did tell my cousin Sam recently," I said, fishing for something positive to offer her. "A couple months ago. I think I'm trying—I just... I wait for the 'right moment' instead of starting it myself."

"That's something," Rada said, her tone softer now. "How did that come up?"

I managed a small smile. "He was decorating my house. I'd had a rough night, took the day off work. We got talking. Next thing I know, I'm spilling my guts. He had no clue it was that bad. It actually felt... good, saying it out loud. He just listened. Didn't judge. Didn't interrupt."

Rada's look said it all: Good. More of that.

We wrapped up the session, and I left her office feeling scraped raw from the inside out. Hoodie up, AirPods in—my usual armour. I didn't want eye contact, small talk, nothing. The music blared, pushing the noise in my head to the background. "None shall pass."

But her words clung to me. Talk to Barry. Talk to your family. I knew I would. Someday.

Maybe.

I drifted through Canary Wharf like a spectre. Rada's voice wouldn't shut up in my head. It grated at me. Was I really making things worse by bottling it all up? Maybe. But facing it felt so much bigger than ignoring it ever did.

Truth is, I was a master at this: compartmentalising. Shoving every horror into a quiet place, slamming the door, pretending none of it happened.

Now, though, those doors? Wide open.

It was like walking the corridors of my own brain, one door after another swinging open without warning.

Smell sewage? Boom—I'm back in the flooded streets, knee-deep in filth and fear.

A stupid line from *Meet the Parents*—"I have nipples, Greg. Can you milk me?"—short-circuits straight to Phi Phi where I watched that movie relentlessly.

Nappy ad—warp speed to me wrapping a stranger's shredded leg in with duct tape.

I'd always called it my memory palace—but unlike the fancy Sherlock Holmes version, mine wasn't for storing useful trivia. It was a panic room for horrors.

Castle Greyskull, my boyhood toy fortress, repurposed as a vault for every trauma I didn't dare unpack. Seal the monsters inside and throw away the key.

It worked for years. Mostly. But lately? Any trigger could unlatch a door. I'd step through, sucked straight back into the Boxing Day apocalypse.

All five senses reliving it like fresh meat. PTSD at its laziest, cruelest setting.

I knew how to tame it once. Drugs dulled the edges, made the palace quiet. Now, sober, the guard was awake and curious. Prying open doors, poking the monsters with a stick.

Rada would say it was healthy.

I wasn't so sure. It felt like living in a house where every room hides a booby trap.

Focus.

Not today. Not now. No more doors. No more memories. I needed quiet.

Real quiet—not the numbed-out version weed had faked for me. Just a moment where nothing reminded me of death, or waves, or guilt.

So I did what I always do. Hoodie up, volume up, world out. Let the next session crack open the next door.

Today, I just wanted quiet.

'Nothing is ever really lost to us as long as we remember it.'
Lucy Maud Montgomery

Thirty Four
Memento

21st August 2021
London

After months of cracking trauma open, I needed to see what else was buried—something lighter. Something that didn't bite back.

There are fond memories hidden inside Castle Greyskull too, sealed in a room behind the tsunami vault.—fragments of my life eroded by the cruel passage of time.

The same shield that kept the worst at bay also buried some of the best days of my life. But lately, I feel strong enough to dig them out. If I can slip past the vault without getting dragged into the tide, maybe I can pull out the good without stirring the bad.

I close my eyes. My bed feels safe. I follow Rada's technique and rewind to 2004, drifting back to a time before everything changed. I hover over that summer, far enough from the tragedy. Flickers appear, offering me a chance to reconnect.

I breathe slowly, let the air fill my lungs, then exhale it all—not just oxygen, but the stale anxiety tethered to that time. Behind my eyelids, a world map blurs into focus. Asia flickers temptingly, but I skip it— too dangerous, a direct line to the epicentre.

I settle on Africa. A spark. The brightest corner of that long-lost year.

2004 was a year for the history books, but while NASA landed rovers on Mars and Zuckerberg launched Facebook, Barry and I were busy chasing our own milestones. Instead of slumming our way around the world, we travelled with some class. We dipped into airport lounges and, on good days, landed in a Sheraton hotel. It's that memory— collapsing onto an impossibly soft bed—that anchors me now, warm in my own bed, letting me rewind without fear.

In my head, that cloud-like mattress transitions into my personal Flying Nimbus—Monkey Magic style—drifting weightlessly over the landscape in a complimentary robe and slippers.

I can see us. Steve, Barry and me. *The three Amigos.*

I had my trusty camcorder strapped to my side, playing videographer like a nerdy Adam Goldberg, recording everything that caught my eye. Half the tapes were stolen during a misadventure in Mozambique; the rest live in a box in my loft, untouched for over a decade. When a trip ends in catastrophe, the build-up becomes hard to revisit.

Fear eclipses joy, and good memories go into hiding.

Maybe one day I'll watch them, when I'm old and distant enough for it to feel like someone else's life. But for now—no tapes, no screens. Just me and my dusty memory palace.

Music was always my tether to a moment, and back then, my whole collection lived in my pocket thanks to the 1st Generation iPod. Thank you, Mr Jobs—that click wheel anchored memories better than any camcorder ever could.

I settle deeper into my bed, Matchbox Twenty's *Yourself or Someone Like You* in my AirPods, drifting over a continent that would surprise us at every turn. Strutting around like the funkiest monkey there ever was, my fantasy attire fades away, replaced by my trusty travel gear.

I land softly in Cairo—thick air, constant horns, a city alive with dust and energy. There's a tension in the streets—not threatening, just edgy. You can't miss the weight of ancient history that hangs in the air. It's the birthplace of one of the most fascinating cultures in human history, a place teeming with archaeological wonders.

The Museum of Egyptian Antiquities hooked me instantly. Mummies, real ones—not Hollywood's Imhotep. Tutankhamun's gold mask shimmered inches away, worth every sweaty hour drifting from room to room. For the first time, antiquity felt alive—more than Indiana Jones competing with Nazis for a shiny relic. Here, real explorers uncovered unimaginable treasure with chisels and maps, rewriting what we knew about a civilisation older than most countries.

At the centre of this fascinating culture: the pyramids.

One sharp turn off Cairo's manic streets and there they were, dumped right beside a main road like a forgotten movie set. From the photos, you expect endless desert and silent awe. Instead, we got honking traffic, camel hustlers, and a lifetime highlight I'll never forget.

As we trudged away from the wonder, a local shop owner waved us up to his roof for tea. We sat above the din, steaming glasses in hand, watching the sun melt behind Khufu's tomb, the Sphinx a dark silhouette at its feet. The city noise faded. The moment felt eternal—mates perched on a rooftop, humbled by something ancient and vast.

The kindness of a stranger indelibly marking my life again.

The memory fades, and just like the great sage, I summon the cloud with a quick whistle and flourish: loyal as ever, ready to carry me across mountains and rivers in a single breath.

South Africa—heavy with scars—comes into view. Walking through Mandela's tiny cell on Robben Island. Some people swear Mandela died in that prison decades ago—the so-called 'Mandela Effect'. phenomenon where people misremember things—like C3PO's silver leg, or the terrorists in *Back to the Future* driving a VW camper van. A fun sci-fi rabbit hole I enjoyed diving into.

We tackled the famous Garden Route in the world's least appropriate car: a Fiat Panda that wheezed at every incline and rattled like a shopping trolley on gravel. By twilight, we rolled into Hermanus: shark country.

None of us slept that night. The thought of dangling in a flimsy cage while great whites circled glued our eyelids open. Dawn came too soon, and the boat trip out felt like a one-way ride to Amity Island. Our guide—leathery skin, wild grin—swore sharks weren't man-eaters. Then he dumped buckets of chum into the water anyway, whistling as the sea turned pink.

We crammed into the cage, hearts hammering. Beneath the surface:

cold, murky silence, broken only by the distant thud of something enormous moving nearby. Then—a blur of white and jagged teeth slammed the bars inches from my face.

I shot up, gasping.

"Back down now, more are coming!" the guide yelled.

Back under. Four of them now, shadows circling, testing the metal. The cage rattled with each bump. I gripped my underwater camera, convinced this footage might double as my last will and testament.

When we finally clambered back on deck, shivering and exhilarated, the guide rubbed one's nose like it was a puppy.

He laughed when we flinched. "See? They're gentle!"

There was no denying the primal fear they evoked. As we sat there shivering—partly from the icy water, mostly from lingering terror—we shared a packet of crisps, exchanging glances that said more than words ever could. Just as we started to settle, the captain throttled the boat, zigzagging wildly. We nearly flew overboard, grabbing onto each other and losing the crisps in the battle.

"What the hell was that?" Barry shouted.

The guide laughed. "Nearly ran into a whale! Captain had to swerve or we'd have capsized."

My heart, which had just started to slow, kicked back into overdrive. 'My my my my—get us outta here!' I thought, nerves frayed to the limit.

We rattled back onto the Garden Route, adrenaline still fizzing. Next came the Bloukrans Bridge bungee—the world's highest at the time. We weren't planning on it; Barry spotted the sign and made the call.

The jump office was closing. Relief washed over me. Too late—brilliant.

But the operator grinned. "Ah, screw it, I'll squeeze you in."

Fuck.

The boys geared up, grinning like kids on Christmas. I dragged my feet, muttering excuses. The bridge walkway was a see-through mesh suspended over a 200-metre abyss—each step felt like it might be my last.

"You sure this is tight?" I asked the operator, pointing at the cord.

"Mate, you'll be fine."

"Doesn't feel right—"

"Trust me it's fine…5…4…3—Oh no! Wait, wait—WAIT!"

Too late. Gravity yanked me over the edge. The scream ripped itself out of me before I could even think. Then the cord caught—the bounce back up brought a rush so pure I forgot the fear. Back on solid ground, I punched the operator's arm, swearing between relieved laughter.

He howled. "That was classic! Got you good there, mate."

We cackled at the prank, fuelled by leftover adrenaline and road-trip banter.

Africa still had one more test for our fragile nerves: Kruger. We hit the park as amateur explorers—no guide, no plan. Just a printed map and our ill-equipped Panda.

The first day, crawling through brush and tall grass with nothing to show until we ran straight into trouble.

"Stop the car Baz. There's an elephant right next to Steve!"

"WHERE?" Barry braked hard.

"Right. Fucking. There!"

Steve's sunglasses slid down his nose as he turned. "Oh, shit."

How he missed it, I'll never know—a giant eyeball inches from the passenger window.

Behind us, another bull stepped out, blocking the track. We froze. One tonne of Fiat surrounded by fourteen tonnes of Africa's angriest traffic jam. The bull swayed its head, testing us. Nobody breathed.

Then it reared up.

"Fucking hell—they will crush us. Don't move. Just stay still," I said, trying to figure out a move. Any move. Play dead, adopt the fetal position!

Something. Anything!

And so we did nothing. We turned the engine off and sat quietly. Afraid to even snap a picture in case, like in *Jurassic Park*, the flash of the camera would be enough to set off a tragic chain of events.

Eventually, the elephants wandered off, and Barry quietly reversed to safety.

That night, under a velvet sky buzzing with distant calls and hidden predators, we argued about dangerous animals and sang along to classic tunes on a battered speaker. Africa felt like freedom—nature, history, the open road, and just enough danger to remind you you're alive.

A Mozambique gang robbed us of the official record from our time in Africa. I may never see those tapes again—but the best ones play fine in my head.

Back in my bed, in the here and now, I open my eyes. The magic cloud dissolves. The good memories unlocked. The bad ones still sleeping. A quiet win. A small victory.

And proof I can do this—one piece at a time.

Thirty Five Explorers

2004
South East Asia

Before Africa, we'd already spent about four months exploring Asia. Starting somewhere familiar helped ease us back into the rhythm—a gentle shift from rat race to road. At first, it almost felt too familiar: Thailand, Malaysia—the same beaches, bars, and backstreets we knew by heart. Still brilliant, still intoxicating, but well-trodden ground.

Koh Phi Phi, though, never disappointed. Our good friend Nok always booked us a bungalow in her village. Nights kicked off at her beach bar: tables in the sand under swaying palms, chilled music drifting through the air. We'd stretch out under the stars until Barry inevitably dragged us off for stronger rum and generic house music.

One night at Nok's bar, we met Lisbeth and Camilla. Maybe it was their first time in Thailand, or just their first time on Phi Phi—either way, they had that wide-eyed look of fresh adventurers. Like us, they were at the start of a big backpacking circuit.

Random encounters like that were the magic of travel: swapping stories, trading tips, mapping out detours. Most flared and fizzled in a day. But some stuck. Lisbeth and Camilla stuck. Thoughtful, generous, planners to the core—they had every route and trick scribbled in battered guidebooks, while Barry and I winged it with a barely thumbed Lonely Planet.

Our 'plan' was loose: The Philippines, Hong Kong, China, India, a few iconic overland routes, and vague dreams of the Great Wall and the Taj Mahal. Beyond that, we trusted luck. Then Lisbeth mentioned orangutans.

"Yes, John—in the jungle. As close to their natural habitat as you can

234

get," Lisbeth said, flipping to a dog-eared page.

"Oh Bazza, we have to do that. I'd love to see an orangutan!"

"Yeah, sounds good," Barry shrugged, as nonchalant as ever.

Meanwhile, I was geeking out. Orangutans! My obsession started in the early 80s when Clyde took a right turn on command from Philo Beddoe in *Every Which Way But Loose*. Unforgettable. Now I could meet Clyde's real cousins in the wild.

"Which one are you visiting?" I asked Lisbeth.

"Sarawak—we'll head there after Kuala Lumpur."

I winked at Barry. "Maybe we'll see you there."

Sure enough, a few weeks later we landed in Borneo—the third largest island on earth. And thanks to Chris 'Finchy' Finch in the brilliant *The Office*, I also knew that it didn't have a capital city.

Reunited with the Danes, we joined a small group heading deep into the rainforest toward Sepilok Rehabilitation Centre. The journey alone was an adventure: mile after mile of ancient canopy, eyes peeled for Asia's only great ape. When we finally spotted them, I forgot the camcorder altogether. Just stood there, under the dripping leaves, watching two females swing effortlessly between branches, followed by a hulking male. Seeing them so close—raw, wild, and unbothered by us—was worth every mosquito bite.

That night we found a bar with karaoke. Fuelled by cheap beer and orangutan euphoria, Lisbeth and I signed up and belted out pop classics, clearing half the bar but losing zero enthusiasm. We even had a homemade mic: a carved orangutan pen from the Sepilok gift shop, christened 'Clyde'. Clyde was front and centre as we screeched through our duet, "That's What Friends Are For." It was ridiculous, funny, and perfect—a snapshot of travel at its best.

With our appetite for adventure fully revived—and our hangovers mostly behind us—we parted ways and signed up for a two-day jungle cruise.

The Kinabatangan River became our highway. Drifting deeper into the wild, we watched snakes slice through the murky water alongside our tiny boat. A huge monitor lizard dropped from a branch, eyes fixed on some unlucky prey. At one point, we ducked under trees and our guide hissed for silence, pointing up.

High in the canopy, a cluster of proboscis monkeys lounged—Borneo's oddest locals with their big noses and beer-belly posture. I stared, awed. Barry, up front, hadn't noticed.

As we drifted closer, droplets started splashing on Barry's head. He fiddled with his hood, muttering, "Think it's starting to rain again…"

The guide snorted and pantomimed a man peeing. "It's pee! It's pee!" he whispered, eyes wide.

I lost it. "That's not rain, mate!" I choked out, doubled over laughing. "The monkey's pissing on you!"

Barry jerked sideways, trying to dodge the golden shower—only to catch another stream square on his mush. "Ahhh, for fuck's sake!" he howled, half-laughing, half-panicking, as the monkey above screeched, shaking its arms for extra effect.

Classic Barry luck: travel halfway across the world to see rare wildlife only to get christened by it. Priceless.

We never did shy away from adventure, but one memory brings with it a wave of terror. A close call that I'd buried deep along with my other ocean-related trauma.

Sipadan. Nestled in the Celebes Sea—the perfect jumping-off point for the mysteries of the deep. We boarded a small boat, skimming across calm waves, watching flying fish skim alongside us like silver darts. We exchanged nervous grins as we reached the site. Novices was an understatement: five dives each, five years ago. But we strapped on the gear, trying to look like we belonged among the seasoned divers.

In for a penny, in for a pound.

The moment we flipped backwards into the water, adrenaline took over.

All the nerves melted as the underwater world opened up: crystal-clear reefs, neon coral gardens, schools of fish flickering like confetti, and a sea turtle gliding past like an ancient ghost. For a while, the risks dissolved in the magic.

Feeling cocky, we went for a night dive. Alone.

Just metres from the shore, the seabed dropped away into an abyss hundreds of metres deep—a hidden cliff that felt like it could swallow you whole. We hovered above the darkness, half-thrilled, half-paralysed by whispers of hammerheads lurking far below. None showed up—but the unseen vastness was enough.

Then I made my rookie mistake. Eager, distracted, overconfident, I drifted deeper than I'd ever gone—almost forty metres down. In pitch darkness, way beyond my training. I lost sight of Barry; when I looked up, the surface was just a faint moonlit blur.

Panic slammed into me, cold and suffocating. I jabbed at my vest, desperate to stop sinking, but the pull of the deep felt unstoppable.

When I finally started to rise, my terror doubled. Too fast meant 'the bends'. Every diver knows: never rush the ascent. But panic bulldozed logic. I forced myself to slow down, clutching at the one rule drummed into me during training: ascend slowly or pay for it.

Each second felt like a fight. I checked my oxygen—the tank draining fast—and made myself rise in tiny, controlled bursts, eyes locked on that distant shimmer above. I didn't dare look down into the black void.

'Does anyone even realise I'm still down here?'

Bit by bit, breath by breath, I clawed my way up until my head finally broke the surface. Relief hit like a drug—but something had shifted. The sea spat me out, but left its mark.

Above water, I gasped—no longer just a tourist, but someone who'd met fear face to face.

That close call stuck with me. I'd touched the edge and got away with it. That felt like enough. Sipadan showed me a world I'll never forget —a perfect mix of beauty, risk, and recklessness—and convinced me to hang up my flippers for good. Never again would I test the ocean like that.

But in a few months it would rear up and come back with another— much more challenging exam.

Our Borneo detour had been totally unplanned: from orangutans to rainforests to underwater realms. On our last day we found ourselves stuck in a remote village—no buses, no tours, roads flooded. So, naturally, we hitched a ride to the port.

A battered Toyota minivan—with a side-mounted door and just enough room in the boot for some stolen plutonium—rattled up at a petrol station.

We squeezed into the back, wedged among bags and giggling locals. Within minutes, the vibe shifted. Chatting with some passengers, we mentioned our plan to catch a ferry to the Philippines.

One woman drew a finger across her throat, dead serious. The driver chimed in with stories of pirates, murders, and gangs who'd love a clueless pair of Westerners.

Brilliant. Thanks for the nightmare fuel, mate.

Barry, fearless as ever—or maybe just wired differently—waved it off. "They're exaggerating. We'll be fine."

I, however, had mental images of ski-masked villains brandishing AK's and Mum holding a ransom note she couldn't afford to pay.

Nope. Not happening.

We debated until dawn and eventually compromised: direct flight to Manila, zero pirate-infested waters, Barry's travel points footing the hotel bill.

Seemed sensible—until the baggage handler at the airport giggled, drew a finger across her throat, and muttered something like "Abu Sayyaf, murder you!"

Christ. Why did everyone love that throat-cutting mime?

Too late to bottle it, I followed Barry onto the plane—for what turned out to be another wild adventure. We steered clear of the gangs, but ended up stranded on an island for nearly a month.

But that's a story for another time.

Phenomenal memories. But somehow, I'd buried them—locked away in silence, serving a quiet sentence. We never talked about those days. They just lingered—starved of attention.

Now, finally, I was dusting them off. One by one. Letting them breathe again.

Thirty Six
Big Trouble In Little China

2004
China

First things first—the title. I know, China is anything but 'little'. It's the world's most populous country, sprawling across deserts, mountains, plains, and mega-cities. But if you've stuck with me this far, you'll know by now: movies are my compass.

Big Trouble in Little China felt too perfect to resist. Like *Falling Down* did for my meltdown chapter, this title nails the spirit of the situation I got myself into.

Movies and music have always been my safety net—a mental escape hatch when real life pushes too hard. Writing this story dredged up plenty I'd rather forget, so pop culture slipped in uninvited, giving me anchors and inside jokes only I needed to survive the retelling.

Thanks for indulging me. Now, back to the big trouble.

China was like a cultural reset button. Overnight, English vanished. Menus were cryptic scrolls of symbols. Our Lonely Planet Mandarin cheat sheet was laughable—one wrong tone and "ma" could mean mother, hemp, horse, or insult. Good luck ordering lunch with Cockney-inflected Mandarin.

Eating became Russian roulette: point at someone else's dish and pray. Some days we won—perfect dumplings or sizzling noodles. Some days? A mystery plate of tripe or god-knows-what that we pushed aside while pretending to be polite. I would later find empathy for the *Idiot Abroad*, Karl Pilkington, and his plight in this challenging environment. I wish, like him, I had packed a case full of Monster Munch.

Trains offered no mercy either. On our first sleeper from Shanghai to

Beijing, we grabbed the bottom bunks and thought we'd lucked out—until our two bunkmates arrived.

That's when the spitting began.

Deep, guttural, relentless throat-clearing. They were dredging up phlegm from the very depths of their lungs. Then gobbing it across the compartment, aiming haphazardly for a waste bin under the window, all too near Barry's head.

We jammed in our headphones—me trying to drown out the horror with Mike Skinner talking about tower blocks and deadbeats. But even his concrete poetry couldn't muffle the splat. By dawn, the wall looked like a biohazard zone. Barry reached for a tissue and came back with his fingers webbed in phlegm. It was rank.

We swore never to book bottom bunks again.

Beijing made up for it. This was the China I had imagined—a city that breathed history with every ancient brick, where the lines between past and present blurred. I felt like I was stepping back in time, surrounded by architecture that stood as a testament to centuries of imperial rule.

The Forbidden City was staggering—centuries of emperors and intrigue still alive in the painted halls and quiet courtyards. Outside, Tiananmen Square hummed with unsaid stories; etched in my memory from news clips in the '80s. I could still picture that famous image of a lone man standing firm against a tank. Had the tank stopped before hitting him? It was one of those haunting images—maybe altered by the Mandela Effect.

When we finally arrived at the Great Wall, the sight stole my breath. Stone and brick snaked endlessly over rugged hills, twisting and turning out of sight. Built over centuries, it once kept out northern invaders and stood as a testament to a people's grit and paranoia in equal measure.

"Excuse me, when did the Mongols rule China?" I joked, channelling my best Ted Theodore Logan. My grasp of Genghis Khan was about as solid as a Bill and Ted history report—but seeing the Wall up close

241

made me want to know more. Some say labourers who died building it were buried within its stones, their spirits wandering still. "Most heinous, dude."

Dark as that is, it adds a certain magic to the wonder.

Back at an internet café, I logged in to send my travel update. My head swam with stories of terracotta warriors and travel gripes, and I was eager to share them.

Tina, in her wisdom, had sent me an outrageously detailed sexual email. Something difficult to enjoy in a public space, so I read it, blushed, and refrained from any risqué reply. I then drafted my group update, planning to cut her message out before sending.

The Mandarin 'cut and paste' options confused the hell out of me.

I didn't cut it.

Next evening, I logged on to over a hundred emails.

Wiggy's sat at the top of the pile: "Mate... you emailed the SEX STORY to EVERYONE!"

'What sex story? What's he talki……….oh SHIT!!'

The penny dropped halfway through my confused thought. I felt the blood drain from my face. My heart hit the pit of my stomach so hard I'm sure I heard it.

'No. No I haven't... have I?'

Friends, family, random people I'd met on the road... oh no. My mum. My nan. Even Tina's dad was on that list.

Steve made it worse by replying all: "Silly Jedi, you sent the sex story to everyone!"

Cheers, mate!

There's nothing quite like realising—with zero way to undo it—that

242

you've just shared a private message with your entire contact list. It was a moment of pure shame, that desperate feeling where you'd give anything for a do-over. I wanted to run and hide.

CTRL + ALT + DEL. Reboot. I'd have gladly thrown the PC out the window if it meant erasing that moment.

Tina took it with more grace than I deserved, but it split us wider than the miles already had. No apology could un-send it. Guilt and shame consumed me. I spiralled. Drank more. Cared less about temples or history. I just wanted to crawl home and disappear under a rock.

Barry dragged me to the Peking Opera to try and snap me out of my funk. Halfway through the show, the music changed tempo and the lead actor pointed into the audience—straight at Barry.

Barry, painfully shy, clung to his seat. I, half-cut on Tsingtao, leapt up instead. One of my all-time heroes, Jackie Chan, had learned his trade in the Opera, so there was something surreal about being pulled up on that stage.

Ten minutes later I was wrestling an umbrella with a tiny acrobat while a packed house howled at my clumsy moves. For a moment, the shame faded. It didn't fix the mess, but it gave me air to breathe.

Of course, shame's a boomerang. The next day I woke up feeling fine for half a second—then it all came crashing back. Barry was making a sterling effort to lift my spirits, but I knew I had to meet him halfway. I needed to break out of this cycle. The more I tried to shake it, though, the more trapped I felt—as if my mind was caught in an endless loop of self-recrimination.

Barry was the kind of friend you need in moments like that—the best of the best.

He never let my worst moments define me, even when I felt I deserved every ounce of the shame weighing me down. When I wanted to wallow, Barry was there, nudging me back into the real world. He didn't pressure me or demand explanations. Instead, he stayed by my side, letting me work through it on my own terms while keeping the door to the present open.

In those moments, I realised how rare and vital true friendship is—the people who hold us steady when we can't find our own footing.

Determined to shake off my slump and stop being a burden, I set my sights on a childhood passion.

"Can we go to the Shaolin Temple, Baz?" I asked, my voice carrying more enthusiasm than it had in days.

"What's that then, monks and stuff?"

"It's the Kung Fu monastery. The original one. Says here in the guide we can stay there, even take lessons."

Barry, easygoing as always, shrugged. "Alright, then. Maybe it'll perk you up a bit."

Legend says an Indian monk named Bodhidharma came to the Monastery in the 6th century, saw monks too weak to meditate properly, and taught them how to harden mind and body. Martial arts and Zen in one.

We didn't sign up for dawn training or lugging water up hills in wooden pails—no chance—but we watched the monks bend pointy spears with their throats and crack steel bars with their skulls. Focus so pure it looked supernatural.

One idea hit me, a lesson I was destined to learn: Wu Xin—empty mind—wasn't about forgetting. It was about letting go. I'd been dragging my shame into every sunrise. So I climbed one of the training poles, struck my best crane pose—half *Karate Kid*, half wannabe monk—and for a moment, everything stilled.

No past. No shame. Just balance.

It was a perfect way for us to sign off on our Chinese experience. I would leave my anguish at the temple gate and live in the present.

'Your life will depend on the strength you have inside of you.'

'The conscience is the instinct of cruelty turned back upon itself.'
Friedrich Nietzsche

Thirty Seven
The Jerk

25th August 2021
London

I'd had a week to reflect on the ground I'd covered. Rada had helped me peel back layers I'd avoided for years, pushing me to face how I'd responded to the trauma—and how I'd buried every feeling so deep that not even the people closest to me could reach it. Looking back, it seemed strange, but back then, it felt like survival.

Since then, guilt, shame, and anger had camped out in the shadows of my memories, convincing me I was to blame—my own worst enemy.

The sharpest guilt still clung to my life with Tina. I'd checked out emotionally long before she walked away physically. Then came 'sex-mail-gate'—careless, humiliating, the final proof of how cowardly I'd been. I hadn't found the courage to end it honestly—to set her free. Instead, I strung her along because I was too afraid to be the villain.

A voice still whispers: Jerk. And it's right.

Over the years, that regret forced me to face uglier corners of my character. It became a turning point. I vowed to be braver, to hold myself to the honesty I claimed to value. I didn't want to be the version of me who talked a good game but hid from hard truths.

This morning, coffee in hand, I sat in silence and replayed it all. Back then, guilt met me every dawn, a heavy stone in my gut before my feet even touched the floor.

I'd failed her. Failed myself.

But I wasn't that man anymore—I'd grown. I clung to that. I could trace it all back to one stupid dinner date: I took the easy way out. And in that moment, a chain of bad decisions began—decisions that would put her in Thailand with me, directly in the path of a wave that nearly killed us both.

A sip of fresh coffee snapped me back to now. These reflections—ugly but necessary—had become a daily practice. I wanted to be proud of the man Meg woke up next to. I'd discovered the seeds of resilience, planted in the arid soil of adversity. Those seeds bloomed into strength —not just for survival, but for the man I wanted to become.

As I handed Meg her cup, a warm wave of gratitude hit me. For her patience. For her love. For holding steady while I unravelled and rebuilt myself. But most of all, for those decisions—the good, the bad, and the weak—that had aligned the stars and brought us together.

"Morning, babe," I said as she settled beside me. "I think I'm going to start practicing mindfulness. There's something to it, y'know?"

"Really?" She gave me a sleepy half-smile.

"Yeah. I once saw these monks at the Shaolin Temple in China…" I rambled about Buddhism, mind over matter. Meg listened, half-amused, half-bemused, as I veered from monks to *Kill Bill* to therapy.

Mindfulness was ancient wisdom, but for me it felt urgent: staying here, now—not lost in old regrets or phantom futures. Simple in theory: breathe, notice. Harder in practice. But I needed it more than most.

It struck me—I'd once stood at the source, and missed the chance to learn.

Gita had told me to start. Rada had reinforced those wishes.

I'd ignored them both.

Now, I was ready.

"…studies show monks can literally change how their brains handle pain," I said, on a roll.

Meg raised an eyebrow, halfway through her coffee. "John, it's too early for a TED Talk." She said, smirking. "What are we doing today, anyway?"

I grinned. "Glad you asked. I want to go to Neasden. There's a temple there—biggest one outside India. Hand-carved wood, all shipped from Calcutta."

She gave me a look. "Neasden? Really?"

"Yeah, come on. It'll be worth it."

She sighed but smiled—indulging me, like always. Maybe all that digging through the past was finally paying off.

Some old mistakes couldn't be undone, but maybe, finally, the lessons could help me heal.

'The world is big and I want to have a good look at it before it gets dark.'
John Muir

Thirty Eight
Into The Wild

2004
Tibet - Nepal

The thin, sharp air of the 'roof of the world' hit us the moment we stepped off the tiny plane. At 12,000 feet, Tibet felt like another planet—every breath strained, every step heavy. Each lungful carried whispers of centuries-old resilience.

Lhasa, the mystical capital, radiated a quiet gravity. Mountains framed the city like guardians, monasteries perched on hillsides, and prayer flags flickered in the wind—colourful echoes of devotion.

Barry didn't last long—flattened by a migraine within hours. While he hid in the dark, mainlining Nurofen, I stepped outside alone and straight into a scene that floored me: hundreds of pilgrims crawling toward a temple, foreheads and knees pressed into the dusty ground, inch by inch, prayer wheels waiting for them at the end. Watching them spin those wheels, releasing centuries-old mantras, I caught myself suppressing a rogue memory of *The Golden Child*—Chandler Jarrell, Brother Numpsa, and "I…want…the kniiife…please."

By morning, Barry was upright and ready to explore. First stop: the Potala Palace. I hadn't even heard of it before landing but instantly recognised its magnitude. Part fortress, part spiritual heart, it once housed the Dalai Lama, its sprawling white and red tiers defying the mountains behind it. We gasped for air climbing the endless steps, lungs burning with every altitude-choked metre. At the top, Lhasa spread out like a dream, its murals and relics whispering stories of faith and politics colliding over centuries.

Back at the guesthouse, a scrawled note on the bulletin board pulled us into our next chapter: two other travellers looking to share a ride across the Himalayas into Nepal via Everest Base Camp. A pint with Andy and Esther later, we were in. No plan. No proper kit. Just the promise of adventure.

We rattled away from Lhasa in a battered 4x4, monasteries flickering past the windows, crimson-robed monks and yak caravans blurring into the high-altitude dust. The roads turned to rock and ruts—exactly the rugged, off-road thrill we thought we wanted—until reality kicked in.

At a remote rest stop—basically someone's living room—the driver's friends served us yak butter tea. The local staple. Black tea churned with butter and salt until it resembled a warm, greasy broth. The smell alone was a dare. Barry shot me a look: We're doing this, aren't we?

No choice. One sip: horror. Two sips: regret. I channelled Richie and Eddie from *Bottom*: "You must! You must! You must drink our tea!" I gagged down another gulp, but in the end, I was defeated.

Two stars for camp. Pathetic.

Barely recovered, we pushed on. Then: a landslide. Boulders blocked the only pass. Our driver and a convoy of local lads decided the answer was... dynamite. Boom, boom, boom—mountain thunder. The freshly blasted gap was barely wide enough for a goat, let alone our jeep. Naturally, he gunned it through at breakneck speed, skidding, rocks clattering off the undercarriage.

By nightfall, we reached a monastery near Base Camp. One dusty stone building, perched under the shadow of the world's tallest mountain. Inside, draughts whistled through the gaps in the walls. A few flickering candles gave the only light and heat. At 16,900 feet, our breath misted in the air, our thermals laughably inadequate for the below freezing temperatures.

I genuinely thought I might freeze to death. Even my midnight dash to the outhouse became a near-spiritual experience in misery: hunched, teeth chattering, muttering pleas for redemption.

I'm a Celebrity, Get Me Out of Here!

But sunrise changed everything. A halo of orange and pink spilled over Everest's icy crown, painting the peaks like a celestial canvas. For a minute, the frostbite, nausea, and claustrophobic cold felt worth it.

The ride down from Everest was a white-knuckle blend of wonder and raw terror. Mountains draped in snow gave way to green valleys, the chill easing as we dipped lower.

But just as I started to enjoy the ride, our driver decided the switchbacks were a racetrack. Overtaking trucks on blind corners, tyres skirting the cliff's edge—my stomach lurched more than once as I pictured our battered jeep cartwheeling into oblivion. At one near-miss, I actually braced to jump out of the car, convinced we were going over. Barry and the others howled with laughter when we didn't.

I didn't see the joke.

Somehow, we survived the descent and rolled into Kathmandu. Dusty, wide-eyed, and deeply relieved to be somewhere warm and human again. The city felt like an old friend—a chaotic swirl of temples, market stalls, and a thousand rooftop cafés tucked into quiet alleys.

A few days later, Steve arrived, unable to resist the pull of the Himalayas.

In Durbar Square, we watched saffron-robed Sadhus drift by— dreadlocked mystics living out lives stranger than fiction: the man who'd held his withered arm aloft since 1973, the Baba who'd only drunk milk for decades, and the notorious Willy Baba, whose questionable talent still makes me wince.

Eventually, we felt the pull of the mountains. Steve and Barry—fitter than me by miles—picked a stretch of the Annapurna Circuit. My packing was comedy gold: a beach daypack, Reebok Classics, flip-flops, a spare pair of pants, and a Spurs shirt.

Perfect kit for hiking the Himalayas, obviously.

Our days found a rhythm: hike four hours, demolish rice and Snickers, hike some more, find a guesthouse. No reservations, no guarantees— just moving forward into a world where each step revealed something wilder than the last.

The Sherpas put us to shame. One bloke passed us carrying a full-sized fridge freezer strapped to his back with a forehead band, barely breaking a sweat while we gasped like fish on dry land.

Even so, we got cocky—on one glorious downhill stretch in Tatopani, we smashed two days' worth of trekking in a single afternoon, practically skipping over ridges and steps.

It felt like a genius move at the time—until the next morning, when my thighs declared mutiny.

I could barely stand. Steve and Barry had to half-carry me to the hot springs, where I sat waist-deep, wincing like an old man, trying to coax life back into my legs.

A sturdy walking stick—more Gandalf than Bear Grylls—became my lifeline. Flatter trails were bearable, but every descent was murder. Worse still, my pace slowed our crew to a crawl.

Somewhere above a deep gorge, we came to a narrow suspension bridge. Steve and Barry crossed first, laughing as I hobbled behind. Halfway across, clutching my staff and camcorder, I spotted a donkey ambling straight for me, saddle bags swinging.

No room to pass.

My legs wouldn't let me backtrack, so I shuffled sideways, praying the beast would show mercy. It didn't. One nudge from its side bag and I was nearly launched over the edge. The bridge swayed—I clung to the rope, my stick clattering into the abyss. I dropped to my knees, breathless, staring through the gaps at the river far below. Barry's hysterical cackling didn't help.

Somehow, I crawled off the bridge, dignity in tatters. That donkey nearly ended my Himalayan story in the most ridiculous way possible.

A few hours later, Steve decided to save us time with a 'shortcut'. He pointed to a gentle valley twenty feet below—"Easy, lads, we'll cut across and save hours!"

Before I could protest, he slid down the bank, triumphant.

251

His shortcut was a trap. What looked like a tame stream turned out to be a narrow, deep river with a fast current. He stepped in confidently —and vanished up to his neck, swept downstream in seconds.

Barry sprinted after him. I hobbled behind—more liability than help.

Steve somehow clambered out, drenched and laughing, as Barry yanked him up by the scruff. Any hope of saving time was lost—we'd added miles instead.

By dusk, half frozen, battered but triumphant, we limped into Jomsom, our checkpoint before Steve's bright idea. He never heard the end of it: our 'head scout' who nearly floated back to Kathmandu by accident.

Against all odds (and with questionable footwear), we'd trekked a good chunk of the Annapurna. We celebrated with haircuts and shaves at a local barber's.

My barber? Six years old, perched on a crate to reach me. His dad beamed with pride as the kid wielded a razor like a surgeon. Fair play: best shave I've ever had—no nicks, no fuss. That moment sparked my lifelong love for a proper barbershop. There's nothing quite like letting someone else tidy you up after you've been dragged through the wilderness by donkeys and dodgy shortcuts.

We left fresh-faced and semi-rehabilitated. The flight was our final adventure: a tin can with wings, a clear view into the cockpit, and every bump a personal insult to gravity. I half-expected Lao Che's goons to burst through the door and force us to bail out on an inflatable raft.

Luckily, no Short Round rescue needed—we touched down in one piece.

For the grand finale, we rafted down the Rapti River, camping on its banks under a sky so thick with stars, it looked fake. Somewhere between the flicker of the campfire and the steady rush of water, I realised just how much this part of the world had cracked me open.

For all the bruises, blisters and misadventures, it carved out a wild, lasting gratitude I'd carry forever.

Thirty Nine
Who Am I?

26th August 2021
London

I'd had a week to reflect—on therapy, travel, and the life I'd somehow survived. Unearthing memories buried behind the tsunami vault felt like opening a chest of long-forgotten treasure—freeing and unsettling all at once.

Rada had shifted my sessions to every other week—a milestone I should have celebrated, but I couldn't help feeling exposed without that regular anchor. Still, I knew it meant progress. Therapy wasn't just a place to unpack trauma anymore—it was helping me simplify this tangled life and understand the man underneath it all.

One big change: I'd stepped away from social media. No more doom scrolling or false dopamine hits. Instead, I was watching my mind— catching the unravelling thoughts and sitting with them, rather than drowning them in distractions.

For the first time in years, I'd let myself revisit the memories I'd sealed away so tightly they felt like scenes from someone else's film. The fun stuff came alive in colour—laughter, danger, adventure—but so did the darker undercurrent of guilt and regret. They came as a package deal, tangled and inseparable.

But this time, I didn't run from it. I was learning to sit with it all: the mistakes, the cowardice, the accidental harm. I wanted to strip myself back to the foundations—decide what to keep, what to rebuild, and what to let go.

Lost in these thoughts, I drifted into a coffee shop in Canada Place. I took a seat in the far corner, hoping to avoid forced small talk. My body language screamed "leave me alone." I ordered a black coffee and a tuna melt I had no appetite for—Rada's stern reminders about not doing therapy on an empty stomach keeping me honest.

The Americano arrived volcanic, of course. It always did. I waited, fuming quietly, then asked for ice as politely as I could muster. On the outside: calm. Inside I was hotter than the coffee. I pressed an ice cube to my temple and tried to breathe through it—in through the nose, hold, out through the mouth.

Too late. Flashback.

This wasn't just any coffee shop. In 2005, just weeks after the tsunami, I'd worked in this exact one. Steve had lined up a gig for me, inspecting their electrical systems.

At the time, I didn't question it—it was something to do while Tina recovered. But now I saw it differently: I'd ended up working there for three months and, oddly enough, never took the Tube, even though it would've been the obvious choice. Instead, I walked everywhere.

Not that I thought much of it then, but now it made sense. The need to be in control. To avoid anything that felt like being confined.

Trapped underground—no escape.

Stirring my cup, I stirred up that whole chapter too: how I'd come home broken, unwilling to admit it, pretending to cope. Too loyal, too cowardly to call things off with Tina. Too scared to heal properly.

One memory summoned the next—and with it, more shame. 'Would this labyrinth ever end?'

I drained the lukewarm coffee, and decided to sit with it: this version of me. Was he strong for surviving, or just scared to do the hard things? All these years later, I could finally name what was missing, integrity—I'd lacked a backbone.

Integrity wasn't just about showing up—it was about honesty. About owning your wants and needs without hiding behind guilt. *South Park's* Randy Marsh popped into my head: Tegridy Farms. That would be my new pillar. Alongside honesty and trust. Late, maybe, but not too late.

With that thought anchored, I headed to Rada's office, bracing for whatever layers still needed peeling back.

Sitting opposite her, I felt the weight of stories I'd never spoken aloud. Hesitant at first, I told her about the bright parts I'd uncovered—the wild travels, the mishaps, the joy. She listened, serene as ever, only breaking her silence to remind me:

"We don't just recall memories—we animate them. Speaking brings them to life. And sharing binds us—to others, and to healing."

She nudged me again: Talk to Barry. Relive the good times with him. Let the laughter loosen the knot of fear that had fused every happy memory with the horror.

Maybe it was time to call Barry.

After all, it was only Barry. If I couldn't tell him, who could I tell?

'Waste no more time arguing what a good man should be. Be one.'
Marcus Aurelius

Forty
Prince of Tides

2004
India

Barry Crenshaw was the calm to my storm—the dependable centre of our chaotic orbit since we were teenagers. I'd always been the restless planner, the worrier, the one spinning ten plates at once, while Barry floated through life as if the universe bent slightly to accommodate him.

He carried it lightly: shaggy blond hair, easy charm, and the kind of face that made girls swarm—but he wore it with such quiet modesty you couldn't even hate him for it.

We met in the summer of '91. He was already one of the large group of Lads who'd become my second family. Barry barely spoke at first, just watched and smirked while I clumsily carved out my place in their circle.

I'll never forget the day he turned heads for the wrong reason—a butchered haircut that looked suspiciously like The Rachel, years before Jennifer Aniston made it iconic. He had to strut through the gym with the whole school howling. Barry just owned it—shoulders back, chin up—the first glimpse of that unflappable grit that would resurface when it mattered most.

Years later, he was there by my side when we buried The Lads—the only time I'd seen him cry. Grief bound us tighter than ever, and when we hit the road in 2004, it was just the two of us against the world. No gang, no distractions. Just me and Baz, discovering how different we really were—and how much I envied his steady core.

In May that year, in Goa, I saw a side of him most never would—a quiet heroism that, six months later, would echo on a beach where the stakes were even higher.

Leaving the calm of Nepal behind, we crossed the border into India on a bus that tested every shred of patience. I clamped my headphones in, shut my eyes, and let Paul Weller's *Wild Wood* drown out my annoyance. Dad had made me promise to give Weller a fair shot—and he wasn't wrong. The Modfather's voice turned that dusty hell-ride into a daydream, each song carrying me far from jolting potholes and stifling air.

At dawn the next day, we boarded the Agra Express. Outside the window, the landscape softened: open fields, dusty villages, the haze of Uttar Pradesh's dawn. In my head, I replayed every cliché about the Taj Mahal, telling myself not to expect too much. But stepping into its grounds before the crowds arrived—that hush, that symmetry—made all the hype feel embarrassingly inadequate.

There it stood: floating above its reflection, veiled in the pale glow of morning. A love letter in marble, impossibly delicate and indestructible all at once. Barry and I wandered slowly, speaking only in hushed bits and bobs, tracing inlays, posing for a few awkward photos we knew would never do it justice.

Agra then destroyed me.

One suspect curry later, I was back in our room, curled on cool tiles, clinging to the bog for dear life. Forty-eight hours of gastric warfare— vomiting, cold sweats, crawling to the bathroom in a half-delirious haze. Relentless waves of intense… let's say "evacuation." Every time I thought I might be in the clear, one sip of water sent me straight back to hell. So much for culture. My big takeaway from Agra: the exact pattern of the bathroom floor grout.

When the worst passed, I emerged blinking into the sun, brittle and cautious. We tiptoed back into the city, sniffing out food I could trust. By pure chance, we fell in with a local shopkeeper, a football nut who waved us into his cluttered stall to watch the Premier League.

Within two beers, we were swapping stories like old mates—until he dropped the kicker: did we fancy a side job smuggling diamonds to New York? "Easy money," he said with a wink, tapping his pocket.

Barry and I downed our drinks faster than ever and bolted into the street. India: never boring, never safe, always three steps ahead. Still chuckling, we slipped away, leaving the Indian Mr Van Cleefe to find some other gullible tourists.

I may sound like Del Boy, but I'd like to think I have a little more nouse.

Then came Goa—our well-earned exhale. A night train south carried us away from India's relentless pace into a coastal paradise that felt half-Indian, half-Portuguese. We slipped easily into a lazy rhythm: mornings on the sand, afternoons lost to fresh seafood and cold beers under swaying palms, nights drifting through beach bars as house beats tangled with the crash of waves. Goa washed the grit of India off our skin and our minds.

One humid morning, we decided to test our 'inner peace' and joined a sunrise yoga class. There, next to a wiry old yogi who twisted like a pretzel, Barry and I fumbled through warrior poses and down-dogs, more sweat than zen. It was a humbling start to a lifelong curiosity I'd revisit years later during lockdown.

But Goa wasn't done showing me who Barry really was.

One afternoon, lulled by sun and the lullaby of gentle waves, I dozed off on the sand. I woke to Barry, drenched head to toe, water dripping from his hair and clothes.

"What happened to you?" I yawned.

He shrugged, barely looking up from his beer. "Oh, just saved a kid from drowning."

Casual. Unbothered.

But later, the child's parents found us. Tearful gratitude, folded hands, a father hugging Barry tight enough to lift him off the ground. Barry just gave them that soft nod he'd perfected—quiet courage, no fuss.

The ocean, with its ever-changing moods, had demonstrated again its power—how it could claim a life in an instant.

Maybe planning had always been my shield. Barry didn't need one—
he just acted.

I wondered if I'd ever find that same instinct. To just act. No fear, no
self-preservation. Just pure decency when it mattered.

Months later, in a very different ocean, we would find out.

'Remind yourself what you've been through and what you've had the strength to endure.'
Marcus Aurelius

Forty One
The Other Guys

26th August 2021
London

I never had the courage to ask Barry what really happened to him that day on Phi Phi. Maybe it was because dredging it up would force me to relive my own nightmare. Between us, there was an unspoken pact: I kept my horrors locked away, and he kept his quiet heroism buried deep. To everyone else, we were the same—the survivors, bonded forever. But inside, we both carried a version of that day we'd never shared.

Rada clocked it instantly. She looked at me, a mix of surprise and quiet sadness on her face.

"How often do you see him?" she asked softly.

"Every couple of months, more sometimes. Our wives are friends, so we hang out. Dinners, kids' birthdays… normal life."

She tilted her head.

I let out a breath that had been stuck in my throat.

"We survived it. We did what we had to do. We know the facts. We just… never pulled it apart, not properly. We've laughed about how it made us live life to the full, but never the raw stuff."

Rada didn't fill the silence. She let it stretch until I had to fill it myself.

"The first time I even heard a hint of Barry's side was from a mate—a throwaway comment, something like, 'Trust lucky Barry to end up on a fridge full of beer!' That was it for years. Then one day, out of the blue, Barry sent me Lisbeth's story."

Rada leaned forward, voice gentle. "Can you share it with me? What she wrote?"

I nodded slowly. "I'll try my best."

The words surfaced like silt from a deep pond. "She starts it in the internet café. She feels it—the floor trembling. She thinks it's thunder at first. Then this roar builds, rolling in from the sea. She glances at Barry. Even he looks rattled—she'd never seen him scared before. He's shouting, 'Don't panic!' but his voice is high, desperate. It shook her. Barry—the calmest man I know—unravelling in front of her."

I paused, chest tight with the ghost of it.

"Then they run. She remembers him pulling her arm so tight it felt like he was the only thing keeping her alive. They get caught in the surge—bodies all around, pushing, shoving, clawing. Barry's yelling, 'Don't push!' but it's chaos. She's scraped raw, barefoot, fighting for breath. They duck under a tin roof, sheltering in a fruit stand. She looks at Barry—he's staring past her, eyes wide. She turns to look, but before she can, the wave hits again. She calls it 'black soup'—the debris, the filth. She said, 'In that moment, my whole life was in his grip.'"

Rada's eyes glistened, locked on mine. "He was her saviour."

"Yeah. Then, floating past them—this fridge." Lisbeth screams, 'We have to get on that!' Somehow Barry climbs up first, hauls her on. They just sit there, bruised, shivering, gripping the handle while the world drowns around them. She told him, 'If I'm going to die, I'm glad I'm with you.' And Barry just looks at her, soaked and bleeding, and says, 'We're still here. We're not going to die.'"

Rada exhaled. "He gave her hope."

"Yeah. Hours later, a Thai man pulled them through his flooded house to safety. Even then, Lisbeth was frantic about the rest of us. At some point, they passed the guitar player from the band. He's just... standing there, hollow-eyed. Lisbeth hugs him, tries to pull him up the hill. He doesn't move. Then he points to a sofa in the street. His brother is lying on it. Dead. That was it. That cracked her open."

A forgotten moment hit me. "I'd passed that same scene without even realising. Maybe only moments apart."

Rada's voice cut gently through the memory. "Please continue, John."

I swallowed.

"When they finally reached higher ground—battered, bleeding— Lisbeth says Barry just scanned the crowd for me. She said he looked broken."

It hit me then: everything I was feeling, he was too. Except he didn't shut down. He kept going until he found us.

Rada nodded, her eyes kind. "He found you. That's love, John. That's brotherhood."

I looked down, throat tight.

"It is. And we've never talked about it—because how do you talk about something so massive? How do you put into words what it feels like to put your life on the line for someone else, and then keep going like it's all okay? How do you sit in a pub and say, 'Remember when we nearly died, and you saved a life on a beer fridge?' It's unspeakable. So, we don't."

She let that hang in the air, then said softly, "Maybe that's exactly what you're doing now, John. Speaking the unspeakable."

'Who looks outside, dreams; who looks inside, awakes.'
Carl Jung

Forty Two
Jury Duty

31st August 2021
London

The record for the most appearances on a jury in the UK is hard to verify. No Guinness World Record. Even the internet draws a blank. But I bet it's not high.

Jury service is a civic lottery—a plain white envelope through the letterbox, plucking your name from the electoral register at random. Some people go their whole lives without being picked. Others might get called once. But three times? I couldn't help imagining Norris McWhirter scribbling it down for *Record Breakers*.

In London, justice has always had a sharp edge. From medieval trial by ordeal to the cold ritual of the Crown Court. Just off London Bridge stands the Southwark Gateway Needle—easy to miss unless you know what it marks: the spike where traitors' heads were displayed after the Tower had done its worst. Wallace. Fawkes. Catesby. In those days, power didn't just punish treason—it made a spectacle of it.

By 1820, that ritual was banned. The death penalty itself finally abolished in 1965. Modern justice runs on paperwork now. Or so we tell ourselves.

My first jury gig was in 2001—twenty-four, fresh out of college, handed a five-week drug smuggling trial. Heroin inside almond shells —clever enough for a Harry Bosch novel, but very real. Weeks of phone taps, CCTV, cross-examinations—then twelve strangers handed a life to weigh. I remember avoiding the defendants' eyes as the verdict was read. It's one thing to judge from afar—another to sit ten feet away, holding someone's future.

Afterwards, we crossed London Bridge to decompress—and ran into the only defendant we'd acquitted.

He hugged us beneath the Southwark Needle, pouring out gratitude so raw it felt almost too intimate. We drank until dawn. I got a tattoo that night—tribal, Southeast Asia-inspired. Years later, my mum would describe it to a crisis hotline, ID in case they found my body washed up somewhere it shouldn't be.

I hadn't planned to think about that on jury duty. But trauma doesn't care about plans. Everything loops back to the tsunami eventually—the axis on which all my stories spin.

My second summons came around 2007—Petty theft, domestic spats. I sat through it, went back to my life, and thought I'd retired from civic duty.

Then lockdown eased, and another envelope arrived. This time, everything was different. Pandemic rules turned the courtroom into an isolation ward: glass boxes, masks, no chat by the vending machine, no quiet solidarity. Each day I sat alone, waiting to be called.

With no case to distract me, my mind put me on trial.

It didn't help that the weekend before had ended in disaster. Meg had planned a trip to visit the Eltham crew at their caravan park down south. I hadn't wanted to go—therapy had left my head pounding with questions. But I said yes, not wanting to disappoint.

The sun was out, kids kicked footballs, music poured from a portable speaker. For a few golden hours, it felt like normal life again.

So I drank. And drank.

At first, the music was balm—memories wrapped in melody. Cans of Red Stripe with The Lads in the park. Pissed in Bundaberg with Wiggy, trying to wrestle a parrot from a tree. But then came "Sweet Child O' Mine." And something cracked.

It didn't take me to Slash. It dragged me back to the Rolling Stoned Bar. Christmas Night, 2004. My Thai friend shredding the guitar.

The last good memory before the island was swallowed.

Panic swelled. The chords twisted in my chest, a dark reminder of what I'd buried. I didn't want to go back—but the music had me.

It reminded me of that scene in *The Goonies*—the bone piano, one wrong note and the floor falls away. Except in my version, there was no treasure at the end. Just demons clawing up from the depths.

Then—blackout. Drowning again in familiar darkness.

I woke face-down in Steve's caravan. Head pounding. Dread in my chest. Meg appeared in the doorway, calm and sad. She told me how I'd turned. Mouthy. Bitter. That version of me I hated—the drunk, brittle one.

So now, in that silent courtroom, sealed in plexiglass, I replayed it on loop. The rage. The switch. The song. Maybe it was PTSD. Maybe decades of numbing had fried something vital. Or maybe I was just *that* guy now—the one no one trusted past his third pint.

It made me sick with shame.

In that courtroom of glass and silence, I passed sentence: no more excuses, no more drink.

I'd done it with weed—clean nearly a year. Why not booze? What did it give me anymore, except blackouts and apologies?

Since fourteen, drinking had been my reward, my armour, my escape. But now it was just a one-way ticket to regret.

Sitting alone, I faced facts I'd dodged for years. Booze didn't suit me anymore. It didn't soften the pain—it stirred the ghosts.

Quitting would break all the unwritten rules of British social life. "Go on, just one," they'd say. "Don't be a wanker." But this wasn't about them anymore. The real trial wasn't in that courtroom. It was inside me—the battle between who I was and who I wanted to be.

And this time, I was ready to accept the judgment.

I'd gotten that tattoo the night of my first verdict—tribal ink for a tribal moment. But this was different. No more markings. No more performances. Just change.

On the train home, I scrolled through photos from the caravan weekend. Smiles. Deckchairs. Enough good moments to keep. But I knew I wouldn't be invited back soon—and maybe that was okay. Maybe they needed space. And maybe I needed it too—so they could remember the version of me they trusted. Not the one still hiding from his past.

This time, I'd hang up my boots by choice. No more excuses. No more pretending the tsunami was the only ghost in my head.

There were others.

And I was finally ready to face them.

Sober. Awake. Honest.

For real this time.

'This place is a dream. Only a sleeper considers it real. Then death comes like dawn, and you wake up laughing at what you thought was your grief.'
Rumi

Forty Three
Dreamscape

1st September 2021
London

The darkness swallows everything. No sound, no feeling—just a suffocating black void pressing in. Breathing feels like forcing air through wet cement. A faint glow teases me forward, but every step is like wading through tar. Panic claws up my throat, but when I try to scream, nothing comes out.

Then, light floods in—and I'm treading water in a shrinking room. The walls close in, the air thickens. I open my mouth, but silence devours the sound.

I jolt awake, half-choking on a sob. Skin clammy. Sheets soaked. Seventeen years later, and the sea still comes for me. I taste brine, hear phantom screams. Every creak in the house slices through me. Only when Meg draws the curtains does the room breathe again.

Swinging my legs out of bed feels like hoisting anchors. My body aches. How much longer could I keep waking up like this?

The dreams—vivid, merciless—felt more real than sleep. Some nights I'd wake clutching Meg, convinced I was drowning. Therapy dredged them up like souvenirs. Each session with Rada added fuel to the fire.

I'd never really grieved. Not properly. I'd carried the guilt like a private curse—survivor's guilt, Rada called it. Rationally, I knew I'd done all I could. But the if onlys never left.

"Let yourself grieve, John. It's okay to mourn the lives lost—even those you didn't know. It's okay to forgive yourself for surviving."

Forgive myself for living—it sounded so simple. But it felt impossible.

268

Still, a part of me wanted to believe her.

"I'm thinking of going back," I said, half-deflecting. "It'll be twenty years soon."

"That's good," she nodded. "There's power in facing the places we run from."

She asked how long the nightmares had been back—how weed had buried them for a decade, and now the dam had burst.

"I'm actually sleeping," I laughed bitterly. "But waking up feels worse than never dreaming at all."

"Numbing only delays pain," she reminded me. "Suppress it long enough and it grows teeth."

She gave me the usual checklist: consistent bedtime, wind down, read a book, breathe, wake up the same time. I heard her. But my mind was still trapped in last night's darkness.

That evening I crashed on the sofa, half-watching Game of Thrones, jolting awake every ten minutes. Meg finally dragged me upstairs. I lay face-down on the bed, bracing for another battle I knew I'd lose.

And sure enough—the ocean came again.

This time I was running—through quicksand—chased by something formless but certain. Legs giving out. Panic drowning me. Meg gone. My fault. Always my fault. Then—towering above—the wave swallowed the light—

"John... John..."

I shot up gasping. Meg's voice pulled me back. She was alive. Warm hand. Worried eyes.

"Just a nightmare. I'm fine, babe."

A lie.

Next morning I stumbled out, unshaven, dead-eyed. Replaying the blackouts, the dreams, the shame. Part of me almost missed the old high—the numb haze where nothing mattered.

At the café across from court, I clutched a venti coffee like a lifeline. Just focus on the cup. One sip at a time.

For the first time, I think I hit rock bottom—sat there, marinating in shame and fear, I wanted to crawl home like a Tibetan pilgrim—penance in every step. But that wasn't an option.

Something shifted.

I reached into my bag and pulled out my Kindle—dead weight for years. One unread book blinked back: *Meditations* by Marcus Aurelius. A suggestion from my chiropractor, the first person who ever hinted I might be carrying trauma.

A Roman emperor, a Stoic philosopher—about as far from Lee Child as you can get. But I had nothing left to distract me, so I opened it.

And it hit. The words landed like I'd been waiting my whole life to read them: Self-awareness. Self-discipline. Self.

What could a Roman emperor possibly teach a working-class Londoner like me?

Apparently—everything.

"Control what you can. Accept what you can't. Virtue is within."

I read it again. Control. Choice. Me.

I'd lived for everyone else—pleasing, apologising, numbing. What if it was time to unlearn that? To build something solid from the inside out?

For too long, control had been external—a performance, not a practice. I'd been the eternal 'Yes Man.' If I wanted to survive, if I wanted even a thread of peace, I had to change.

Not just quitting booze. Not just talking to Rada.

I had to confront the person I'd become. And start again.

As I sat there in that courthouse, surrounded by masked strangers, something cracked open.

One page. One thought. One breath at a time.

Maybe, beneath the armour of my past, there was a version of me still worth fighting for.

'Half of the troubles of this life can be traced to saying yes too quickly and not saying no soon enough.'
Josh Billings

Forty Four
The Yes Man

10th September 2021
London

The weeks in my self-imposed dock—brutal, but necessary. For the first time in my life, I was properly cross-examining myself— no excuses. No blaming fate. Just me, the choices I'd made, and the dents they'd left behind.

Like the night I flung myself out of a moving car just to dodge an argument with Meg. How insane is that? One second a heated exchange—the next I'm rolling down the road like Lee Majors.

The worst bit? I was driving.

Between those humiliating reruns, I devoured Stoic philosophy. Every line peeled back a layer of bullshit I'd wrapped around myself for decades. The basics weren't complicated: be decent, own your behaviour, control your reactions.

But living it? That was the hard part.

Growing up where I did, 'morals' were flexible. The closest thing to a philosophy lesson was "finders keepers, losers weepers." We weren't outside the tuck shop debating Plato—we were nicking Dib Dabs and dodging fights. My code was survival: watch your back, trust no one, hit first.

Even friends turned fast—sometimes with fists, sometimes with silence. No wonder my temper lived on a hair trigger. I'd been jumped, chased, threatened more times than I could count.

But now, thanks to a long-dead Roman and a very alive therapist, I was seeing another way.

I didn't have to be the wildcard anymore. Maybe I could shed that skin and build something better.

So I read. Slowly. Hungrily.

Each page sparked memories I'd buried deep—and this time, I faced them. See it clearly, Rada's voice echoed. Some memories made me grin—outrageous antics, the chaos, the camaraderie. But this wasn't nostalgia. This was about the parts I'd ignored: the volatility, the recklessness, the compulsive need to say 'yes' to everything.

Underneath it all, I knew I had a good heart. But I also had work to do—temper, people-pleasing, the way I'd burn myself out trying to keep everyone happy.

Over the past year, I'd made changes—but mostly by accident. I quit smoking, but only because lockdown made it hard to score. My diagnosis came because work intervened, not because I sought help. Even sobriety was a response to shame, not strategy.

That had to change.

No more stumbling into progress. I had to be intentional—draw a line, and commit to becoming a man I could stand behind.

Religion had never stuck—especially after people told me "God had a plan" while we buried The Lads. But Marcus Aurelius? He made sense. No gods, no threats—just wisdom: stay calm, live well, control what you can.

Travelling had introduced me to faiths from everywhere: Buddhism in Tibet. Islam in Brunei. Hinduism in India. Judaism in Jerusalem. I hadn't thought much of it back then, but now I saw it differently. Maybe it wasn't about divine will—maybe it was about human truth passed down through time.

One line in *Meditations* punched me in the gut: "Focus on the present. Stop wasting energy on what you can't control."

I laughed. The present moment—that elusive thing I'd always traded for worry or regret.

And then came the real kicker: the power of No.

Saying 'yes' was my default setting.

Wiggy had nailed it years ago:

"Brommers, you're always in. No half measures. Full-blooded two-footed challenge every time."

It was a badge of honour—until it wasn't. It had given me some of my best stories—wild nights, globe-trotting madness, the kind of memories that feel too big for one life.

But it had cost me too. Drugs. Near-death stunts. Toxic relationships. A marriage I never should've entered.

Being the Yes Man came at a price.

And it kept me running from truths I didn't want to face.

Not anymore.

I could feel it—the brakes screeching on my autopilot.

I closed my eyes. Took a breath.

Made a promise: I won't say yes so easily anymore.

As if my mind rewarded the honesty, a buried memory jolted to life—late '80s, one reckless yes that nearly cost us something far worse than broken bones.

Oh God.

The time we almost got groomed…

'There's daggers in men's smiles.'
William Shakespeare

Forty Five
The Predator

1989
London

It was maybe '89—the year slips away, but music always pins it down. *Bad* had just come out, Michael Jackson's big follow-up to *Thriller*. I'd played that album to death, memorising every beat. I was too young to realise "Dirty Diana" was about a prostitute. And stupid enough to think "Liberian Girl" was about some book-smart chick in a library. I won't admit how old I was when I learned that MJ wasn't serenading Plain Jane Super Brain down the non-fiction aisle.

By then, I'd shifted to Bobby Brown. That smooth swagger. Love songs with an edge—perfect for a long, hot summer on the estate, where you either grew up fast or got left behind.

I was twelve. Nick, a year older. That summer, we cooked up a car-washing hustle to earn money for the essentials: Joe Bloggs jeans, Kickers, shell suits. We'd sweat under the blazing sun, stripped to our shorts, chests bare, skin slowly browning. Too young, too innocent to notice we'd caught someone's eye.

Our final job that day was Nick's older brother's car—a bright red Renault 5 that had to gleam like showroom stock. He was like Chet from *Weird Science*—all bullish orders and belittling insults. He called us "Spunk 'n' Sperm." It was meant to be a joke, but it stuck—crude, mean, older boys' humour.

We scrubbed hard, passed his military inspection, then legged it, laughing as we went.

"Oi! You two! Up here!"

Third-floor flat. Window open. Squinting against the glare: Vincent.

They called him Vince the Nonce. Back then, just a nickname—the weird uncle of a kid we hung with. Skinny, shock of white hair, thick NHS specs—a cross between Jimmy Savile and Bricktop from *Snatch*. Nobody questioned it. He was just around.

He offered us a cleaning job. Said other kids had done it. We checked —they had. Came back with plenty of readies.

It was kosher. So we said yes.

The first time felt harmless. Crammed into his battered white Escort van, rattling down to Croydon. Office block sweep, McDonald's on the way back, twenty quid each.

Week later: another gig. Same drill. Alarm code. Dust. Polish. Burger. Cash. It felt legit.

Spunk 'n' Sperm Enterprises was booming.

Afterwards, Vince said we could eat at his place. Watch TV "like grown-ups." It felt like a promotion—like we were earning trust.

His flat stank of stale smoke and secrets. Brown-orange wallpaper, threadbare shag carpet, overflowing ashtrays, heavy curtains that swallowed all light.

He put on *Escape from New York*—Snake Plissken growling across a ruined Manhattan. We were hooked. Barely noticed Vince watching us. Measuring.

Then the shift.

Once the wrappers cleared, he leaned in.

"Got a special job for you two. A proper one. But only if you can keep your mouths shut. Shtum, you understand?"

A tale followed: safe-cracking, jewels, cash. He needed small, strong lads who could swim the Thames and slip through a window. "You're special," he said. "Different." Then:

276

"Let's see those muscles, boys."

We flexed. Posed in his smeared mirror. It felt… off. A chill crawled in my gut, but Nick laughed—called me a weakling. I laughed too.

"Next week—wetsuit fittings. Strip down, get measured. Two hundred quid each."

Two. Hundred. Quid. We didn't even blink.

Then he turned to me, too casual:

"You like this movie, Johnny Boy?"

"Dunno. Never seen it before," I muttered, eyes locked on the screen.

"But you like films, don't ya? Haven't taken your eyes off it."

His voice dropped. "Got loads more. Anything you want—Vincent's your man."

I edged closer to Nick. Something in the air had curdled.

Vince sensed it. Smiled wider.

"Hang on. Got something you'll really like."

He disappeared. We sat frozen. Nick said nothing. My mouth was dry.

Vince returned, knelt at the VHS player, slid in a tape.

"Don't tell your mums I let you watch this, alright?"

We nodded. Nick glanced at me, something in his eyes…

Then the tape flickered—porn.

Not like the torn-up mags in the woods. Full-blown, graphic porn. We froze.

He watched us squirm, his grin stretched wide.

"Pass me fags, Nick. Maybe next time I'll let you watch more."

Nick flicked him the pack without speaking.

"Next week, boys. We'll sort it all then."

His smile was all stained teeth.

Nick shifted. Jaw set. If Vince made a move, I knew Nick would go for the glass ashtray.

He elbowed me. "Come on. Now."

We left without a word.

We never went back. Nick never spoke of it again. And I wouldn't understand for years what we'd brushed up against: a predator hiding in plain sight, wrapped in a stupid nickname and our childish trust.

A chill crept over me now, sitting in the courtroom, that memory snapping back into focus.

The ticker on the TV rolled: No more jurors needed today.

I gathered my things and stepped out into the London air, grateful—for once—for the daylight.

> *'The chains of addiction are generally too small to be felt until they are too strong to be broken.'*
> **Samuel Johnson**

Forty Six
Nowhere To Run

23rd September 2021
London

I was an alcoholic. The man in the mirror—sunken eyes, five-day stubble, skin years older than it should've been—knew it too. I barely recognised him anymore.

I certainly didn't like him.

I gargled tepid water from the tap, spat into the sink, and the stench of vodka rose back up the plughole—sharp and sickly. Brushing my teeth set off my gag reflex, and I spat out a small, vile mix of spit and orange fluid. Stomach acid, probably.

My latest attempt at sobriety had lasted almost a week. Six days for the shame of the caravan blackout to fade, just one hundred and forty-four hours to bury all the painful introspection I'd unearthed in court.

I'd convinced myself those lessons would be life-changing—a roadmap out of the cycle I was trapped in. But I'd discarded the tools almost as quickly as I'd picked them up.

I splashed cold water on my face, forced down a bitter instant coffee, grabbed my rucksack and stumbled out the door. I was running late. Nothing new.

London was mercifully mild—warm enough to skip a coat, cool enough that my brisk walk to the station wouldn't turn me into an even bigger mess of sweat stains and creases.

I sprinted the final metres, clattering through the doors as they hissed shut. The carriage was nearly empty. Good. No witnesses to the state

I'd become—panting, chest pounding, sweat soaking through my collar.

Two stops later, my breathing calmed—but not my shame.

'Go home,' a voice in my head hissed. 'Call in sick. Cancel therapy. Hide.' But I didn't move. I sat there for twenty-eight minutes, watching my reflection in the window and hating every inch of it.

Why do I keep doing this to myself? I've really got to get my shit together.

Mike's ghost was riding shotgun. One song last night—a shared favourite—and I'd drowned myself in grief and cheap vodka.

It was always music that undid me, the secret code Mike and I spoke fluently.

Now silence replaced him, and it ached in every cell. Our friendship hadn't even reached its full stride.

Fuck, I was a mess. I hoped Meg hadn't heard me blubbing in the kitchen.

By the time the speaker barked "Victoria," I was wound so tight I could've snapped steel.

Late, tired, stressed, upset.

I just needed to get off.

Nineteen platforms, and yet every bloody day, for as long as I'd been commuting, we had to stop outside for five fucking minutes. Did they not know this train was coming? I could feel the other passengers glancing my way.

'Nosy cunts,' I thought, my anger winning out.

I should've stayed home.

"For fuck's sake!" As soon as it left my mouth, I regretted it. Too loud.

Too exposed. But I let the stares wash over me. Let them.

Doors hissed open. I merged into the flood—shoulder to shoulder, funnelling toward the barriers like cattle in a slaughterhouse. Bodies pressed against mine: hot, damp, unyielding.

Then I wasn't in Victoria anymore.

I was back on that pier.

Sunburnt faces. Ragged clothes. Screams. Salt in the air. A crush of bodies fighting for a spot on a lifeboat that couldn't hold them all.

Panic choked me.

Nowhere to run. The wave would come—it always did.

Blackness.

I came to on a bench in the concourse, bent double, gasping, sweat dripping onto my shoes. No clue how I'd got through the barriers. Just grateful I hadn't collapsed. I squeezed my knees, forced my lungs to obey.

Not now, John. Not here.

"F.E.A.R. Forget Everything And Remember." Ian Brown's voice rattled in my skull as I clung to the bench, reminding myself to forget my past and remember to breathe. Musical mantra. Inch by inch, the past retreated.

I made it in—fifteen minutes late, my hair plastered to my forehead. I skipped the fake hellos, poured a strong black coffee—just how Reacher drinks it—and hid in the corner behind my laptop.

What had happened to me? That was new.

Usually, I'd keep myself busy on the train—crafting a post, building a story, anything to distract me and keep the demons at bay. Normally, I'd have waited for the platform to clear, easing into the day.

Instead, I'd walked straight into a trap I'd set for myself.

I was regressing, slipping deeper, and this morning, the facade cracked.

For the first time, I couldn't deny it. I wasn't well. Not at all. And I was watching it happen, helpless to stop it.

Rada's eyes pinned me gently to the chair. "Rough morning, John?"

I hated how she saw me—hated needing help more. My lungs fought me. My chest a locked box. But slowly, her voice cut through the static. The edges of the panic dulled.

After a while, her question landed softly but didn't let me hide.

"Tell me about the train platform. About the flashback."

The word tasted clinical, but the reality was anything but. A crack in the dam. An old nightmare made real.

"I thought I was doing better," I said, my voice sounding hollow even to my own ears. "But it's like… every time I try to get it together, something comes along and just…" I trailed off.

"Let's take a moment, John. Just breathe. You don't have to say anything. Just… be here. You're okay. You're safe. Slow breaths. That's it, stay with it… in, and out."

She spoke gently, but I could feel her studying me.

Have you ever tried to calm yourself down when someone's watching you like a hawk, analysing every twitch, every breath? It's impossible to relax.

My mind went into overdrive, latching onto the smallest details. I closed my eyes, feeling each breath like a chore. My chest tight, muscles locked. But I followed her words. Slowly, the edges of my mind softened.

I could hear the hum of the heating vent above us, and Rada's quiet breathing—a reminder that I wasn't alone.

My heartbeat slowed. I felt steadier, more present. Not trapped in the half-realities I'd been fighting all day. Rada waited, letting me arrive at my own pace. I'd not thought about that moment since it happened all those years ago.

'If you're going through hell, keep going.'
Winston Churchill

Forty Seven
The Rescue

December 27th 2004
Thailand

The walk back down the mountain felt endless. Each step heavier than the last. Our adrenaline drained, replaced by a dull, bone-deep exhaustion. We were numb, driven by one goal: reach Gypsy Village, find shelter, cling to whatever scraps of normal remained.

Others trickled down behind us—silent, hollow-eyed—stumbling through a world that no longer looked like theirs. The air stank of ruin and decay. Cries of survivors drifted through the canopy—desperate calls for the missing, mostly children.

I caught Lisbeth's eyes. We didn't speak. If I let the grief in now, I'd break. Later, I promised myself.

Where the mountain path met the dusty road, the island revealed its wounds: collapsed shops, broken bottles, wreckage scattered like confetti. We scavenged a crushed case of bottled water, passing it around in silence.

The heat rose with the sun, baking everything in misery.

Some whispered that help must be coming—governments, aid, helicopters—but we couldn't see it yet. It felt like the world had been scrubbed clean of everything but us—though just beyond the horizon, entire fleets were already mobilising.

At Gypsy Village, the huts still stood. A gift from the ocean, sparing scraps of our lives. Tina and I ducked into ours. Her clothes lay soaked and ruined, strewn like garbage. My backpack, unbelievably, sat upright and zipped—untouched by the wave that had drowned everything else.

My laziness saving my belongings.

"It had to be my clothes, didn't it?" she snapped, too exhausted to hide the edge.

"Forget them," I muttered. "Grab your bag, let's go. We can't stay here."

Back outside, Barry latched onto rumours: speedboats to Phuket for a small fortune. Hope flickered—then vanished when someone outbid us.

New plan: get to the pier. Maybe rescue would find us there.

The closer we got, the clearer the scale of the destruction. The beachfront was gone—boats wedged in shops, timbers stabbed through walls. Corpses surfaced in the corners of our vision. Broken limbs poking from rubble.

Don't look. Just walk.

We passed the shop where it all started, the yellow Kodak sign still dangling above the ruined doorway. No words. Just the shared, silent question: What if we'd hidden there instead of running?

At the pier, news spread—a ferry was coming, bound for Phuket.

As it docked, hush turned to chaos. People pressed forward onto a wooden skeleton built for dozens, not hundreds. The wood groaned, swayed with every shove.

"Wait! It can't take this weight!" Lisbeth and Barry pleaded, but panic drowned them out. Mob instinct took over. Better to risk the pier snapping than be left behind.

I was trapped in the middle—suffocating, no room to breathe— terrified I'd survived a tsunami only to die here, crushed by fellow survivors, falling to jagged rocks below.

By luck or fate, the pier held. We boarded one of the first ferries. I collapsed on the upper deck. Below, people still scrambled for a spot.

Guilt stabbed at me. I'd made it out. Why me? Why not them?

Trying to bury the thoughts, I pulled out my camcorder—some part of me still needing proof this wasn't a fever dream. But the lens drew fury from below. A shout. A finger pointed. Rage and grief aimed squarely at me—the survivor filming the misery they were still trapped in.

Shame flooded my chest. I snapped it shut, ducked below the railing.

What an inconsiderate bastard.

I haven't turned it on since.

The two-hour crossing was a heat-scorched blur. I wrapped my head in a shirt, pressed myself small against the deck, trying to block it all out: the sun, the noise, the guilt. Everything.

Years later, that pier still lives in my chest. The crush of bodies echoes in every tight space, every commuter platform, every crowd.

"I should never have got on that boat," I told Rada, my voice a raw whisper in her quiet office.

She didn't flinch. "Why do you believe that?"

"There was nothing wrong with me. I was strong enough to stay and help."

Her eyes didn't let me hide.

"You did the best you could in an impossible moment, John. You didn't run. You survived."

I wanted to believe her. But the truth burrowed deeper than comfort: I'd abandoned something in myself that day. A standard I thought I'd never break.

No amount of logic could wash that stain away.

I let myself down.

By the time I left Rada's office, darkness had fallen. The air outside bit at my skin, sharp and sobering as I crossed the canal bridge and descended into the station's hum. My AirPods were jammed deep, volume cranked high—anything to drown out the guilt.

The tube rattled under the Thames, pulling into North Greenwich with its familiar screech and sigh. I made it through the crush, resisting the pull back into the dark corners I'd just unearthed.

Outside, my bus waited. I climbed aboard, sinking into my usual seat by the exit doors—an instinct I'd never questioned until now:

Always know the escape. Both exits in sight. Both exits within reach.

The engine's low hum worked like a sedative. For the first time all day, I felt a flicker of quiet—fragile, fleeting, but enough. I watched the streetlights blur by, half-watching the other passengers. Old habits intact: scanning faces, clocking movements, staying ready.

Just in case. Always just in case.

Then the driver tested my patience—jumped a red light, blasted past stops, left people stranded, their arms raised in futile protest.

I turned back, frustration tightening my gut. Bit it back.

I had nothing left to spare for someone else's problem.

But then, outside the hospital, an old woman boarded—frail, careful as she tapped her card. Before she could settle, he yanked the bus into motion. She went flying down the centre aisle—dull crack of bone on metal, a gasp from the crowd.

Reflex overtook exhaustion.

I was on my feet before I knew it, hauling her up with another passenger, guiding her to the nearest seat as she winced and cradled her wrist. Luckily not broken.

Then he jumped out of his cab—had the gall to blame her.

Mean, defensive words spilling out.

The red mist came instantly, burning through every last scrap of restraint.

"How dare you blame her? This is on you. You couldn't wait thirty fucking seconds, could you? You've driven like a prick since North Greenwich—now get back in your seat and do your fucking job properly."

He flinched, stammering something half-formed. I cut him off, voice low, dangerous.

"Shut the fuck up and drive us home."

He shuffled back behind the wheel. Nobody spoke.

A few passengers caught my eye as they disembarked—a nod, a murmur of thanks, a hand on my shoulder I barely felt.

But inside, I was shaking. Regret coiled tight with leftover rage. I wanted to vanish. Instead, I sat there, staring blankly out the grimy window, my reflection ghosting back at me:

A man unravelled, snapping threads one by one.

That night, the nightmares didn't bring images—just a thick, formless dread pressing on my lungs, squeezing the air out until there was nothing but black. I clawed at it in my sleep, but there was no escape.

Only a vision—clear and surgical, slicing through the dark: A knife hovering at my throat. So close I could feel its cold promise.

I jolted awake, breathless, hand at my neck. No blood. No wound.

Just the ghost of the thought, coiled tight around my heart.

That image stayed with me, sharper than any dream. Something had shifted in the dark. A line I couldn't uncross.

'Not until we are lost do we begin to understand ourselves.'
Henry David Thoreau

Forty Eight
The Way Back

24th September 2021
London

Eyes squeezed shut, I tried to push the thought aside—the phantom ache of a nightmare that had pulled me under and left its poison seeping through my veins. Not suicidal. Not really. More like a primal urge—to carve something dark out from inside me.

I forced myself up, feet heavy, limbs leaden. I didn't want my routine today—the familiar sweat, the forced calm. But I did it anyway. The sauna had become my only sanctuary, a place where the noise could thin out for a few precious minutes. I lay back on the cedar bench, the heat clawing at my skin, hoping it might cauterise the raw fear still ringing from the night before.

I thought of Marcus Aurelius: "You have power over your mind, not outside events."

Easy for him to say. But maybe there was something in it—a scrap of control in a life that had felt anything but.

I know how pretentious this all sounds. A guy with a home sauna, quoting Roman emperors while he meditates in yoga pants. What a prick.

I get it.

But this wasn't some overnight transformation. It had been years in the making. I'd picked up titbits about well-being—never used them.

I blamed procrastination, but the truth was simpler. I was a lazy drunk.

The flashback. The bus rage. The nightmare—all of it pointed to one

290

truth I kept pretending wasn't true: the alcohol had to go. I could spout Stoic wisdom all day, do yoga, punch pads, chant affirmations till my throat gave out—but none of it would stick if I kept sabotaging myself the moment I picked up a glass.

Mike had known that. Mike had fought it. And I'd ignored it, thinking we were different. That binge drinking didn't count. That "alcoholic" was a label for someone else—someone on a park bench, clutching a can of Super Tenants.

I knew better now.

'I miss you mate,' I thought, letting the heat blur my vision. 'I'm so sorry I wasn't there at the end.'

Cold water slammed my skin awake. It stung—but the sting felt clean. A scrap of penance, maybe.

Wrapped in a towel, I thumbed open WhatsApp—The Breakfast Club.

"Morning lads, sauna done, cold shower done. Happy Friday."

No mention of nightmares or phantom blades. Just a simple check-in with the boys who'd become my life coaches.

We were all grappling with our own demons, not least the absence of Mike. So we had a pact to stay connected and support one another's progress.

I dressed and headed for the barbers—one small ritual I could rely on. The chair, the buzz of clippers, the familiar banter.

Abs offered me a beer.

I asked for Turkish coffee instead. He raised an eyebrow but didn't push.

Twenty minutes later, a peel-off mask made me look like a Discount Zorro. I snapped a selfie, sent it to the group. Barry would love it. Maybe that was the point—reminders that life could still be light,

291

sometimes, if I let it. Maybe it would remind him of our Himalayan adventure, and the child barber who kickstarted this addiction, back when the days were still full of potential.

In the mirror, my face looked clearer.

Not healed. Not fixed.

But a man with lines and bruises who might still find his way back.

Too late for Mike. But maybe not for me.

'First you take a drink, then the drink takes a drink, then the drink takes you.'
F Scott Fitzgerald

Forty Nine
California Man

August 2004
America

"Call him then," Barry urged, dropping his battered backpack at the base of the phone booth.

"Alright, alright..." I muttered, flipping through our dog-eared notebook to find Mike's number scrawled in the margins.

Barry promised a pint every night if this bloke spared us from another Greyhound trip.

The LA bus station was the end of the line—literally and spiritually. After months living on those buses, we'd had enough. Endless cracked seats, fogged-up windows streaked with old rain, and the unmistakable smell of recycled misery.

I punched in the number. Crackle. Click.

"Yo!" A voice boomed through the static.

"Is that Mike?"

"Yep. You must be John. Bobby said you might pop up. Where you at, LAX?"

"Nah, mate. Greyhound station."

"Get the fuck outta here!" He laughed, a big hearty rattle down the line. "You British cunts are crazy! There's a pub called the King's Arms nearby. Go there. I'll grab you in an hour." Click.

"He's on his way," I told Barry, who looked like someone had handed him a winning lottery ticket.

As Barry dug out the guidebook, I scanned the station. The place was a far cry from the glitzy arrival we'd pictured. Greyhound terminals always carried the same mix of desperation and decay, but LA's had a special kind of bleak.

We'd learned to keep our heads down—staying on the fringes, avoiding eye contact. Like that night in Louisiana, when I wandered half-asleep into the toilets and saw a man washing his privates in the sink. Pants round his ankles, cupping himself in one hand, working the timer tap with the other in a kind of grotesque rhythm.

Barry nearly died laughing. But by then, we were mostly numb to the surreal.

Back in LA, the station stank of old burger grease. We found the pub —stale beer and frayed carpet, but it felt like home. We'd barely touched our first pint when the door flew open.

"Barry! John!"

Mike was huge. Booming. All bear hugs and sarcasm. In minutes, we were in his truck, the city blurring past in a haze of stories about Bobby and Vietnam.

His condo felt like paradise—clean, quiet, cockroach-free. Within days, we were swept into his world: pool parties, poker nights, lazy mornings with South Park. He called us "his London project" and treated us like brothers.

Mike got me. Dark humour, obscure references, emotional shorthand. For once, I wasn't even the nerdiest guy in the room. Our conversations ran deep and dumb and brilliant all at once.

Even now, when I hear "I'm sorry… I thought this was America!", it's Mike's voice I hear, not Randy Marsh's.

LA was magic—but also the start of something darker. They were all stoners, not pissheads like us. Weed was everywhere: bongs, pipes, vaporizers. I barely knew what half of it was, but I didn't hesitate to join in.

Harmless fun, I thought. That was the moment drugs became a doorway. Nobody told me the door swings both ways.

Back then, I was just a boy saying yes to everything—no idea how hard it would be to say no later. My memory of those months holds a version of myself before the shadows crept in. Before addiction changed everything.

I think about Vegas, 2014–Meg's 30th. Mike showed up stone-cold sober while we drowned in cocktails. Still the loudest in the room. Still the funniest. No drink in hand, and he didn't need one.

I was proud. And ashamed.

Watching him proved it was possible. But it also reminded me of the 'Fun Bobby' curse—that fear you're only lovable when you're lit. Mike carried that fear too, hidden behind our shared jokes and one-liners.

It's clear now: the tsunami didn't create my addictions. It supercharged them. The wiring was already there—I was always primed for excess, for saying yes when I should've run. PTSD just dressed it in a sharper suit and turned up the volume.

If I'm honest, I've been trying to get back to a version of me from before LA. Not to erase everything—but to reboot. Back to basics. Reclaim the innocence I lost somewhere between the Greyhound and the wave.

We survived, sure. But what the fuck were we supposed to be now?

"This is 29 Acacia Road. And this… is John, a boy who leads an amazing double life. For when John gets triggered…"

Cue the transformation:
Name: John Bromfield
Alias: Tsunanaman
Reality: Earth-1610
Occupation: Adventurer
Base of Operations: The Dreamscape
Special Abilities: Hyper-vigilance, black humour, quick reflexes.

Weaknesses: Water, crowds, noise, pollen, anger, molluscs, booze, drugs, cats, eczema…

Eczema? Really? (If you got that *Office* reference, you would fit right in.)

That's me—using pop culture to keep from drowning.

Therapy cracks you open. You see the truth. You swear you're cured. Then you slip. Again. And again.

But I can't keep slipping. Not after Mike. He fought to the end. He deserved better.

Maybe I owe him more than memory.

Maybe I owe myself a rescue mission.

But first, there's one more story buried close to the wave—when everything split into before and after.

Time to stop circling it.

Time to finish the reckoning.

Time to face it all.

'The leaves of memory seemed to make.'
Henry Wadsworth Longfellow

Fifty
The Dead Zone

October 7th 2021
London

I was close to the finish line of my story. I was ready to finally piece it all together and face the truth—not just fragments, but everything I could remember. Sharing it all wasn't about dumping my past on Rada and hoping for a miracle cure. If these sessions had taught me anything, it was this: the real work had to be mine.

I'd been using our sessions to dissect the tsunami and its aftermath, then spending the rest of my time dredging up old memories, applying what she'd given me. Chipping away at the calcified layers, trying to find the boy who'd once been easy to love—by others, and by himself.

So much had shifted. When I'd first walked through the doors at Mind, I couldn't name a single thing I still enjoyed. Gita had pushed me to rediscover old passions, and I'd come up empty. The wave hadn't just washed away my life—it had taken my identity. My spirit. Withered, like Sadhu Amar Bharati's arm, forever raised and frozen in time.

But what better test than a night with my best mates? We were getting the gang back together—Wiggy and his wife were hosting—Bobby, Barry, Steve and their wives were all coming. The girls did the impossible: synced diaries, bribed babysitters—made it happen.

It felt like a final exam for the progress I'd made.

I felt a flicker of dread. It'd be the first time seeing them all since the caravan club fiasco. Part of me wanted to cancel, hide, let time soften the awkwardness. But I was done running. And the moment Steve hugged me at the door—warm and forgiving—the fear vanished. Among these people, my flaws didn't matter.

Barry arrived late, and Rada's advice rang in my ears: You have to talk to him. My pulse spiked just looking at him. How do you casually say, 'remember that giant wave that nearly killed us? Fancy revisiting it over canapés?' The thought made me sweat.

But the moment passed, and I let it.

For a few golden hours, the heaviness fell away. I didn't care that I hadn't brought up the wave. That could wait. Tonight I just wanted to remember who I was before.

A few days later, I was back on Rada's couch. She didn't have to say a word—her disappointed silence said it all.

"John," she sighed.

"I know. I know. I didn't bring it up. It wasn't the right moment. I will. I promise."

She nodded, unconvinced.

"Alright then. Let's pick up where we left off—do you remember?"

Of course I remembered. It had never left me.

It was waiting—right there in the corner of my mind, ready to pull me back in.

Arriving in Phuket offered no escape. Devastation met us at the pier and followed us inland like a curse. Whatever calm the ferry ride had provided evaporated the moment we stepped into the orchestrated chaos of the rescue effort.

Volunteers moved with frantic purpose, directing crowds of stunned survivors who, like us, had washed up from the islands. Buildings I'd once known were flattened, streets a mess of rubble and grief.

When the tsunami reached Phuket's shores, it unleashed waves up to ten metres high—wiping out entire villages, leaving behind a coastline littered with debris and death.

We were herded away from the pier, down roads so warped I barely

298

recognised them. But amid the nightmare, there was relief in someone else taking charge. For the first time in twenty-four hours, my guard dropped—just a fraction. I dared to hope, briefly, that we were safe now.

Deep down, I knew better.

No one spoke. We sat in silence, staring out at the ruin.

They dropped us at a building still miraculously intact—a school or government block, now a makeshift rescue hub. Outside, survivors huddled on patches of grass, some crying quietly, others staring at the ground, vacant.

We found a spot and sat, too drained for words. One thought beat through my head: I needed to call home. My family didn't know if I was alive—every second of their not knowing was another second of agony I'd caused.

Barry and I locked eyes. No need for words—we both knew. Inside, we found a lone payphone bolted to the wall, a queue of anxious faces snaking toward it. As we waited, I rehearsed what I'd say, stomach tight with dread and relief. Each caller seemed to take forever.

When it was finally my turn, Barry gestured for me to go first—always the gent.

The line clicked.

"Hello?" My mum's voice—raw, trembling.

"Mum." That single word broke her.

"It's him! He's alive!" she shouted to the room behind her. "John, oh thank God. I knew, I just knew—"

I blinked hard, forcing calm into my voice.

"I'm okay, Mum. We're all okay. Me, Tina, Barry—we made it."

She wept. I kept it short—told her we'd be home soon. As I hung up, a weight lifted. But guilt gnawed underneath: I should've done this sooner. I'd trusted that SOS text. It never sent. I should've insisted.

That was on me.

While Barry made his call, I drifted down a corridor, and stumbled onto something that nearly brought me to my knees.

A large hall—maybe a gym once—now a silent morgue, lined wall to wall with bodies. Neat rows of white sheets, some flecked with blood, some pristine. People moved between them—searching, lifting corners, gasping—breaking down as their worst fears crystallised under fluorescent lights.

The sight punched the breath from my chest. My resolve cracked, replaced by a tide of sadness and guilt. 'Why them? Why not me?'

I tried to back out but something rooted me there—a sick need to witness it. On one wall, a grid of Polaroids: faces of the unnamed, each marked with a number.

I stepped closer, drawn by something I couldn't name. Each face was a life, abruptly stopped. So many nationalities, ages, stories that would never finish. Death didn't discriminate—it levelled us all.

I don't know how long I stood there. Eventually, Barry's reflection joined mine in the glass. He didn't speak. He didn't need to. We just stood, side by side—a silent prayer for strangers, and for the fragile line we'd danced along.

When we finally turned away and walked back to the others, the enormity of it weighed on us like an invisible shroud. This was survival, yes—but it was also a ghost we'd carry forever.

And deep down, I knew: some part of me had died in that hall, replaced by something I'd be trying to understand for the rest of my life.

'I am not what I am.'
William Shakespeare

Fifty One
Homeward Bound

October 7th 2021
London

The skin on my neck prickled, goosebumps rippling down my arms like a silent alarm. I hadn't faced this memory in years—if ever, not fully. It lurked beneath a broken streetlamp in some back alley of my mind, buried under layers of avoidance.

Now, it had been dragged into the light—violating every fragile defence I'd built.

The faces came back. Ashen, frozen in brutal clarity—Polaroids taped to the morgue wall. Each tagged with a cold number, matched to the sheet-draped body behind it. A cruel lineup of lives cut short, waiting to be claimed. Whole families wiped out in an instant. My mind recoiled, helpless, like a child staring at something too vast to grasp.

As my avatar stared at those photos, dread surged through time. Just as visceral now as it had been that terrible day.

Death. All around me.

I gasped—present again. Rada's ice-blue eyes held mine, unwavering. She'd guided me here with quiet persistence, stopping me when panic bubbled over.

My Spidey Sense was tingling, my pulse thundered. But Rada's steady breath grounded me, her gaze anchoring mine until my chest rose and fell in sync with hers.

In—two, three, four. Out—two, three, four.

Be here. I dug my fingers into the cushion, clenched my toes into fists. This isn't real anymore. Stop.

301

The memory hit like a flood—pain, confusion, shame, sorrow. But no anger. Not this time. My trusty Garbage Pail Kid sidekick, 'Greaser Gregg', all leather-jacketed rage and snarling bravado, had vanished. He'd left me that day on the pier when I thought I'd be dashed to pieces on the rocks below. That furnace of fury was gone, carried away on a futile scream.

What remained was a hollow ache, vast and formless. No more rage. Just Damaged Don. All I had left was exhaustion. Despair. And tears —long-stalled since 2004—that finally broke through in 2021.

"I think I stayed with Tina out of guilt," I blurted. My voice cracked under the weight of it. Rada didn't flinch.

"Explain," she said—no-nonsense, steady as ever.

"I didn't want to be with her, Rada. Not for a long time. But after that day… it felt like I owed her. It feels so mad that we were married."

She flipped through her notes. "Married? You said she was your girlfriend John."

"She was—then. Later, we got married. Then divorced, obviously. So surreal, really. Like it happened to someone else."

Surreal didn't quite cover it. It was like recalling a parallel life. I drifted, but Rada reeled me back in with her endoscopic persistence. Always probing, always asking me to stay with the story.

Breathe, John. Just breathe.

Eyes closed, I slipped back into that morgue skin—standing amidst the frozen silence, those endless rows. Barry's voice echoed across time:

"Don't look! Shut it down!"

And I did. I shut it all down—for good.

Back then, I wrapped myself in Colossus's steel skin from my childhood comics. Unbreakable. A layer of organic steel flesh unfurled and created an impenetrable layer between me and my emotions. I could feel it reverberate through the years making me invulnerable to what was raging inside.

I felt it as I stared back at Rada, realisation taking hold. I'd locked my emotions behind a mutant shield that day! Completely and deliberately.

Rada called it emotional numbing—a survival tactic, meant to be temporary. For me, it became a way of life. A prison. A shell that locked out joy and grief in equal measure. Her words made sense, but I preferred my version: a self-made X-Man, impervious to feeling.

Like a ghost, I detached. From passion, purpose, people. I didn't make decisions—I drifted through them. I pulled away from friends, from family. Safer not to feel anything than to feel it all.

After the session, I staggered into the street, collapsed behind a wall, and gagged—retching up fragments of my emotional fortress. A horror movie moment: possessed protagonist vomiting up black bile.

Something ancient. Fetid. Evil.

The reality was worst: Middle-aged man, sobbing into a gutter. Ring a bell. Walk me naked through the town. SHAME! SHAME!

I wiped my mouth, composed myself, and merged back into the London crowd—trauma neatly hidden behind a polite smile. "The power of Christ compels you." Smile. Pretend. The good old British way. Stiff upper lip. Demons be damned.

I'd lost a decade to that numbing. A slow erosion. Fuck, fuck, FUCK. CTRL+ALT+DELETE. Reboot required. John 5.0 is defective.

The tube screamed under the Thames—a banshee howl that shredded even the best noise-cancelling AirPods. It made me want to scream with it. I didn't. I breathed instead.

Johnny Five is alive, I thought in my best laser-lips voice.

Alive. Somehow, we'd all made it home. That's something, right? But

303

only parts of us made it back. We left something behind in those waters.

At some point the screeching stopped. I was on the escalator, staring into space, sightless. On autopilot. Drifting.

Yesteryear pulled at me again. The three of us—Barry, Tina and me —waiting on the lawn by the morgue. Watching every other nation gather their people—all sorted, helped, lifted away. But us? Nothing.

We hugged our Danish friends goodbye. Just like that, they were gone.

"Someone will come for us too," I said.

But no one did.

No Virgin aircraft. No Richard Branson in a hot air balloon. Just gallows humour to keep the spirits up.

Then someone pointed out a British consulate guy. Crumpled suit. Lost expression. Our last hope.

Mr Bean would've been more help. No planes. No plan. No clue.

My fury returned like a heat-seeking missile, zipping across Phang Nga Bay to bind itself to my new armour. It wrapped around me, exposed and untamed, my very own alien symbiote. An exposed nerve in a broken steel suit.

"So what the fuck do we do, then?" Barry asked, quiet but iron-willed.

The man shrugged. Sit tight. Figure it out.

'Fuck that. Useless twat.'

Barry clenched my arm. "We don't have passports."

The man reached into his briefcase, pulled out emergency documents.

Tina was babbling about New Zealand again. Gone, checked out. I had to get her home. That was my mission now.

Strangers got us there—Thai volunteers, bus drivers, airport staff. We ended up at Phuket Airport somehow.

Waiting, drifting.

Then it came—not the Thai Airways jet I expected, but a C-130 Hercules. A beast of a warplane. We filed in like POWs, strapped down against the walls. No words. No tears. Just quiet gratitude.

Bangkok was a blur. Kindness. Organisation. Hotels and medics and well-meaning hands. But I couldn't slow down. Movement was my only tether to sanity.

Barry stayed behind. I didn't blame him. But it still sits uneasily—like unfinished business between brothers. Another thing I need to broach when my courage shows up.

At check in, I handed over my soggy debit card. Explained who we were, where we'd come from. The woman behind the desk gasped. She barked orders in Thai. Heads turned.

We were the first wave.

They treated us like family. Bowing. Apologising. "Please don't blame Thailand."

ประเทศไทย ฉันรักคุณและจะขอบคุณความกรุณาที่คุณแสดงให้ฉันเสมอ
(Thailand, I love you and will always be grateful for the kindness you showed me)

The card worked. Two seats to Heathrow. Boarding passes in hand. They seated us alone at the back. Tina barely moved. I drifted in and out of nightmare sleep, waking to my own voice screaming, "Run! RUN!"

Once, I woke to a stewardess mopping my brow, holding my hand. The sorrow clung to me like static. No monsters in the wardrobe—just trauma, reshaped, recast in every dream.

Forever.

I don't remember the drive home. One moment, the car door slammed.

The next, I was in bed.

Sleep dragged me down. Nightmares came on like a thunderstorm. As strong as on that flight so long ago. I jolted awake gripped by panic, not knowing where or when I was.

In the darkness, shadows took shape. Bodies on the ceiling. Draped in white sheets, writhing, reaching out to pull me under, to where I belonged.

Meg's voice pierced the dark. Her hand on my head. Grounding me.

When I could speak, I whispered, "I'm okay, babe. Just need some water."

I crept down the stairs, gripping the banister like a lifeline. That buried part of me had clawed its way out again.

Don't let this be back for good…

But trauma doesn't work like that.

It waits.

Always waiting.

'When we are tired, we are attacked by ideas we conquered long ago.'
Friedrich Nietzsche

Fifty Two
Aftermath

January 2005
London

Given the sheer magnitude of what we'd survived—the danger, trauma, and life-threatening chaos crammed into forty-eight frantic hours—the aftercare we gave ourselves was pathetic. With hindsight, it's obvious we set ourselves up to fail. If there were a checklist titled "What Not To Do After Surviving a Natural Disaster," I'd have ticked every box.

Complex PTSD feels inevitable.

Back then? I thought we were fine. Arrogance sealed the vault. Not an excuse, but I'm a product of the "Man Up" generation.

Put on your big boy pants. Stop complaining. I didn't know any other way.

The plane touched down on December 29th, 2004. We stumbled off, half-conscious, running on snatches of plagued sleep. The flight crew let us disembark first, showering us with hugs and good wishes—embarrassing but kind. Other passengers watched in awkward silence. Nothing to see here, I wanted to say. Just two damaged souls dragging themselves to the jetway.

At baggage claim, I nearly abandoned my bag—just a wet, mouldy pile of clothes—but some weird instinct kept me attached. We all survived—no one left behind.

Reaching customs, I felt relief. Family will be on the other side. It's over. I can let go. Breathe.

Then reality broke the spell.

307

"…Sir? Excuse me, Sir. Will you stop? I'm talking to you!"

A hand gripped my bicep. A young customs officer blocked my path. For half a second, I thought she was there to help—someone official, finally.

I turned to her, dirty, barefoot, forcing a hopeful smile.

But no.

She looked straight through me. "Where have you travelled from, and what's in that bag?"

It almost dropped me to my knees. Was this real? I wasn't going to comply. Not today.

"Are you serious?" My voice came out ice-cold. "Look at us. Where the hell do you think we've been? We're barely alive, and you want to search my bag?" My anger—my symbiote—hissed. "Half of Asia's been wiped out, and you want to know what's in my fucking bag? Here—look!" I hurled it to the floor, unzipping the rotting mess.

She didn't look. Maybe she saw how close I was to breaking. Maybe she just didn't want the hassle.

"That's okay," she murmured, backing off. "Zip it up. I don't need to look."

Dragging the bag behind me, leaving wet footprints in my wake, I pushed through the green sign for Nothing to Declare.

"We are Venom."

My entire interaction with British officials after surviving the tsunami was diabolical. No help in Phuket. And now: a bag check. The audacity cut deeper than any search ever could. I needed comfort— and almost got the rubber glove treatment instead.

On the other side: men in black jackets with scribbled signs, families hugging, taxi drivers prowling. Normality. Strangers going about their day. As if nothing had happened.

Then our families found us. Relief in their hugs and tears. I don't remember much—just that I let go. Let them steer me home.

Finally, I surrendered.

The next few days? A blur. The vivid memories vanished. Not erased —just inaccessible. No images. No feelings. Just sleep and silent meals, hidden in my childhood bedroom—my fortress of solitude.

Unchanged. Safe.

I emerged only for food or to reassure my mum: I'm fine. Leave me be. I'd done my job: got us home. Now there was nothing left to focus on.

Nothing but the echoing hollow inside me.

Next morning, breakfast was a bacon sarnie and a proper cup of tea —staples in the Bromfield household. We ate in near silence until Dad switched on the BBC. Survivors trickling home. Footage of Phuket: cars swept down streets, buildings devoured.

Phi Phi barely mentioned—a ghost island nobody seemed to want to show.

Banda Aceh dominated the news. Thirty-metre waves. Entire cities swallowed whole. 167,000 dead there alone. My ordeal felt tiny by comparison. Like it didn't count.

I left most of my sandwich untouched and slipped back to my room, claiming fatigue. I was hungry—but appetite felt obscene.

Then the call came—Tina's dad. She couldn't keep food or water down. She needed a hospital.

Good. A distraction. A mission.

I grabbed Mum's tiny red Micra and raced to Woolwich. Straight to A&E—what we should've done the moment we landed.

Four hours waiting. Five. She looked worse with each passing minute: gaunt, yellow-skinned, drifting in and out. I pestered nurses. You're in the system. Be patient. At last, we were called.

Tests. Blood. More waiting.

The doctor confirmed it: Salmonella. Probably from swallowing sewage. Plus Campylobacter—likely from a cut exposed to foul water. No wonder she was delirious. Shock and fever rewriting her reality.

Me? No one asked if I was okay. Or if they did, I waved it off. No visible wounds—so nothing wrong, right? Another brilliant decision from yours truly.

Then nothingness.

This stretch of my life is a black hole. It's infuriating.

A gap in my Rolodex.

Not just weeks. Years. A glitch. A corrupted file I never dared try to restore. I see it now: classic *Red Dwarf* syndrome—"Thanks for the Memory." I did it to myself. Erased the grief. Wiped my own mind.

What a smeg head.

The tsunami, my life with Tina—filed under Forget and Move On. It felt smart at the time. Now I know better. I didn't just shelve a painful chapter. I buried my own history.

Maybe there's still a way back. The way Rada showed me.

In my mind, I picture a dusty library, a secret lever behind a bookshelf, a hidden staircase spiralling down to a forgotten speakeasy. I can almost smell the stale cigars, hear the echo of old stories.

If I can just find the right book… maybe I can finally remember.

'What you resist not only persists, but will grow in size.'
Carl Jung

Fifty Three
The Man Who Wouldn't Talk

October 10th 2021
London

"I want to talk tonight, 'bout how you (sort of) saved my life."

Simple words. Easy, when sung by Noel Gallagher on *Oasis'* criminally underrated B-side "Talk Tonight." But reality? Anything but simple.

We never talked about it. Never addressed what had happened, how close we'd come to meeting our maker, or how it had twisted our melons. Instead, we drifted forward in silence.

Part of me wanted her to open that door. To look me in the eye and say, "That was mental, wasn't it? Thank you for coming back for me, John. Scary as hell—but you did it."

I didn't crave praise, not really. Just a nod. A shred of understanding of the monumental task of running back into a tidal wave. But it never came. So my pride stepped in, laying a wall between us, brick by silent brick.

Trauma doesn't vanish. It burrows in, finds a dark alcove, and waits. Deep inside my mutant steel flesh, my old buddy Damaged Don kept that ember of rage alive—waiting to resurrect Greaser Gregg.

So, we became experts at avoidance. Skirting the truth like it was a fragile ornament we'd shatter if we got too close. Conversations stayed shallow: "Good day at work? Shall we get on it?" Just enough to keep pretending.

Sometimes I'd catch her eye when a loud noise set me off, or when the ocean flickered on screen. I'd search for a sign that she remembered. That she carried it too. But she'd look away, as if the wave had swallowed it all—and I'd swallow my words along with it.

Nights were the worst. We drifted to opposite sides of the sofa, each isolated in our own version of the same nightmare. She'd drift off fast, her breathing calm—a master of forgetting. I envied her. I resented her, too.

I won't lie about that.

I told myself I didn't need her to say anything. 'Be a man. Get over it.' But inside, the other voice whispered: 'She could have said thank you. Just once.'

Then came the guilt: 'Oh, poor you, John. Want a fucking medal for doing what anyone would? You're not Mutley, you wanker.'

'It was your fault she was there anyway!'

I'd burn with shame alone in the dark. Resentment and guilt piling up like kindling.

Looking back, my silence was cowardice dressed as pride. Stoic philosophers call it 'courageous endurance'—the strength to stand firm in discomfort, to speak the hard truth. I failed miserably at that.

I let the distance grow until it turned to quiet loathing. Rada praised my instinctive bravery—pulling Tina from danger. But that was primal survival, not courage. Real courage would've been facing her, facing myself, and naming what sat rotting between us.

But I didn't. I left the ball in her court and blamed her when she never served it back.

Whatever connection we had before the tsunami unravelled. We stayed together out of guilt, habit, laziness—anything but love. Everyone said, "What doesn't kill you…" So we thanked whatever god kept us alive and pretended survival was enough.

I patched up my battered old backpack—my so-called lucky charm—

and prepared to run again.

Tina wanted to finish the world trip the tsunami had so cruelly cut short.

She'd not stopped talking about it, even as we sat stunned on that rooftop.

I didn't want to go.

Guilt steamrolled instinct. Obligation overruled intuition. So I queued for new passports, renewed working visas, filled out forms. One step at a time until I had no excuse left.

Families hugged us at the airport, probably wondering why we were so desperate to run away again. I didn't think about them. Not once.

Selfish much, John 2.0?

I. Am. Alright. Jack.

Looking back, that round of travel feels maddeningly vague—a blank space where adventures should be. My earlier trips play back like a buddy movie: laughter, mishaps, pure joy.

But this chapter? PTSD didn't just scar my emotions—it stole my memory. I'm left sifting scraps, trying to rebuild moments I don't want to admit are missing. Maybe it's re-entry amnesia. Maybe it's for the best.

But my reality isn't full. The one I've built my existence on—it doesn't have all the facts. So here I am, dredging them up. No rose-tinted glasses. Just raw edges and awkward truths.

It feels necessary now. Unavoidable.

Bear with me. This is somewhere I never thought I'd need to go. But now, it seems imperative. Inevitable.

Memory upload complete.

No wonder I buried it deep. No wonder it still feels shameful now.

Well, shit.

One thing's clear: I can't unsee it now. The memories are back, real as ever. No more running. No more silence.

Start your engines...

'The truth will set you free, but first it will make you miserable.'
James A Garfield

Fifty Four
Without a Paddle

2005
New Zealand

I can see the past through the murky windscreen, welcoming me back with open arms. Auckland Airport, rental car keys, open road. I eased into the driver's seat, hands gripping the wheel. Anchored again.

My own DeLorean—no roads required.

With a final glance at the skyline, I turned the ignition. The hum of the engine was a small comfort. As we navigated through the city's waking streets, *Bachelor Girl's* "Blown Away" bled from the speakers—a lyricist's summary of my state of mind.

The road stretched out, a ribbon of asphalt winding through rolling hills and sunlit countryside. Tina, already asleep beside me, had dropped the map to the floor. Her brief stint as chief navigation officer: over. Alone behind the wheel, music filling the steel cocoon—my temporary fortress from everything clawing at me.

This would become routine: Tina asleep, me and my iPod, my real companion. Each song a fragile tether to who I used to be.

Mr Chekhov finally stirred just as we neared the Bay of Plenty. Our digs for the week: a scruffy caravan behind a crowded hostel. The owner, Kevin, promised the basement lounge for the Champions League final—a small slice of normality that sparked a flicker of excitement.

But Tina had other plans.

"We're going white-water sledding tomorrow."

"What? Tomorrow's the final! You just heard Kevin?"

"Already booked it. They're picking us up at six."

Another thing steamrolled. Another chance to say no. Another one I let pass.

It's just a game, you'd say—but back then, it was more. A flicker of familiarity I needed.

"Fine," I muttered.

25th May 2005. Liverpool's miracle comeback in Istanbul—and I was hurtling down Grade V rapids on what was basically a baking tray.

Our 'ride': a battered white van. Side door slid open—young Māori bloke, comically large spliff, "Three Little Birds" blaring "Don't worry about a thing," indeed.

The Kaituna River was bone-achingly cold. We suited up in damp wetsuits, strapped on laughable helmets, then got a thirty-second briefing: Kick left. Kick right. Good luck.

What followed was a battering. Grade V Rapids slammed us into rocks and dragged us under. Then came the waterfall—Tutea Falls. One of the highest commercially rafted falls in the world. Except we had no raft. No practice. No sanity check. Just: "Aim for the middle, dive over!"

I glanced at Tina. For once, my concern mirrored in her eyes. Too late to back out. Only forward. Kick, brace.

I went over. Free-fall. Icy darkness. Violent slam to the riverbed. Surfaced gasping, scraped raw. Fear prickled my spine.

Clambering out, soaked and shaking, I shot Tina a look. Inside, the anger roared. The pyre inside me was almost ready.

That night, huddled in the heater-less caravan, sleep was fleeting. Each time I drifted off, I was yanked back under—churning water, struggling for breath.

By morning, we were packed and gone. Fleeing, as if distance could erase the ghosts.

By Tongariro, the cold I caught had turned serious. Five days in a foggy hostel. No hike. No view. Just fever and a TV loop of *Lost*.

Wellington felt like salvation. Tina's friend Zowie had invited us to stay, and I clung to the hope of a stable environment. But by morning, the bug owned me. Delirious. Barely functional.

They left me—went sightseeing, giggling over cocktails while I shivered under a blanket. Hours passed. No food. No water. Nothing.

When they returned—twenty hours later—they were drunk. Reeking of cigarettes, laughing, teasing. They thought force-feeding me vodka was the solution.

I drank just to shut them up. Salt on a wound.

That night, bitterness dug deep. As sleep finally took over, the resentment inferno almost blew.

Next morning: worse. So I drove myself to the local doctor. Tina incapable of getting out of bed and showing some compassion.

Doctor said pneumonia. Antibiotics and rest—in a draughty flat with two drunkards. Great.

Every cough rattled my chest. Every lonely hour cemented one truth: When shit hit the fan, Tina checked out.

I'd been by her side for weeks during her recovery. In my hour of need, she'd fucked off.

Not smart enough to slow down, not brave enough to confront her, I turned inward. The voice in my head got louder.

Drinking became escape. No longer social—now survival. Hostel to hostel, bottle to bottle.

Which is why Queenstown—land of adrenaline and late nights—was the worst place for me.

I said yes to caving. A jagged hole in the forest. Abseiling into black nothing. Inside: pitch darkness. Then, headlamps off. A trust jump into an unseen underground river. Free-fall. Suffocating dark. Icy shock. I surfaced gasping, feeling dread in every cell.

Jet boating down the Shotover—cliffs, icy spray, and a looping mantra: 'this is how I die.' Tina squealed with joy. I faked a smile through clenched teeth.

Then: the Nevis Swing. The death drop. Hung over a canyon, clinging to a steel pole until my grip failed. The scream ripped out of me before laughter could catch up. Brief pride. I'd beaten my fear demon. But I knew—I was losing the larger battle.

Fear was infiltrating every decision.

That night, I woke abruptly, heart pounding. Nightmare again—but something else. A spreading dampness.

What the hell?

I shifted. Realised.

I'd pissed myself.

Mortified.

Thank God Tina was in the top bunk. Imagine her waking to a drip from the sopping mattress. A disgusting twist on Chinese water torture: "I'll talk! 4737 Carlin, sir!"

I crept to the showers, dumped my clothes in the bin—a burial at sea for my dignity. Crawled back onto a dry corner. 'Just an accident, John. Forget it.'

But I couldn't. The shame clung like the damp. 'Why now? Why me?'

Alcohol. That's the excuse I reached for. I thought of Dangerous Dave and the only adult case of bed wetting I'd known. Dave had a bottomless appetite for booze and class A's—but it came with a side effect.

Dave had pissed himself weekly on the Bondi flat's sofa. Nine blokes in close quarters—it became a running joke.

Eventually, Dave's issue reached its climax. One night, a party in full swing, the soaked MDF base collapsed—dragging two girls into the sofa's storage pit.

A Benny Hill moment if ever there was one.

Back then, we laughed. Now, lying in my own shame, I got it. Too well.

Next incident came days later. No hiding this one. Tina woke to find me rigid on the bed, staring at the wet patch. She laughed it off.

I started to dread dorm rooms, terrified someone would discover my issue. I took to stealthily disposing of evidence in the dark of the night.

New Zealand had unlocked a Pandora's box. 'Wee Wee Willie' joined the growing gang of Garbage Pail numbskulls.

Shame. Shame. Shame.

So the drinking worsened. Not just "escalated." It evolved.

No addressing the psychological unraveling. Just numbing it.

I kept thinking of Dangerous Dave—but this wasn't funny anymore. The fear wasn't just in dreams. It was waking. Creeping.

I'd forgotten this chapter—and I understand why. But now, going through it, I'm stunned by what I find:

Nightmares. Rage. Guilt. Fear.

Accidents. A war inside.

The Franz Josef Glacier—blue ice, towering crevasses—should've amazed me. It didn't. I was too hollow to care.

Even White Island Volcano—surreal, sulphurous, dangerous—couldn't compete with the inner chaos.

That island later erupted in 2019. Twenty-two people killed.

When news of disasters breaks—A volcanic eruption on a spot I stood on. A tourist death on a river diving off a waterfall with a flimsy sled and a faulty helmet. Birds flying into the engine of a propeller plane above the Himalaya plateau. Vehicles tumbling down the mountainside. Children, trapped in a cave system, running out of time —My fear, ever the opportunist, taps me on the shoulder. "See? Told you."

Then a forgotten memory emerged.

A reconnection with the Kiwi couple from our escape. We stayed with them. Drank with them. Did we talk about it? Compare stories?

I don't know. I can't see their faces. Did I soil their linen? The thought yanks me away like a dog on a leash.

Move on. Move on.

Abruptly, we left New Zealand.

I was different.

Angry. Guilty. Drunk. Pissy Pants.

Fear, my new best friend.

Shackled to my armour.

'Pain is certain, suffering is optional.'
Buddha

Fifty Five
Wrong Turn

2005
Australia - USA

And so it was, armed with my newly acquired 'quirks', that we landed in Australia. Fear circled my mind like a vulture—relentless and sharp-eyed—refusing to release its grip on the past few weeks. 'It's not permanent,' I repeated. 'I'm not Dave. Just a few accidents.' That mantra became a broken record. But even as I whispered it, the vulture kept pecking at my dignity.

Now, on the road with iPod, I turned away from my relationship and into music. I needed the noise. I clung to it like a lifeboat in an ocean of anguish. Each song drowned out the choir of tormenting voices: "Pissy pants… you loser… it should've been you under that wave."

Now those same songs show up on my mindfulness playlists—anchors from a storm I barely survived.

Coober Pedy. *Mad Max* territory. Donning my imaginary fedora, I entered this alien world like a weary explorer on another doomed mission.

Arriving felt like stepping into a dystopian sci-fi novel. The air shimmered off the desert, heat bouncing back into our faces. To escape it, the locals had carved homes, shops, even churches into the earth. It was like discovering a secret Womble civilisation thriving below the harsh outback.

Inside the subterranean hotel, the walls were cool to the touch, smooth like fresh clay. The silence was profound—the kind that wraps around you, pressing on your ears. Our room had no windows. No natural light. No sound.

A sensory void.

I slept. Hard. Eighteen hours. But the darkness turned on me—no visual cues, no familiar noises, just pitch black that blurred dream from nightmare. I felt pinned down by a formless terror pressing from the ceiling. Limbs locked. Brain screaming Wake up, John!

When I finally clawed my way back, sunlight felt like salvation. I staggered topside. Dragging new shadows with me.

I remember the date now: July 7th, 2005. Unforgettable. Tina went horse riding—I stayed back—beer in hand, cheap paperback in lap.

I'd declined—not just to avoid time with her, but to avoid the activity itself. Maybe just tired. Or maybe it was Nervous Nelly whispering about the girl I once knew who fell off a horse and broke her back. Whatever the reason, I stayed behind.

A small TV flickered in the corner with one of the 24-hour news channels.

Then: **BREAKING NEWS.** London Terror Attack. Explosions on the Tube—stations I'd walked a thousand times. I gripped the remote like a life raft. Details were scarce. The footage was harrowing.

Our friends and family used those lines. Panic.

Now I was on the other side of disaster, waiting helplessly. It rattled me in a way I didn't admit. Though the situations were incomparable, the role reversal was quietly unsettling.

I called home—answered on the first ring. They were all safe.

Months earlier, I'd been avoiding the Tube. Not consciously, but instinctively. The thought of being trapped underground was unbearable. As the images played on Foxtel—commuters fleeing smoke-filled tunnels—I felt vindicated.

Nelly again: 'See? Told you, John. That could've been you.'

I don't know when I stopped pissing the bed. But it wasn't that night.

Stupid boy.

Years later, I learned the science. PTSD flips the fear switch. Amygdala screaming. Cortex AWOL. Nightmares as time machines, dragging you back. The body panics. Control collapses.

I never told anyone. Just flipped the mattress, cracked jokes, and carried on. But each damp mattress corroded my dignity just a bit more.

Night after night, the cycle devoured me: dread → nightmare → shame → fear → repeat.

So I found a solution—pathetic, but effective.

Insomnia.

If I didn't sleep, I couldn't dream. If I couldn't dream, I couldn't drown. No more accidental shame. No more ghosts in the dark.

Just me. Awake. On guard. And slowly unraveling.

I refused to face what I was becoming. I turned headfirst into my problems, chiselling minor cracks into gaping chasms. If I couldn't extinguish the inferno inside, I might as well throw a jerry can of kerosene on top and watch it rage.

Touching down in the new world, insomnia followed me like a shroud. I carried a dangerous mindset—unwilling and unable to break the patterns that had taken root.

The details of where we went and how we travelled blur together, but the music remains vivid. The sun was just beginning to climb when Tina clambered into the passenger seat of the hire car—backpacks, Big Gulps and M&Ms—and we hit the road.

The Mojave rolled by, "Mr. Brightside" on full blast. The Grand Canyon couldn't crack through the concrete wall around my mind. At Santa Monica Pier—the symbolic end—the road was done, but inside, I was still lost.

Tina had slept through most of it. I hadn't even tried to wake her. Sleep well.

Standing at the edge of the pier, the music still playing in my head, I felt a flicker of optimism. Maybe reconnecting with the LA gang would reset something inside me—break the cycle, bury the worst parts of myself, and become the version they remembered: loud laugh, last one standing, the easy "yes."

We piled into Mike's truck for a road trip to Joshua Tree. The landscape was otherworldly—twisted trees reaching skyward, rugged rocks like desert sentinels. A U2 album cover turned climbing frame. Mike, our resident action hero, led the ascent. I wanted to prove something—to him, to myself.

The first few feet were fine. Then the crevice stopped me cold. Palms sweating, heart racing—the ninja version of me long gone. Replaced by a trembling imposter.

Nick would've disowned me instantly, revoking my Shinobi credentials without ceremony.

Tina climbed with a grace I'd never seen from her. Humiliating. I made a second attempt, pure stubbornness. Forced each step, legs shaking. At the top, the view felt like a threat: Palms sweating, adrenaline buzzing, gravity humming beneath me—I teetered.

I climbed down, hollowed out but alive.

In the stillness, I realised how far I'd fallen. The fearless version of me had abandoned his post. In his place: someone brittle. Afraid.

That night, the heaviness lifted. Me and Mike killed a bottle of vodka, howling at old SNL skits. Barry Gibb Talk Show on repeat—him nailing Fallon's falsetto. It would haunt me years later in a voice note: "Talkin' 'bout issues… real important issues… talkin' 'bout chest hair" —toothpaste flying from my mouth during lockdown.

That was Mike—a mixtape of old jokes and belly laughs.

That night was special—friendship in its purest form. And now, all I have are the memories.

We'd uprooted everything so quickly, we hadn't realised we were drifting. What began torn in New Zealand had unravelled further in Australia. Now, in California, I buried it under the guise of recovery.

Addiction had taken root. The wrong turn wasn't in the vehicle.

I never saw the signs.

Bedwetting? I told myself it was just a phase. Too drunk, too stoned, too tired to notice when it stopped.

I didn't know I was scarred. I only knew I was scared.

The fear stuck. It coiled around my armour, provoking the symbiote.

Help wasn't an option. Escape was.

Weed. Vodka. Pills. On repeat.

I can't get no sleep.

Fifty Six
Return Of The Living Dead

2005
South East Asia

Inappropriate title? Maybe. But somehow, it felt right. Revisiting the place that nearly killed us—horror and absurdity all tangled up. A nod to a genre that shaped my imagination: zombies stumbling on despite rot and ruin.

Zombies always fascinated me—not just as monsters, but as mirrors of human dread. Romero's *Night of the Living Dead* and *Dawn of the Dead*— each one a different lens on society's decay. My first zombie film was *Return of the Living Dead*, and it stuck. Irreverent, grotesque, funny as hell. Just like life at its worst.

As I prepared to recount this return to Phi Phi, it felt like I was stepping back into the graveyard of my past, bracing myself to confront the ghosts I'd left behind.

I'd been drifting across Southeast Asia—not living, just existing. Insomnia, booze, endless reruns on a battered portable DVD player— my own flickering afterlife. 2005: a jumble-sale jigsaw—edges torn, pieces missing.

I couldn't piece it together until recently. Fitting, then, that I borrow from the genre I've always loved. Zombies may be mindless, but they're bloody persistent.

In Vientiane, we spent four straight days locked in a room, devouring *24*. Jack Bauer became my spirit animal: relentless, compulsive, unstoppable—except I was the opposite.

Vietnam? Swapped Jack for *Seinfeld*. Pirate DVDs stacked high—the same stores where I once plundered CDs. Costanza's rants, Jerry's quirks, "Serenity now…"—all distractions from the beautiful, unforgiving truth outside our window. It was pathetic.

Nights were the worst. Desperate for relief, I turned to an old, familiar companion: Valium. Cheap and accessible, it became sidekick to the rum, granting me a deep, empty blackness. A deadly duo where I could rest without fear.

We wandered through temples and markets, beaches and forests, but I saw nothing. The world around me was vibrant—inside, I was a dull, unlit chasm.

It reminds me now of a music video—the lead singer in sharp focus while the world behind him moves in reverse, disconnected. "The Scientist." Chris Martin, alone in the madness—a visual representation of my internal dislocation.

I can't fully speak to how Tina felt during this time. I can only assume she was grappling with her own challenges. The unspoken weight of our shared trauma loomed large—an elephant in the room neither of us dared address. What I do know is she faced everything with a daredevil spirit I couldn't summon.

Like the time she almost got eaten by a tiger. Yes, you heard me. Eaten. Tiger.

We visited a monastery promising an unforgettable experience—or a lawsuit. Tina sat with a massive male tiger on her lap, fur under her fingertips. In a blink, it turned, jaws open, saliva stringing from its canines. A monk dove between them, saving her by an inch.

She laughed it off. Went back in for the photo. Fearless or reckless— hard to tell. I couldn't understand it. The same jaws that had nearly torn her apart… and she just smiled.

I didn't feel brave. I didn't feel amused. I felt something I couldn't name—like I was watching someone I knew from a distance I couldn't cross.

Bangkok, post-tiger madness, we drifted down Khao San Road. I spotted Arthit—the singer from the Rolling Stoned Bar. I should've

327

looked away. I didn't.

"Arthit! Mate, it's me—John, from Phi Phi."

Recognition flickered, but so did something else. He'd lost his wife in the wave. Fled to Bangkok to escape the ghosts. His world, once filled with music and promise, had been levelled. His pain wrapped around my throat like a choke chain.

I'd fled mine too, but here I was—dragging it back into the light like it was a reunion show.

I knew then: Phi Phi was inevitable.

The ferry cut across calm water, but my insides bucked like a storm. A year since the wave. Tina bounced at the rail, eager, hopeful. I trailed behind, leaden. As the island's jagged cliffs came into view, they no longer felt like the sanctuary I'd once yearned for.

The new pier was sturdy—unlike the rickety mess that almost gave way beneath a screaming exodus. I stepped off and the sensory nightmare began: saltwater and fish mingled with the tropical sweetness of frangipani, instantly transporting me back to the moment the ocean turned malevolent.

The calls from shopkeepers—"Massage, massage"—took on a sinister edge.

She pointed at new hotels, shiny shops, neon signs of 'recovery'. To her, rebuilding meant healing. To me, it mocked what was gone: the children we played football with, the bar owner who lost all eight kids yet still poured Chang for tourists too drunk to care.

The quaint shacks had been replaced by concrete—sturdier structures rising from the rubble, ready to capitalise on tragedy. All made possible in the wake of Poseidon's wrath.

They even had a tsunami siren now. Drills at dawn. The first time it shrieked, I froze in bed, pulse pounding, transported straight back to Boxing Day. Tina flipped the curtain, calm as anything. "Just a drill."

My brain didn't care.

Zombies don't just die. They stumble forward, one mangled step at a time. So would I.

I can't ignore these memories anymore—no matter the pain.

'Fore it's the memories, isn't it, sir? The memories that make us who we are.' * (Kryten - *Red Dwarf* - "Thanks for The Memory" 1988)

> *'We cannot solve our problems with the same thinking we used when we created them.'*
> **Albert Einstein**

Fifty Seven
The Pursuit Of Happyness

October 14th 2021
London

I hadn't realised how broken I'd been that year. Back then, I'd have sworn I was thriving. But looking back now, it's painfully obvious: I was broken. The booze, the drugs, the white-hot rage—how did I miss it all?

The isolation. The anger. Jesus—how could I have missed it all?

Maybe it was textbook trauma—my brain doing damage control, shielding me from the weight of what I'd lived through. But still.

Rada and Gita's diagnosis, though hard to swallow, now feels undeniable: I have PTSD.

Fuck. Fuckity fuck fuck.

I hate the version of me I've uncovered through this brutal mirror of therapy. 'PTSD isn't an excuse to be a cunt, is it, John?' Rada hadn't said it. I had. And it echoed, loud and merciless.

If anything, it's the reason to work harder. To catch the slide before it starts. To protect the people I love from the blast radius.

This raw, soul-stripping process has to mean something. It has to leave me better—for Meg, who's stayed through every fractured version of me—never demanding, just gently holding space. For my family and friends, who never gave up even when I had.

Today is the only thing I can control. My job now is finding those marginal gains. Rebuilding trust, one quiet act at a time.

The journey's been brutal. But maybe—just maybe—it'll be worth it.

Because in the end, hope is all I have left in the box:

In the dark of trauma's night,
Where shadows blend and fears take flight,
Anger sparks, a flickering gleam,
Tainting the soul with fragile dreams.
PTSD, a stormy sea,
Crashing waves, a tortured plea.
But hope's light, though faint and shy,
Guides me on, lets my spirit fly.

My mind was a swamp that autumn day—thick, stagnant, and impossible to wade through. I showed up to work late, unshaven, eyes sunken, radiating an aura of 'stay the fuck away'.

Sleepless nights bred self-loathing. And insomnia whispered sweet nothings about the comfort of old vices.

I'd resisted—for now. But the pull was growing stronger.

Weed was calling.

Alcohol had already made itself at home. Binge drinking had crept back in like an old friend with a fake smile—wine, vodka, whatever I could grab. Evenings melted into *Seinfeld* reruns, the cheap laughs masking truths I couldn't bear to face.

It felt familiar. Too familiar.

The dull numbness, the empty rituals—this was how I used to disappear. And I hated that guy.

But now he was staring back at me.

Today was my final session with Rada—and honestly, I couldn't wait for it to be over. Her therapy had helped, no doubt. But lately, it felt like too much. Like digging too deep, foundations crumbling.

Rehashing every fear and failure was stirring up more than I could handle.

The drinking, the sitcoms, the painkillers—they weren't habits anymore. They were anaesthetics.

I couldn't keep spiralling like this. I couldn't go back to being that man.

But what more was there to say? How much more could I dissect, reframe, reprocess? When does therapy stop healing and start hurting?

I didn't know. I was still just a novice.

The walk to Rada's office gave me space to think—or overthink.

One question kept rising: 'What do you want, John?'

I didn't know. I wasn't sure I ever had. I wanted to be happy—but what did that even mean?

The autumn air was crisp. I let my playlist carry me through the backstreets of Shoreditch. The grit, the graffiti, the pulse of it—a good match for the mess in my head.

What is happiness? Everyone wants it. But most of us follow the same predictable signposts: love, money, success, freedom.

For me, it had always felt just out of reach—like trying to grasp a mirage.

I searched my past for clues.

Childhood joy: running wild on the estate with Nick. Laughter, mischief, freedom.

Teen years: before The Lads died. The world had seemed infinite back then.

Travel brought tremendous joy. But even before the tsunami, something was always missing.

Purpose? Meaning? Was I chasing a shape I couldn't define?

I was still lost in that loop when a mural stopped me.

Bold, stark letters: OBEY.

Shepard Fairey. Obey Giant. *They Live*. Roddy Piper. The sunglasses. Iconic.

The messages: CONSUME. CONFORM. OBEY.

It hit me like a punch to the gut. Freedom.

That was the key. That's what I wanted. Not status, not money—freedom. To live on my terms.

My working-class roots taught me to graft hard—but also to endure, to survive. Somewhere along the way, I'd traded freedom for security.

Traded the blank canvas for a checklist. And now I wanted it back.

Love was still the cornerstone. The one thing I knew for certain. From our first date, I'd known Meg was different. She became my anchor. My reason to keep going, even when I couldn't see the road ahead.

Through her, I caught glimpses of what happiness could be.

But love alone wasn't enough. Not for the life we wanted. I needed to shed the chains—addiction, burnout, that endless corporate hamster wheel—and build something better.

A life that gave us both space to breathe. The clarity was liberating. And terrifying.

By the time I reached Rada's office, my stride had purpose. For the first time in weeks, I didn't dread the session. I welcomed it.

This chapter was ending—and I was ready to slam the door shut.

All those past versions of me, Johnny 1.0 through 5.0—flawed, broken, messy—had led me here.

Without them, there'd be no Meg. No Rada's couch. No growth.

I wasn't those men anymore.

I was older. Wiser. My memories no longer blazed—they glowed like embers, warm with lessons learned.

Like a phoenix, I could feel myself rising.

"Hello, John. Did you walk all this way again?"

Rada's voice broke through the hum of Adam Duritz still echoing in my ears. Her tone was soft, familiar—head tilted just so, scarf fluttering in the breeze.

"Hiya." I tugged out my AirPods. "Yeah, you know me—can't resist a walk."

She smiled and motioned toward the door. "Let's get you inside."

The room felt like it always did—neutral, grounded. She handed me a bottle of water as I sank into the couch, loosening my tie, sleeves rolled.

The walk had left me flushed.

She sat across from me, eyes sharp but kind. Then, almost playfully: "What's that on your arm?"

I looked down, momentarily thrown. "This?"

I turned my left forearm so she could see the faded ink.

"Yeah. What is it?"

"A tattoo. Got it in Thailand. A few years ago," I said, eyes scanning it like I hadn't really looked in ages. "It's Sanskrit—says 'Big Wave Tsunami.'"

She tilted her head again, face unreadable. The silence stretched until

334

I filled it.

"I was on holiday in Phuket with Meg. Just… decided to get it done. One of those bamboo ones. They do them everywhere out there. Didn't think about it much. Just did it. On a whim."

Rada scoffed. "I don't think so, John. I think you thought about it quite a lot."

I frowned. "Really? I don't remember planning it. I just… did it."

She folded her arms. "You know that's not true. A tattoo like that doesn't just happen. It means something."

I paused.

I'd told the story so many times—always framed as casual, impulsive, meaningless.

"Huh." That's all I could manage. I pursed my lips and looked upward, like the answer might be tucked away in the rafters of memory. I wasn't lying; but was I being honest?

Maybe my subconscious had done the heavy lifting—branding something I couldn't say out loud.

The Goo Goo Dolls floated in. 'Scars are souvenirs you never lose…

Maybe that was it. A scar, etched in ink because my body bore none. No bruises, no broken bones—just the invisible kind.

The silence stretched. Heavy.

Then Rada gently shifted gears.

"Last time, we were talking about Tina," she said. "You mentioned you were married. Let's talk about that time."

I exhaled, grateful to drop the tattoo but unsettled by the questions it had raised.

335

"Right," I murmured. "Tina…" I wasn't ready for what came next. But maybe it was time I finally looked back—properly.

Fifty Eight
I Love you, Man

2005-2008
London

By the end of 2005, so too ended our strange trip. We returned home just in time for Christmas—and more importantly, to be as far from the scene of the crime as possible for the first anniversary.

But coming home didn't bring relief. It brought displacement. I was lost—and whatever mental wreckage I'd carried had only deepened. Nine months of roaming hadn't dulled the trauma—it had magnified the disconnection.

Back in London I faced one bleak fact: "My name is John. I'm unemployed, and I live with my parents."

Loser.

I felt nothing. Just numbness.

Maybe our families saw it too. Survivors shambling through life like extras in a zombie flick. In some twisted way, we were the resurrected from the *Pet Sematary*—bodies intact, souls conspicuously absent.

The fear that had followed me around the world found a megaphone in the silence of home:

Would I ever work again?

It sounds pathetic now, but I was convinced my hard-earned skills had vanished. Who would take a chance on me? Was I destined for a permanent life in the spare room, signing on, fading into failure?

I grabbed the first lifeline I could—I needed proof I wasn't broken.

But the job came with a soul-destroying catch: the commute.

On an average day? Three hours. Each way.

Less than a year in, the routine was killing me. Hours alone in the car. A job I hated. Nothing left of me by the end of each day.

Harder than the job was the loneliness—a kind of quiet erosion no one talks about.

The boys had all moved on with their lives. Most were in long-term relationships. Nights at the pub were rare, replaced by dinner plans and baby talk.

And Wiggy? He'd fallen hard—head over heels and all in. He skipped the trip with me and Baz to stay with the love of his life. Smart move. He missed the tsunami and found what we'd always wanted.

I missed him terribly, but I couldn't begrudge him. We'd always been soft-hearted saps, really—soppy twats with our hearts on our sleeves, both secretly craving real connection. Growing up in the '90s meant hiding that under layers of bravado.

Nights out 'on the pull' were the norm, but truthfully, we both hated that scene. Every outing felt like a competition. Every failure chipped away at already brittle confidence.

His happiness only underscored how strange my own relationship had become. I wanted what he had. I wanted to feel chosen. Instead, I felt replaced.

So I turned to something that had always pulled me back from the edge—music. The Arctic Monkeys had just exploded, and their debut, *Whatever People Say I Am, That's What I'm Not* wasn't just an album—it was therapy.

Their raw energy, sharp lyrics, northern swagger—my daily armour. Some mornings I'd scream along just to stop myself screaming at the maniacs on the A40.

Then Joey reappeared. Old mate, familiar voice. We started chatting during my commutes, trading gripes and jokes. Those calls kept me sane. I'd laugh again—not often, but enough to remind me I was still in there somewhere.

One evening, crawling home, my phone rang. "I've got something for you," Joey said. His tone had weight. "Come work with me."

I pulled over, hands trembling. "Are you serious?"

"Deadly. You hate that job. We need someone. You in?"

"YES."

The new job was a godsend, and more importantly, I had a wingman again. My shoulders dropped. My jaw unclenched. For the first time in months, I felt like me.

But the relief didn't last.

I couldn't outrun the shadow the tsunami had cast.

Joey had been on Phi Phi the week before, so he knew. But the rest of the office? They found out quick. The rumour travelled like gossip always does—pint glasses to break rooms.

"Hey, you were in that tsunami, right?" someone would ask mid-tea-bag dunk, like it was trivia. Worse still, my director began using it in sales pitches.

"John was there, you know," he'd boast to clients. "Go on, tell them your story."

I'd freeze, then rattle off the script I'd built: "Yeah, I was there... on an island... escaped from a shop... got home eventually."

Clean. Emotionless. Bulletproof.

But sometimes the shield cracked. Words slipped through. Images of dead babies. Shattered legs. Memories I never meant to share. I'd drift through meetings in a daze, smiling mechanically, fighting off the rising panic.

339

My body at the table. My mind underwater.

Hard to believe my trauma was used like that—a time where emotional wellbeing came second to client orders.

But I didn't speak up. I was still too conditioned. So I did what I always did.

I reached for the bottle.

By Christmas, I was done. The job, the drinking, the pretending—it all caught up with me.

Then life threw me a curveball.

Tina's best mate Julie invited us to a last-minute New Year's Eve party. I didn't want to go. The season stirred a storm inside me that I wasn't quite adept at recognising.

The lights, the songs, the forced cheer—it all felt like mockery. I tried to bail, but one look from Tina ended that idea.

We threw together half-hearted costumes. Mine? A sarong, flip-flops, and a "Same Same But Different" tee. All I needed was a label:

Tsunami Survivor.

At the party, I drifted. Smiling through gritted teeth.

That's when Julie's new boyfriend, Matt, appeared. "Here, mate. Come with me," he said with a knowing grin.

In the bathroom, he racked up a line on the cistern and handed me a rolled-up tenner.

I stared at the mirror—at the stranger in a ridiculous costume, clinging to the past. Then I bent over and snorted.

We made small talk, rode waves of coke-induced chatter and paranoia. The tsunami came up more than I liked that night. Friends, strangers—digging for details.

But Matt? He stayed light. He didn't pry. He pulled me from the fire. "Let's go for a doobie," he said.

I'd never heard the term, but I liked it. My brain flicked to *The Doobie Brothers*, then the giant lizard in Sydney—anything to escape the weight of the past. Outside, the cold bit through my sarong, but the joint's warmth was familiar. A taste of California.

"You ever seen a blue-tongue, Matt? Big fuck-off lizards in Australia…"

We laughed. Genuinely.

Something clicked. The drugs, the banter, the absurdity—it all came together. We stayed up till dawn: music, stories, smoke, laughter.

New Year's Day arrived with a vengeance. No sleep. A head full of coke. A stomach full of regret.

Matt offered us a lift home. Still half-cut, I got a bit too lippy from the backseat. With a devilish grin, he dropped everyone else off first. By the time we reached my street, my hangover had bloomed biblical.

He parked a hundred yards away. "You'll be fine," he smirked.

I wasn't.

I staggered from the car, clutching my stomach. Each step was a countdown. My pace quickened. Sarong slipping. Flip-flops off. Y-fronts flapping in the wind.

I burst through the garden gate, collapsed by the hedge, and let it all go.
As I wiped my eyes, I saw Matt slowly driving off, laughing his head off.

It was absurd. Undignified.

But for the first time in a long time, I didn't care.

That evening, the fog lifted. A monstrous hangover remained. I stumbled downstairs to the smell of roast dinner. My mum, used to my states, said nothing. Just piled my plate with roasties and Bisto. The cure-all.

We gathered round the telly. On came Your Shout—one of those "feel-good" local fillers. But this one hit different.

A family. Devastated. Their son, early twenties, lost to the tsunami. Through tears, they described identifying his body. Moving forward seemed impossible.

My fork froze.

The face on the screen: James.

He'd spent Christmas night with Tina and me. His first trip to Thailand.

Then the screen cut to his best mate: Tyler.

The same Tyler who'd wandered Phi Phi with Barry, searching.

Two best friends. Two stories. Opposite endings.

"I knew him," I whispered, slipping upstairs to close the door.

I sat on the bed.

Flashes: Barry's face. Tyler's hope. James' smile.

Swinging in a hammock, listening to his hopes and dreams. The excitement in his voice lingered in my mind.

Was I the last person to see him alive?

I grabbed the vodka. Tried to quiet the pain. Slipped into uneasy sleep.

Rebuilding life in London felt like walking a tightrope with an anvil strapped to my bollocks. I was doing the right things—working, forming friendships—but the wave still nipped at my heels.

So I focused on what I could: real connection.

Reconnecting with Joey steadied me. But meeting Matt? That saved me.

Urban Dictionary defines bromance as "a brother from another mother." A bond between heterosexual males never seen as romantic —though it's joked about. Grounded in pop culture shorthand.

You meet a bloke—say, named Brian—and mutter "Welease Wodewick." He replies, "Stwike him, centuwion, vewy woughly."

Boom. Bromance.

Matt had nothing to do with the tsunami. He didn't know the 'before' me, so I didn't have to pretend. He met me as I was—and that was enough.

He was also a seasoned stoner. I was a rookie. It started innocent—a puff here, a toke there.

Then I noticed something: the nightmares eased. I could sleep.

Weekends became Sundays. Then weeknights. Then every night.

"It's therapeutic," I said. "They all do in LA. It hasn't hurt them."

Truthfully? It was a crutch. A nightly ritual to hush the screaming ghosts.

Still, those nights brought peace. Gaming. Weed. Dumb telly. Stillness.

It wasn't healing. Not really. But it was something. And sometimes, something is enough.

But 'enough' slowly turned into 'essential.' The line between coping and dependence blurred.

I wasn't the tsunami guy. I wasn't broken. I was just John. His mate. Matt appeared when I needed someone most. He helped me navigate the void when I couldn't see the road forward.

Tina, I assume, was finding something similar in Julie. We were always together as a group, but emotionally? Separate islands.

I told myself it was a phase. That I was fine.

But the truth? I was an addict.

Still, those years were pivotal. Not because they fixed anything—but because they kept me alive long enough to eventually face what needed to be faced.

I hadn't been looking for a best mate. I'd been looking for nothing at all. But friendship found me anyway—the kind that asks nothing, sees everything, and stays.

I wasn't healed. I wasn't whole. But I wasn't alone.

'If it is not right, do not do it. If it is not true, do not say it.'
Marcus Aurelius

Fifty Nine
The Proposal

2008
London - Phi Phi.

The next five years weren't a decline—they were a free-fall. I didn't just retreat from my problems. I retreated from everything. Life outside became a hostile minefield, full of reminders of who I wasn't and what I'd failed to be.

It was all too much. So I shut the door, closed the blinds, and dulled the world's sharp edges with a constant cloud of weed.

At first, it was a way to quiet the storm. But over time, the escape became a prison. My days revolved around the next high, the next drink, the next moment when the past couldn't reach me.

London—once loud, bright, full of life—became another planet. The things I used to care about—ambitions, passions, even simple pleasures—faded into grey. In their place: apathy.

I let myself go. My diet became a cycle of junk food and anything that required minimal effort. It wasn't food—just fuel. The consequences stacked up: weight gain, phantom aches, constant exhaustion. Even getting out of bed felt like a battle. My reflection became unrecognisable—sallow skin, unkempt hair, dead eyes. A stranger.

Weed dulled the pain and helped me sleep through the insomnia choking me each night. Without it, I was irritable. Explosive. It jumped to the top of my hierarchy of needs. But even that wasn't enough. Alcohol was key to the mix, amplifying the haze. Days blurred into nights. Weeks into years.

Time lost its shape.

The gym, once a haven, became a monument to the discipline I'd abandoned. My strength withered. My stamina disappeared.

Social interactions became unbearable. Every conversation felt like a trap—a chance for someone to see what I'd become. Even my family, reaching out with concern and compassion, couldn't break through. Their calls, their visits, their offers to help—I met them all with polite deflections.

It was easier to be alone with my misery than admit how far I'd fallen.

Then a wake-up call arrived—brutal, uninvited, and impossible to ignore.

We had decided to buy a house. It should've been a milestone—a fresh start. But it came with a condition: I needed a medical exam to qualify for life insurance.

The results hit hard. Liver damage. Sky-high cholesterol. Blood pressure through the roof.

I was thirty years old with the internal stats of Mr Creosote. And without the insurance, we couldn't get the mortgage.

The fear was immediate and visceral.

I quit drinking—not for me, not really. I was doing it to avoid prescriptions and the slow march toward becoming a statistic. Weed stepped in as my full-time caregiver. I cleaned up my diet, swapped crisps for kale, downed milk-thistle pills with religious commitment.

And it worked.

Three months later, the insurance was approved. The mortgage followed. On paper, everything was back on track. But inside? The rot ran deeper than blood tests could show.

A month later, I was off the wagon—like the whole thing had never happened. The fear had passed, and with it, the urgency. I'd ticked the box, passed the test, fooled the system. But I wasn't fooling myself.

Progress, it turned out, was just another mask I'd learned to wear.

Homeownership didn't ground me—it suffocated me. Mortgage payments, maintenance, DIY—it all felt like punishment for a life I didn't want.

While I was regressing, my mates were moving forward—proposing to soulmates, having kids, building lives I envied but couldn't replicate.

And me? I felt the pressure. The unspoken obligation to keep ticking boxes: house, marriage, family.

So I doubled down on the worst decision of all.

The decision to not walk out of the restaurant. When I didn't end things before travelling with Barry. When I stayed after the tsunami instead of letting her go find herself.

I didn't course-correct—I turned into the skid.

The setting for my ultimate bad decision couldn't have been more ironic: Koh Phi Phi.

Despite everything, we convinced ourselves we were happy to return. Maybe we thought we could overwrite the horror with new memories. But really, we were being pulled back into the trauma, subconsciously drawn to the epicentre of everything we'd never processed.

Was it Boxing Day? I don't know. It was definitely the Christmas holidays, but surely not that day. Surely I wasn't that deluded?

Whatever the date, I remember the anger. I was seething. That alone should've been the red flag.

Tina took hours to get ready. I paced around the beach hut, stewing. Each minute dragged. This wasn't just lateness—it was a pattern that always got under my skin.

That night, it lit a fuse.

I should've called it off. But I didn't. We walked to the beach. Yes, that beach.

The sunset I'd imagined? Gone. The moment had passed, swallowed by darkness and outfit changes. My disappointment curdled into contempt.

'Fuck it,' I thought. Little Don was in charge of a towering inferno—and he'd abandoned his post.

I fumbled for the ring box, hands shaking from frustration more than nerves. I dropped it. Panicked, I dropped to the sand—just as Tina turned.

And that's how it happened.

The angriest, most inappropriate proposal in history. No speech. No romance. Just me, seething on a haunted beach, holding out a ring neither of us should've accepted.

It was doomed from that very moment.

The wedding was surreal.

Tina threw herself into planning. I sat on the bench, nodding in all the right places. My only real contribution? Naming the tables after tracks from *August and Everything After*. A lonely signal from a man already checked out.

The night before, the boys all gathered—Joey, Barry, Wiggy, Bobby, Matt, Steve and Mike. Mike, being Mike, showed up with new THC-loaded edibles. I took one. Thought it'd take the edge off.

It didn't.

It launched me into a spiral—high, paranoid, and choking on the weight of my choices. I woke up the next morning still buzzing, unsure of what universe I was in, let alone who I was supposed to be.

Me. A husband. Too late to back out now.

And then—of course—Tina didn't show up. Not at first. Classic Tina.

Turns out the car broke down on the M25. Some sympathetic coppers picked them up on the hard shoulder and gave them a lift—blue lights and all.

My 'out' disappeared to the tune of *The Bill*. 'This is happening, John.'

At the wedding breakfast, her dad gave a speech that stopped me cold. "If you two survived the tsunami, you can survive anything," he said, choking up.

Just like that, the shame returned.

I'd asked for a litre of Smirnoff on my table instead of wine. And I drank it. Fast. Her dad's words rattled me, and vodka became the dam holding back everything I didn't want to feel.

Somewhere during the first dance, the night went dark.

I woke up in the wrong room. No funny business—just the nearest bed my friends could drag my blacked-out arse into.

Not how a groom should behave.

No excuses.

It gets worse.

Mauritius. Ocean winds blowing wild. Every gust smelled like the past. I should've embraced the beauty. Instead, I locked myself away. Curtains drawn. Bottle open. Numbing myself with sitcoms while Tina sat alone in the sun.

Ten days in, I broke. I told her I wanted to leave.

She didn't argue.

The hotel staff were devastated. Apparently, no one had ever left early. Let alone honeymooners. But for me, there was no other option. It was already over.

Who does that? Who walks out on a honeymoon?

Someone broken. Someone scarred so deeply that even joy felt dangerous. I wasn't well. But I wasn't ready to admit that. To anyone.

She must've felt abandoned—alone with a stranger who couldn't even name his pain.

I hate looking back at this chapter. It's a raw, gaping wound. I wish I'd had the courage to say, I'm not okay.

I didn't. I retreated further into denial. It must've been awful for Tina.

I hope it wasn't as bad for her as I now imagine. Maybe there were still pieces of me that made her smile. I want to believe that.

Maybe I'm exaggerating the worst. Maybe there were good days I've forgotten. But what sticks now is the weight of depression—the hollowness of going through the motions in a marriage I didn't believe in.

I found comfort in the blur—weed, drink, TV, and the quiet companionship of Matt. It wasn't happiness, but it passed for something close enough.

Numb was better than broken.

I convinced myself I could live like that forever.

But I wasn't living. I was slowly dying.

And in the end, it was Thailand that pulled the thread. Again.

The same country that had given us our beginning—our trauma, our survival—became the place where it all unravelled. There's a cruel poetry in that. A symmetry I can't ignore.

The circle closed, not with a bang, but a slow, quiet collapse. Maybe it had to end that way.

Maybe the island needed to finish what it started.

'You can't go back and change the beginning, but you can start where you are and change the ending.'
C.S. Lewis

Sixty
The Break-Up

2010
Thailand

I've realised lately that I've always framed my emotions through strange characters from childhood. Most references are familiar—except maybe the Garbage Pail Kids. A grotesque parody of the Cabbage Patch Kids, they were a playground phenomenon in the mid-'80s.

The cards were crude, cartoonish, brilliant. Kids with names like Jay Decay, or Nasty Nick, drawn with leaking orifices, exploding heads, or dangling eyeballs. Revolting and hilarious in equal measure. At 50p a pack, they were affordable rebellion. I was obsessed—collected them all.

In 1987, I sold the lot at a car boot sale for £2. At the time, it felt like a deal. Now? A mint collection would be worth a small fortune. I try not to think about it.

Funny thing is, those cards became more than collectibles. They're a weird way to visualise my emotional states. Anger? Not just Greaser Gregg—but Adam Bomb: fire in the brain. Guilt? Leaky Lou. Shame? Cryin' Ryan. My feelings now seem warped and cartoonish—distorted by trauma and years of avoidance.

Back in 2010, though, most of those emotions were buried. Only anger remained. Passive-aggressive. Toxic. Always simmering.

It was Christmas. We were in Thailand. Again. The place had a pull we couldn't resist. This time, Matt and Julie joined us, adding an odd dynamic to an already strained relationship. Technically, Tina and I were still a couple. But we moved like strangers sharing an itinerary. The gap between us had grown too wide.

351

The tension began even before we left. At the airport bar, Bloody Mary in hand, Tina casually dropped a bombshell: she'd arranged for her 18-year-old nephew, Rich, to house-sit.

No discussion. Just, "Oh, by the way…"

I was livid. Not just because of Rich, but because of everything I'd swallowed over the years. This was the final straw.

Despite the rocky start, the holiday played out fine—on the surface. We travelled through Malaysia and Thailand, ending up on Koh Lipe, a remote Andaman island. It was paradise: white sand, turquoise sea, cool nights. The kind of place you're meant to feel healed by. But beauty doesn't fix disconnection. It only throws it into sharper focus.

At 2 a.m. one night, just after Christmas, Tina's phone buzzed. Rich. Panicked. There was a leak at the house.

My first thought: 'It's your fault he's there, you deal with it.' What came out wasn't better.

"What the fuck am I supposed to do? It's 2 a.m., and I'm 12,000 miles away. He'll figure it out."

Cruel, yes. But part of me justified it—Rich was a trainee plumber. Still, it wasn't about solving a leak. It was about shutting her down.

Tina turned and walked out onto the veranda. Her voice came back through the dark: "It's over."

I sat upright in bed. Her words echoed.

And I felt… relieved. Not upset. Not shocked. Relieved.

Like I'd been waiting for her to say it out loud. Like I needed her to end it, because I never could. It felt like an epiphany.

Looking back, the signs were everywhere—from the wedding morning mirror moment to the Phuket airport screw-up. But it started earlier. It started the day I mumbled, "I'll think about it."

I didn't love her. Not the way she deserved. I think part of me always knew that—but I hoped proximity would breed something real.

My sarcasm, my cruelty, the quiet contempt—it was truth leaking out. It must've been obvious to everyone but me.

What a Mean Gene.

We said nothing for days. Moved around each other like strangers at a wake. The silence wasn't awkward. It was heavy. Inevitable.

By New Year's Eve, the island came alive. Fireworks, music, and beach bars. We went for dinner with Matt and Julie. Tina and I barely spoke.

Later, we lit Chinese lanterns. A ritual for reflection. I whispered something vague—a hope for happiness, for both of us, apart. My lantern lifted… then caught a gust and dropped. Crumpled into the sea.

Poetic.

I can't remember what I wished for. But that ruined lantern said it all. Crashed. Burned. Surrendered to the ocean.

The itinerary was finished. The trauma map complete.

And yet, beneath the wreckage: a flicker of hope. A quiet promise that maybe we'd find better lives, apart.

But I'd stayed silent too long. Bottled anger. Swallowed resentment. Let the worst parts of me take control.

The Jerk.

To protect myself, I buried it all. Filed away our history. Deleted a whole chapter of my life. Fifteen years later, I know that was wrong. Avoidance doesn't erase. It just lets the pain rot in the dark.

While Tina chose healing, I chose escape. She moved forward. I trod water. She sought redemption—and I respect her for that.

353

Seneca would've been proud.

But even in confusion, I found clarity. Maybe I could find that half-decent version of me, lurking somewhere within my past.

Fifteen years on, the battle wasn't over. It was just beginning.

But this time, I wouldn't run. I'd face the pain. Face myself.

I owed it to the person I used to be. And the one I still wanted to become.

"It's not you, it's me. If it's anybody—it's me."

'Our greatest glory is not in never falling, but in rising every time we fall.'
Confuscius

SixtyOne
Point Break

November 11th 2021
London

It was over. My secondment to a mental health expert had come to an end. The relief was overwhelming—but dulled by exhaustion that clung to me like a lead jacket.

Therapy had been brutal. Not because of Rada—she'd been nothing short of exceptional—but because it had forced me to confront parts of my mind I'd long since boarded up. I was drained beyond words, barely able to summon the energy to leave her office.

Walking to the tube felt like a marathon. I stumbled onto the escalator, letting it carry me downward, legs like lead. Twenty-four metres below the glass and steel of Canary Wharf, the train screeched in. I closed my eyes, trying to block the rising sense of fragility. It took so much precision to keep the world above from collapsing.

The tunnel's hum only amplified the chaos inside me. I cranked my music, hoping the chords would drown it out. The train was nearly empty. I collapsed into a seat. Two stops—even that felt too far. As we jolted forward, my eyes drifted to the ad panel above the window.

My breath caught.

"Don't fear the Poonami!"

The word lodged in my brain. Its playful absurdity twisted into something sinister. My stomach turned. An invisible tide dragged me under. I leaned forward, head in hands. Heart racing. Shallow breaths. I didn't know what a "Poonami" was, but I knew exactly what it implied.

I clung to the music, trying to anchor myself.

At North Greenwich, I stumbled off, legs trembling. But it followed—chasing me up the escalator, echoing across the concourse.

Poonami. Bright purple posters. Laughing in my face.

Apparently, some *Mad Men* thought it clever to turn "tsunami" into a cutesy term for baby diarrhoea. Funny—if you hadn't nearly drowned under a wall of sewage and saltwater. If you hadn't seen what a real tsunami leaves in its wake. Including babies.

But I had.

This wasn't marketing. It wasn't funny.

My brain didn't see nappies and toddlers. It saw the fight to breathe. The taste of filth. The man wading through ruin, clutching his lifeless child. A nappy hanging from that tiny body. Another used as a bandage, wrapped around a half-severed leg.

The images erupted—vivid, violent.

Thanks.

I know it wasn't their fault. They couldn't have known. But the word tsunami deserves more respect. For all those affected by the thousands of tsunamis that have decimated coastlines through history.

Now, that word's a joke.

Japanese: tsu (harbour) and nami (wave). A deceptively gentle term for a force of unimaginable destruction. In deep water, tsunamis are nearly invisible. But near land, they rise—walls of water, obliterating everything.

Today, it's universal. But I remember when it was barely known.

And now? It's diluted. Co-opted. Punch-lined.

It's everywhere—billboards, headlines, talk shows. Not just marketing—metaphors, lazy analogies.

Take these actual headlines from just the past year:

- The Starmer tsunami – a political landslide.
- Behind the 'Zuma tsunami' in South Africa.
- Tsunami of drugs and violence in prisons.
- UK's 'e-waste tsunami' – MPs.
- A tsunami of ACL injuries in women's football.
- Pendleton rescue overwhelmed by 'tsunami of dogs'.
- Luis Rubiales kissing Jenni Hermoso unleashes social tsunami in Spain.

I'll stop there. You get the gist.

Lazy reporting? Clever metaphor? Maybe both. But I'm not the average reader. When I see tsunami, I don't think surge. I feel it. And before anyone calls me a hypocrite—yes, I've used water language in this book. But deliberately. This is a book about a tsunami. The warning label's built in.

Still, I know—this is my issue. My trauma. But knowing doesn't stop it. One word, and the wave crashes in. No warning. No buffer.

It's why I have to stay hyper-vigilant—headlines, websites, Tube ads. One careless phrase, and I'm back under. A floodgate opens. And while it might sound poetic to others, for me, it's not a metaphor.

It's memory. A survival fight.

Maybe we tame terror by dragging it into the mundane. I don't know.

Rada helped me find the cracks. But right now? I'm wide open. And in a word? Fucked.

I gripped the handrail at the bus stop, like it might anchor me to reality. A flicker of Rada crossed my mind—the woman who'd pulled these buried things to the surface. I shoved the thought away. I wasn't ready to acknowledge what she'd helped me see. But one thing was clear: surviving wasn't enough anymore.

I needed to thrive.

That word felt alien. Overreaching. But it clung like an ember refusing to die out.

As I walked toward the bus fragments of Gita's voice resurfaced. Softer than Rada's. Her homework. The exercise I never did. "Write it down."

Rada said the same: "Get it down, John. If you let it fester, it will own you."

I'd dismissed it. What good could come from reliving it on paper?

But now, standing at the bus stop, their words lingered. Maybe they were right.

I boarded the 486, sank into my usual seat, and stared out the window as the city blurred. My mind drifted—to their astonishment when I told them how long I'd carried this alone.

The memories of that day still lingered—like a gift from the Dementors. Soul-sucking creatures that fed on happiness and left you hollow. Their skeletal hands never fully out of frame.

Maybe it wasn't about letting someone in. Maybe it was about letting it out. What would people find if I ever told the truth? Would they recoil? Or understand?

After Tina left, the clouds broke. The storm arrived. Repressed anger isn't just emotion—it's a bomb. Suppression warped everything. A distant storm fed by silence and denial.

And when it came back? It didn't knock. It smashed through.

In the form of an email. Out of the blue. It self destructed after the first read. But it wasn't cruel. It was... sincere. She thanked me for the good times. And said that every time she heard Adele's "Someone Like You," it hurt—because it reminded her of me.

At the time, I was livid. I didn't understand then. But I do now.

She wasn't trying to wound me. She was trying to make sense of it—using music, like I always have.

Because really, what is this book, if not a mixtape? Helping me heal in my own strange way as I worked through this monumental homework assignment.

But it wasn't just emotion. There were physical consequences too. My nervous system was in overdrive. Cortisol flooded my system like poison. Headaches. Brain fog. Painkillers became daily essentials.

Exhaustion was my baseline. Thirty-four, single, and running out of time.

My wardrobe shrank as my waistline grew. My immune system gave up. Sleep was fractured. Thoughts intrusive. Eventually, I began hiding—from people, light, myself. Not to protect me—to protect them from the outburst I couldn't predict.

By mid-2011, I was empty. I could describe that year in detail, but by now, you know the terrain: neglect, addiction, resentment, fear, silence.

I wasn't living. I was enduring.

But even in the dark, something shifts. Not a grand revelation—just a spark.

Hope.

A yes.

San Francisco. 11/11/11. Mike and Keisha's wedding.

That trip reignited a spark I thought was dead. Reminded me who I was—before the tsunami, before the trauma, before the darkness. And on the flight home, I couldn't stop thinking about one thing.

Meg.

She was the thread that tugged at me. The one person who made me believe I might still have a shot at something real.

As the bus rolled through city streets, I checked the time on my phone.

11/11/21.

The numbers froze me. A shiver—nothing to do with the cold.

Ten years. To the day.

Synchronicity? You couldn't make it up.

That trip gave me the courage to say yes—to risk, to life, to love. It gave me Meg. She pulled me from the wreckage with quiet strength and stubborn kindness. She believed in me long before I could believe in myself.

And I still had her.

The challenges were different now. No dramatic collapses. But the battles? Still real—old habits, creeping doubts, quiet self-destruction.

That fire I found in San Fran never went out.

It smouldered.

Waiting.

As the bus pulled to my stop, I stepped into the night. The cold stung my face. I welcomed it. Meg had been my reason then. But now—with her still beside me—I realised something bigger:

I could be my own reason, too.

And for the first time in a long time,

That felt like enough.

'Healing is a matter of time, but it is sometimes also a matter of opportunity.'
Hippocrates

Sixty Two
True Romance

2011 - 2013
London

The night Meg told me she liked me was the start of my salvation. Her words felt like the universe offering me one last chance. In the streak-stained toilet mirror, through a haze of vodka, I stared at my own reflection channelling Lloyd Christmas: "So you're telling me there's a chance?" This changed everything.

'Don't fuck this up, knobhead.'

As we left the pub, her hand in mine, I tried to mask my nerves. This wasn't going to be a fairy tale. She was a spotlight, illuminating the dark corners I'd spent years avoiding. I used to think true romance was bullshit—something from a movie where passion, danger, and love collided in a whirlwind of drama. I didn't realise my own life was about to start mirroring the silver screen.

There were laughs, excitement, a spark I hadn't felt in years. But beneath the surface, I was still broken, still hiding, still afraid my anger would find a way out. Our nights out were electric—wandering London's streets, wrapped up in each other. But like a Tarantino film, the tension simmered underneath, waiting for its inevitable outburst.

I lived in fear. Fear of screwing it up. Fear of her seeing who I really was. But Meg didn't flinch. She stood by me, even when I fell back into self-destructive patterns. I knew she deserved better. That knowledge became both my biggest motivator and my deepest shame.

Meg was everything I wasn't—kind, emotionally open, engaging. Where I'd buried my feelings beneath layers of sarcasm and silence, she arrived with warmth and persistence. I'd built walls. She rolled up in a siege tower. Her family was her source of strength—the kind of closeness I couldn't fathom. Daily phone calls. Easy "I love yous." Hugs that didn't feel forced.

It baffled me.

It made me question why I'd kept myself so closed off for so long. My family wasn't cold, far from it—but love was implied, not spoken.

I loved that about her. Slowly, her influence chipped away at my armour. I found myself wanting to connect—properly—for the first time in ages. I started small. Telling her I appreciated things. Saying how much I enjoyed being with her. It was awkward at first, like learning a new language. Each moment of connection loosened something in me. Like ice cracking. I began to feel again, just a little, as if spring were coming after a long, frozen winter.

I called my mum just to talk—told her I loved her. She laughed and asked if the aliens had returned her son. That stung, but it was fair. I'd come back from travelling distant, empty, carrying a sadness I didn't realise had infected everyone around me.

I hated it. I couldn't have loved or respected my family more. I just couldn't show it. Love had always felt like kryptonite. But Meg was dragging me back into the world—one small gesture at a time. Quietly helping me battle demons I hadn't yet dared name.

The path wasn't smooth. That first year was turbulent—my anger still simmered, spilling out in ways I couldn't predict. The Christmas Eve punch-up incident is burned into my memory— "all the Persil in the world couldn't shift it."

The shame of losing control in front of Meg—seeing the disappointment in her eyes—was unbearable.

I'd stood there on Platform 5, pleading: "Don't walk away." And she hadn't.

That moment drew a line in the sand. I couldn't keep ignoring my volatility. Meg deserved better. So I began doing the work I'd been too afraid to start. I cut back on drinking, especially around her. When the rage bubbled up, I talked instead of shutting down.

It wasn't easy. There were setbacks. Crowds, booze, my undiagnosed symbiote—sometimes the mix was too volatile. I snapped again. London Bridge.

I broke my hand. Broke my progress.

The red mist evaporated as fast as it had arrived, leaving me hollow and ashamed. I was still a loose cannon—an angry autopilot dragging me further from who I wanted to be. "Get out of my head, man! I don't know what's wrong with me." Even then, Meg stayed. Not with judgement, but quiet resolve.

The 'Adam Bomb' rage. The 'Venom' reflex. It was all piling up—and it had to stop. Meg was my Alabama in a sea of chaos. I couldn't lose her.

"I believe you," she said softly as I returned from A&E. "But you need to change. I won't live like this."

That incident had happened at Christmas too. Drinking was expected, going over the top was normalised. Scrapping? Fairly common. But for me, the holidays had become a dangerous cocktail: drink + trauma + fear = Joker in the pack. "Wait'll they get a load of me."

I used to love Christmas. But it turned into something sharp-edged—a time that only magnified my turmoil. One evening at a market, Last Christmas drifted from a nearby stall, and I froze mid-step.

Meg turned to me, concern in her eyes. "You okay?" she asked.

I nodded, swallowing hard. "Just… the song."

She tilted her head. "It reminds you of it, doesn't it?"

I hadn't expected her to piece it together.

"Yeah," I said, barely above a whisper. "We sang it that night…"

I trailed off. Meg squeezed my arm. We stood there a moment, the world bustling around us, her presence a quiet shelter from the storm in my mind.

The songs, the lights, the crowds—they were triggers hiding in plain sight. And I didn't even see them coming. But Meg did. She was my lighthouse. While Tina and I had been distant, Meg and I were side by side. Fully in it. She saw what I couldn't, even when I didn't know I needed saving.

Travelling became our thing. That epic road trip across the States cemented our shared love for adventure. Then came Southeast Asia— a region I knew well and Meg had always wanted to explore. We wandered through Bangkok's vibrant streets, Angkor's ancient hush, and Laos' peaceful hills. I loved every moment—except for one place we skipped entirely.

Phi Phi.

I couldn't face it. Just the thought turned my stomach. Instead, we stayed a few days in Phuket. But even there, the ghosts lingered. Just across the bay.

It was there, trying to reconcile my past with the present, that I got the tattoo. It was spontaneous—at least, that's what I told myself. But there was meaning in the pain, in the permanence. As the needle tapped, spelling out my trauma in neat Sanskrit, I felt something lift. Like I was claiming my story instead of being haunted by it.

Meg held my hand through it all. Her grip steady, her warmth grounding me as I marked a new chapter on my skin—and in my life.

By 2013, our relationship was unrecognisable. Everything I'd done wrong with Tina, I did differently. Where silence had once been my sword, communication became my shield. I stopped avoiding intimacy and started leaning in. Meg taught me love wasn't something to fear— it was something to share.

I took the 'opposite' strategy. Like George in *Seinfeld*—do the reverse of every instinct, and life might actually work out. It sounds ridiculous, but it helped. I refused to let anger fester. We argued, yes—but we worked through it. The silence of my past gave way to something honest, vocal, real.

When we decided to get married, it wasn't a big production. No elaborate proposal. No drama. Just a conversation—like we always had.

Joint decision, mutual respect. The opposite of my first marriage in every way. My wedding ring has never left my finger. I didn't wear one before.

Read into that what you will.

My trauma had driven much of this bizarro behavior. I became hyper-aware, determined not to repeat old mistakes. But instead of treating that as a burden, Meg embraced it. She understood why I needed to do things differently. Why every choice had to be rooted in love, not fear. She never doubted my motives. She stood by me, even as I played the part of her anxious, overthinking Art Vandelay.

Meg didn't just save me—she showed me how to save myself. Her belief gave me the courage to face what I'd buried. She made me believe I wasn't doomed to be the sum of my past.

Our story isn't perfect. But it's ours. Every stumble, every step, every dream.

I look back now and understand what true romance really is.

It's not grand gestures or perfect moments. It's building something real, even when it's messy.

It's the daily graft. It's choosing each other—especially when it's hard.

'The greatest glory in living lies not in never falling, but in rising every time we fall.'
Confucius

Sixty Three
Everything Everywhere All At Once

2013 - 2017
London

I'd risen from the ashes of a failed marriage. Meg and I had built something grounded in honesty and trust.

But even then, the cracks were visible.

Meg had become the centre of my world—the only bright light in it. All I wanted was more time with her. More moments. More future. But one thing kept me up at night: money. Or more accurately, my reckless relationship with it. After the tsunami, I'd spent without thought—credit cards, loans, things on tick I'd long stopped tracking.

No point dying with cash on the hip, right?

Now, the weight of it was suffocating. The noose tightened each month.

I was stuck in a job I loathed but couldn't afford to leave. Fear followed me everywhere. For years, I'd believed my breakdown began in 2018, as I described in *Falling Down*. But that wasn't the start—just an episode in a longer decline, one I now see might've started as far back as 2005, stuck in Australia, betrayed by my own body.

The cracks. They'd always been there—patched with Polyfilla and blind optimism.

I've come to believe happiness needs multiple pillars. Love alone isn't enough. I had that in Meg. I had friendships, too. But without financial stability, the whole thing wobbled. If I could reinforce that one weak structure—thread some rebar through it—maybe I'd have a shot at something sustainable.

So I built a roadmap. A five-year escape plan. It would take time, discipline, automation, relentless focus. But if I stuck to it, I could emerge debt-free. A real custodian of our future. A grown-up at last.

We married in 2016—small, intimate, close to home—and honeymooned in Mexico.

It was magic. Adventure, history, calm. And no thoughts of bailing this time. Even when she suggested swimming with whale sharks—the opposite indeed.

Mornings were lazy poolside rituals. Afternoons meant adventure—Meg indulged my obsession with ancient sites. At Chichen Itza, I felt the same quiet wonder I'd known at Angkor, Machu Picchu, the Pyramids.

Evenings ended in hammocks, watching sunsets paint the sky in impossible colours. We talked, dreamed, planned. For a moment, the weight of debt and responsibility subsided.

I came home with quiet resolve. I wanted to bottle that feeling, bring it into daily life. We wanted more—purpose, escape, permanence. But freedom has a price, and the mountain of debt stood firm.

Hard labour, intricate spreadsheets and the magic of compound interest were all I had.

The dream would have to wait.

Back in the grind, I found it impossible to function. The commute became an unrelenting test of patience. Trapped in overcrowded carriages, tempers flared. "Move down inside!" "Fuck off, there's no room!"

No toilets. No air con. No relief.

Some days, the train would crawl, then stop just outside the station like it had been surprised by its own arrival: "Oh dear, Gordon's in my platform again…"

Each journey chipped away at what little stability I had left. I muttered expletives under my breath and dodged judgemental glances.

London's rail network, once a marvel, had become a parody. Privatised and profit-driven. And here I was, face mashed against a stranger's armpit in a sweltering tin can, wondering if we'd be derailed by wet leaves.

One day, desperate, I spotted a row of hire bikes outside the office. Summer heat. Temper frayed. I strapped my laptop to the front and pedalled two miles to Canary Wharf. Then caught the tube one stop and a bus home.

It wasn't perfect. But for those two miles, I was free. The breeze on my face, the rhythm of movement—it gave me peace the trains never could.

But the bike only soothed symptoms. I was trapped in a life that didn't feel like mine. And something else was rising. Something I couldn't name, but it felt impossibly heavy.

As the manager at a new landmark building, I received daily security briefings:

THREAT LEVEL: SEVERE.

London had become a target again. The July 7 bombings still lingered in memory. But then something hit closer.

I was driving when the LBC bulletin broke: "A man has been beheaded on the streets of London."

Be-head-ed!

My grip tightened on the wheel. Lee Rigby, a young soldier, had been run down, then attacked with a cleaver. The killers remained on the scene, calmly spouting ideology as they stood there drenched in blood.

It had happened in Woolwich—less than a mile from where I was.

A cold sweat bloomed. My chest clenched. Panic coiled tight. I pulled over. Sat frozen. The news replayed in my head, on loop. I couldn't drive.

Could barely think. My body was on high alert.

When I finally made it home, I sat in the car for what felt like hours.

Meg didn't ask questions. She just held me.

The fear didn't fade. It sat idle. Waiting.

Weeks later, in traffic with Meg, a driver took exception to my lane change, jumped out of his car and started walking toward us. The look in his eyes turned my blood cold.

Who does that on a motorway with good intentions?

Without thinking, I swerved onto the hard shoulder—nearly hitting him—and floored it. It lasted seconds, but it shook me to my core.

By 2016, the fear was constant. The daily grind felt like a threat. Then came October. North Greenwich station. A suspected IED. Controlled detonation.

That was it.

I slipped into full hyper-vigilance. Every day became a siege. I smoked, drank, loaded up on caffeine, skipped sleep. I plotted exit routes, imagined attacks, rehearsed what I'd do.

It was irrational. But I'd already lived through disaster. Why wouldn't it strike again?

Then, one morning before Christmas, I took the secure elevator down to the sub-basement. It felt eerie. Exposed. I couldn't shake the feeling: This building's a target.

No plan. No warning. I packed up my stuff—and walked out.

The fear had consumed me. My boss, shocked but supportive, helped transition me to manage clients in sleepy towns and villages.

No sirens. No crowds. No targets. Just long roads and calm.

Driving became my therapy. The hours alone gave me time to feel how deep the fear had rooted. No epiphanies. Just quiet. And in that, I found something like safety.

But quiet became stagnation.

My routine became a joke: bed, car, booze, codeine. The true devil's cocktail. I gave up walking, cycling. Replaced momentum with stillness. And the physical toll followed fast.

Some mornings, I couldn't get up. Then I didn't. I called in sick. Lied. Said it was bugs. Old injuries. Anything but the truth: I couldn't keep going.

Looking back, I wish I'd given myself space to breathe. But life doesn't offer room for vulnerability, does it?

"What's wrong? When will you be back? Can you just log in for this one thing?"

Recovery felt impossible. The pressure never stopped. And the thoughts came more often.

I was frayed. Unravelling.

2017 was the year fear finally caught me.

March—Westminster Bridge. A car ploughed into pedestrians. A police officer stabbed. Chaos in the heart of my city.

May—Manchester. A suicide bomber at an Ariana Grande concert. Kids. Parents.

June—London Bridge. A van. A stabbing spree in Borough Market.

Even amid the horror, there were stories of extraordinary bravery. A man armed with a narwhal tusk, a detail so surreal it bordered on the absurd, had confronted one of the attackers. Elsewhere, a gang of Millwall fans channeled their hooligan instincts into heroism. Protecting their territory, their people, from the knife wielding attackers.

Meg and I could've been there. Our place. Our pub. Our streets.

The news became inescapable. Each attack carved deeper into my sense of safety.

I started staying home. The whisper of fear had become a scream.

I was slipping. Avoiding life. Imagining threats in every shadow.

Clinging to control.

I couldn't see a way out. But soon, something would arrive—not a breaking point, but a miracle in the form of an old friend.

'When we are no longer able to change a situation,
we are challenged to change ourselves.'
Viktor Frankl

Sixty Four
My Best Friend's Wedding

June 2017
Croatia

Barry was getting married. We were heading to Croatia, and I couldn't wait. I needed a distraction—something to jolt me out of free-fall—and a week with friends felt like a lifeline.

He'd chosen Hvar, a stunning island along the Dalmatian coast. I hadn't been involved, but thanks to Meg, I didn't have to be. Honestly, without her, I'd have shown up at the wrong airport. No passport. A far cry from the capable traveller I used to be.

Bobby, Steve, Wiggy and our wives had all decided to share a villa. Magic. It was ridiculous—cliffside, sea views, outdoor kitchen, fire pit, a pool that shimmered.

That night we lounged by the water, cocktails in hand, while a private chef cooked us a feast. For the first time in ages, I felt something close to peace. No stress. No responsibilities. No imagined disasters. Just friends, food, and the sense that maybe I could hold it together.

The next day, Barry hosted a beachside get-together. The energy was buzzing—house music, cocktails, laughter. I let myself get swept up in it.

"There's Lisbeth," Wiggy said, nodding over my shoulder.

"What?" I spun around, startled. Somehow, it hadn't crossed my mind she'd be here. Obvious in hindsight—her and Barry were forever tied —but I'd been too lost in my own head.

"Didn't you know she was coming?"

I didn't answer. I just weaved through the crowd, dodging a wild stag party, heading straight for her.

"John!" she beamed, pulling me into a hug. We held on a little too long. For a moment, time folded in on itself.

"I can't believe you're here," I said, dazed. "It's so good to see you."

"Same. I've been looking forward to this. And guess what… I still have Clyde!" she laughed.

The name hit like a cartoon mallet. My mind went straight to Sarawak—cheesy duets, late nights, her voice, our Orangutan mic. Clyde. Before I could stop it, the memories crashed in.

It wasn't just a memory—it was a glimpse of who I used to be, back when joy still came easy.

And I melted.

Not a discreet tear—full-body sobbing. Loud, messy, gasping-for-air sobbing.

Lisbeth didn't flinch. She gently guided me from the crowd, around a corner, and sat me down.

"What is it?" she asked softly. "I'm so sorry if I upset you."

"You didn't," I managed, wiping tears with the heel of my hand. "Just… seeing you… remembering… I don't know."

She sat patiently, calm, her presence like a pressure release valve. I couldn't articulate the pain, but she saw it anyway. I learned she'd left the police and now worked in psychology, speaking openly about the tsunami. Her steady voice anchored me as my mind ping-ponged between Borneo and Phi Phi. Eventually, she pulled me back.

"Try this," she said, taking my phone. "It's an online test I did recently. I think it might help." She typed in a link.

"Thanks," I said. "Promise I'll do it."

Back at the bar, I ordered the largest cocktail I could find—more fruit than a Carmen Miranda hat. I drank fast, slunk back for more. Three or four rounds later, the lights went out. Mange Tout.

"Morning, you." Meg's voice cut through the hangover. Emphasis on 'you'—never good.

I blinked in the sunlight. Right bed, right villa. No memory.

"Do you remember last night?" she asked, voice light but loaded.

I shook my head. Just flashes: Lisbeth, cocktails—then blackout.

"You couldn't even talk. We took you to a harbour restaurant, thought food might help."

The words landed like a gut punch.

"Who's 'we'?" I asked, dreading the answer.

"Wiggy and Kate. Barry and Rach."

Bonnet de douche. Relief and embarrassment clashed. At least it was our 'circle of trust.' Still, I hated being that guy. Again.

"What happened?" Meg asked gently.

"I'm sorry," I said, voice cracking. "I don't remember anything after the bar."

"You were knocking those cocktails back," she said. "Idiot." She smiled and pulled me out of bed. "Come on. Let's get some sun."

The villa was quiet. I collapsed on a sun-bed, sunglasses on, shame wrapped around me like a wet towel.

"Morning, Kate," I muttered. "Sorry about last night."

She laughed. "You were no worse than usual John! Just a bit gobby." She handed me a vodka soda—hair of the dog. Bless her.

The day came alive—laughter, buzzed day-drinking, ball games. Curious, I checked my phone: Enneagram Personality Test.

It clicked. The test Lisbeth made me promise to take.

Simple questions. Fast answers. I did it.

Type: 9
Name: Peacemaker / Mediator
Vice: Sloth
Virtue: Action
Trap: Seeker
Basic Fear: Loss, Separation
Basic Desire: Wholeness, Peace of Mind

Some of it hit like a punch. Loss, Separation? Check. Sloth? Absolutely. I'd made inactivity an art form. Junk food, fat pants, TV marathons—"His brain is mush. If you shine a flashlight in his eyes, he'd probably die of shock."

And then it went deeper. Type Nines crave peace but avoid conflict—even with themselves. We merge with others, suppress our needs, and let issues rot in the dark.

That was me.

I wasn't just lazy. I was shutting down. Choosing comfort over growth. Denial over healing. And now I was paying the price.

No time to dwell.

The wedding was perfect. A sunlit dream in a cove overlooking the sea. Barry and his bride exchanged vows as the sky melted into gold. For a moment, I was present—laughing, toasting, dancing. Friends. Family. A rare sense of belonging.

But joy, for me, was fragile.

Later, I sat with Lisbeth. Her calm acceptance of our trauma struck like lightning. She talked about the tsunami like it was part of her—

not buried, just there. I'd sealed mine away.

Her words made it surface again. Too raw. Too close.

I drifted from the party, physically there, mentally miles away. Watching Barry surrounded by love should've lifted me. Instead, it reminded me how far I'd slipped.

I resolved to get better. But resolutions under fairy lights and Prosecco rarely last.

Anxiety crept back. I lit a joint. My go-to fix. But it didn't soothe—just blurred. When I returned, the group photo had been taken.

A picture of love and history—and I wasn't in it.

It crushed me. Stupid, maybe. But symbolic. Always nearby. Never in it. Present but absent. Watching life instead of living it.

The wedding showed me what I'd lost—connection, purpose, myself.

Lisbeth hadn't judged. Just reflected me back at myself. A mirror I'd avoided. The Enneagram cracked something open. I couldn't ignore it anymore.

Type 9. The avoider. The peacemaker who avoids his own pain.

It explained everything—the drift, the dissociation, the self-sabotage.

I'd been coasting. Pretending.

And pretending hadn't worked.

As the plane descended over southeast England, Meg's hand in mine, I felt something shift. Not peace through avoidance—but the kind that comes from acceptance. I didn't have all the answers. But I was ready to start finding them.

I'd tried everything—new jobs, new places—but nothing worked. The trauma remained. The depression followed.

I needed to stop. And that, I realised, was the scariest part of all.

The truths revealed in Croatia started the cascade that would lead to my *Falling Down* episode—and to the real healing.

Thank you, Lisbeth. I owe you one.

'No one ever told me that grief felt so like fear.'
C.S. Lewis

Sixty Five
The Iron Lady

1st March 2022
London

It had been forty-nine months since my long, drawn-out breakdown reached its climax. Roughly 1,492 days since what I'd framed as a calculated "play"—became something else entirely.

The symptoms I'd dismissed for years had a name. PTSD.

The diagnosis became a reckoning. A slow reckoning, but a necessary one. Rada's work, building on the foundations laid by Gita, pushed me past the obvious trauma of the tsunami and into deeper waters—my anger, my anxiety, the roots of my pain.

It was like unearthing a long-lost map of myself. Slowly, I was charting a new course, moving toward a version of the future I could finally believe in.

But I wasn't done. I'd made two promises.

One to Gita: get it out of my head and onto the page.

The other to Rada: tell my loved ones the story. Not just Meg. Not just Barry. My family.

I thought about it constantly. The idea of sitting across from my mum, cup of tea in hand, laying it all out was frightening. The words felt impossible—too sharp, too weighty. I imagined it a hundred ways. Once, at a family BBQ it almost came out, she gave me a look. It said, "I'm ready, John. Whenever you are." I chickened out.

"Soon," I promised myself.

Thanks Mum. Roger that.

Things were really good between us. Closer than we'd been in years. Meg had helped rebuild the bridge. We weren't fully back, but we were better.

I cherished that.

A call from my sister Louise shattered everything:

"Are you home? Can you go to Mum's? She's collapsed. Dad's giving her CPR. Ambulance is on the way!"

My stomach dropped. I was in Green Park—one of the rare days I'd gone into town for work. Ninety percent of the time, I was at home. But today—of all days—I'd come in for a pointless meeting.

I sprinted for the Tube, dodging commuters. The doors were closing. I dove through without breaking stride.

Twenty minutes to North Greenwich. Another twenty by Uber. Best case.

'Why the fuck did I come into London today?' I clenched my fists, teeth grinding. Another breath. I needed to stay calm. Ready.

The train emerged into light. Waterloo. Sixteen minutes to go.

I focused on the pips of the doors—used them as a metronome. Breathe in. Breathe out. I wanted to kick open the drivers cab, drop the dead man's switch and drive it through every station like Jason Bourne.

But I sat. Waited.

Then the memories started up—a lifetime of emergencies bleeding together.

Mum, slurring on the phone: "John I'm having a stroke."

"What! Where are you?"

"In the garage having a fag."

"For fucksake, hang up and call an ambulance. I'm on my way."

Me at twelve, hearing she'd been carted off in an ambulance while I was climbing trees with Nick.

That was her first cancer diagnosis. Partial gastrectomy. King's College became a second home. Waiting. Fear. Antiseptic.

Dad trying to hold it together, hands shaking in the waiting room.

Two heart attacks. A blood disorder. A stroke. Coma. She came back different from that—but she came back.

I texted Sam when she woke: She's awake.

His reply: No doubt. Nothing can take her down.

Suffering from Aphasia, she taught herself to walk and talk again, with almost no assistance. She did it with a smile and a newfound way of laughing at the muddled sentences and mixed up names. It was a childlike quality that I'd never seen before, both endearing and hilarious.

No therapy. Just East End grit. The Iron Lady.

We believed it.

The train pulled into Bermondsey. Six minutes to go. Her birthplace. Post-war Bermondsey girl—tough, loyal, fearless. Images of her childhood flashed behind my lids. This time felt different.

Through all the illnesses, I never once believed she wouldn't pull through.

But this time...

I bolted up the escalator at North Greenwich. My Uber was waiting. I wanted to assume that *Bourne Identity* and push the hapless driver out of his Prius, take the wheel and speed home as quickly as the electric engine would allow. But some part of me remained in control.

"I'm sorry. My mum's collapsed. Please, just get me there. Fast. Safe. Please."

The driver nodded. He made every amber light count. Twelve minutes later, we pulled into the street.

"Anywhere near the ambulances," I blurted.

Of course he knew.

I sprinted up the path. A paramedic met me at the door. "I'm the lead paramedic. We've been working on her for about an hour. Your dad did CPR until we arrived..."

Her voice trailed off. The truth hung in the silence.

I sat with Dad and Louise, listening to the rhythm of compressions from the next room. Lou went in. I couldn't. I didn't want to see her like that. I couldn't add one more image to the gallery of death in my head.

Eventually, they stopped. Pronounced. Gone.

Just like that.

The paramedics filed out in yellow jumpsuits and face masks. Just the three of us now. Stunned.

Outside, Sam had been waiting. As I stepped outside, he looked at me, his face searching mine for an answer. I shook my head. Slowly. Deliberately. He crumpled, sobbing into his sleeve. I put my arm around him, holding him tight. Moments after losing my mum, there I was, consoling someone else.

It surprised me—my own reaction. The strong one, the calm one. I didn't feel strong. Inside, I was crumbling. But if I broke, the whole family might fall apart, so I pressed on, exuding a controlled persona that didn't match the storm inside.

I made tea. Couldn't let Dad see me cry.

Then came the neighbours. One knock. Then more. Tears. Questions. I wanted to scream. 'Her body's still in the next room. Can we have a minute, please?'

But I smiled. Nodded. Made more tea. Said the right things. "Do you want a biscuit with your PG Tips?"

There are other versions of Johnny boy that would've told them to fuck off, instead of asking how many sugars they took. But instead I breathed, and I thought empathically. I understood the good intentions, but could they have given us a bit more time? I think so.

Meg arrived. She found me in the kitchen, staring blankly.

"How are you?" she whispered.

A child's voice cut through: "Nanny's gone!"

My nephew. Three years old. Palms up. Confused.

His words sliced me open. Meg wrapped her arms around me. I turned away, swallowed it.

Not now. Shut it down. Phi Phi style.

I regret that. I wish I'd let it out. But my body made the call. Survival mode. Again. That organic steel fortress. It wasn't conscious, it was survival.

Grief tightened around me. A silent weight. It felt like fear. Fear of life without her, fear that I'd never recover. I wish I could explain it better, but its painful in an empty kind of way.

Sadness. Loss. Devastation. Colossal.

And then, right on cue came the anger. It simmered, quiet at first, but growing in intensity. The visitors, the forced politeness, the unrelenting condolences.

So I went to Jiu-Jitsu. Wednesday night. Routine. Structure. She'd paid for my yellow belt the week before. "Brilliant, so proud of you," she'd texted. "I knew you would smash it luv xxx."

Her Aphasia meant she pronounced it Jin Jinsy. I love that.

I fought for her. It helped.

And when I got home, I reached back for the bottle.

The weeks that followed were a brutal blur. A barrage of logistics. No time to grieve. Just forms, phone calls, decisions.

Her absence haunted the house. Her chair. Her teacup. The pinny and gold slippers she wore like a uniform. My sister stepped up with quiet strength—planning, organising—while me and Dad floundered.

It hit Lou hardest, but she carried us. And I'll never forget that.

The funeral was everything she would've wanted. Flowers blanketed the driveway and the cars. The neighbours lined the pavement as the cortege passed. By the time we arrived at the crematorium, there were more faces than I could count.

Even Nick made an appearance. I hadn't seen him since I was fourteen, but the years disappeared when he hugged me.

The service was a haze—eulogies, hymns, goodbye. I sat in silence, paralysed by grief, full of pride. I wanted to speak. I didn't. I couldn't.

Weak. Afraid.

Louise and the kids spoke beautifully. I let them speak for all of us.

And I hated myself for it.

Afterward, we gathered at the local club. My one contribution: a slideshow—seventy years of her life in photos. I worked on it obsessively. It was something I could do alone. My way of saying goodbye.

The music was my choice—a soundtrack of her life through my ears.

My duty.

Nick cornered us to share stories from the estate days.

"Remember when the police brought us home? And your mum chased us down the alley?"

We laughed, even through the pain.

"Those sovereign rings used to sting, didn't they?"

Then he said something that stopped me cold.

"Remember that time you nearly drowned? With your cousin Jake? He just stood there. In Mallorca right?"

"Portugal," I said, stunned.

I'd buried that memory. But Nick remembered. A stamp of validation on a long-lost fragment of truth. Of my ailing memory.

He didn't know about the tsunami. Few people did. But that day in Portugal—surviving something so terrifying—made me realise how much our childhood escapades had shaped me. The climbing, the jumping, the lido, the games of ninja—it all helped me stay calm under pressure. Even underwater.

When it mattered most.

"You know," I said, changing the subject, "I probably owe you a thank you. All that nonsense we got up to—I think it saved my life. I was in Thailand a long time ago when…"

And just like that I told my story. Just like Rada had told me to. It wasn't to the right person but it felt like progress.

Later, my cousin Sam found me, his face etched with quiet understanding.

"You alright, John? You all did well today."

"Thanks, Sam. It's been hard, but what can you do?"

The tsunami was fresh in my mind. I hesitated, then admitted something I'd never voiced.

"I wish I'd told her, Sam. I wanted to—but I didn't make it happen in time. I'm gutted."

He looked me in the eye.

"I told her."

"What?"

"I told her everything John."

"You serious…?"

"She knew. She knew something big had happened to change you so much. And she was proud."

Relief surged through me. The words I couldn't say—she'd heard them anyway. Through Sam. Through love.

She knew.

And that meant everything. I could take comfort in knowing she didn't die with that part of me hidden.

In the end, my mum's story is one of grit and grace. A woman shaped by hardship who never let it define her. A protector. A provider. A mother who gave everything—even when she had so little—and asked for nothing in return.

I regret not spending more time with her. I hate that my own illness robbed us of so many years—years of fleeting visits where I couldn't even sit still for a cuppa and an episode of EastEnders.

I was aloof and distant after the tsunami, lost in an undiagnosed storm of pain. We were just starting to rebuild the bond, and although it wasn't as much time as I'd have liked—it was something.

Even now, I feel her love, guiding me. Anchoring me.

And I miss her every day.

Sixty Six
Clean and Sober

24th March 2023
London

My mum's funeral should've been a time to reflect and honour her memory. Instead, I used grief as a green light to self-destruct. What was meant to be one night of release, became nearly a year of self-sabotage.

I'm embarrassed by how easily I let it happen.

I couldn't let her death defeat me. It had to mean something. Losing her knocked over the fragile tower I'd spent years rebuilding—like a Doozer construction in *Fraggle Rock*, obliterated by Red's careless paw.

And yet, I had to find a way through. Mum had always believed in me. Now it was my turn.

I'd made promises before—to cut back, take control—and broke them every time. A tough day, a bad memory, a reason to celebrate.

Any excuse would do.

Work threatened to smash through once again—reminding me just how fragile it all was. I'd just stepped into a café when I got the message: "Call me."

My boss didn't waste time. "Thomas threatened to cancel the contract."

"This is ridiculous," I said. "I can't keep doing this."

"Don't overreact. Take the weekend. We'll regroup Monday."

"No. Fuck this. Find someone else to manage this account. I'm done."

And just like that, I was falling again, the sequel no one asked for.

By Monday, the spiral was tightening. I had two options:

Behind door one: the same man I'd been for years—drowning in a vodka-soaked pit of self-loathing. Behind the second: someone unrecognisable—stronger, sharper, braver.

So, with my best *Big Trouble in Little China* swagger, I kicked open Door Two.

"Okay, you people sit tight, hold the fort and keep the home fires burning. And if we're not back by dawn… call the president."

I'd glimpsed the life sobriety could bring—habits built, sleep restored —but it never lasted. I never fully committed. I convinced myself moderation was possible, that I could be someone who had 'just one.'

But I'm not that person. I never have been.

I am all or nothing. Simple. Alcohol has dictated my progress for too long. It's the weight around my ankles every time I try to climb. I can train hard, set goals, build routines—but if booze is still in the equation, I'm dragging dead weight.

This time, I'm done. Not just with drinking, but with the half-life I've been living. This time, I'm choosing ownership. Extreme Ownership.

Growing up, alcohol was everywhere. It was the glue of our friendships, the centrepiece of every gathering. Sobriety? That felt like betrayal. A rejection of everything we were raised to believe.

But then Bobby quit. No big announcement—just action. And he thrived. Clearer. Fitter. More driven.

"You'll achieve more in six months sober than in ten years drunk," he told me. At first, I laughed. Then I started to see it. Not just in him— but in me.

Alcohol had been holding me back my entire life.

This is my line in the sand.

I know the road ahead won't be easy. There will be temptations. Weak moments. Old excuses whispering in the background. But I'm not giving them space. Not this time.

This time, I choose discipline.

I laced up my trainers. Above them, the sign I'd pinned months ago:

What would David Goggins do? Stupid question. He'd run a marathon before sunrise and hydrate with his own tears.

Still, I channelled a fraction of his insanity. Ran. Sauna. Ice bath. Reset. By 8 a.m., I was showered, dressed, feeling like a new man. One who may or may not have sobbed in the tub.

That's how it is—resistance training for the soul. Every time I don't give in, I grow stronger. I silence the bitch in my head. Not forever, but for today.

Still, I saw the pattern. Hope, challenge, burnout. I used to believe the grind was noble. That ambition meant sacrifice. But it only delivered more stress, more emptiness.

Maybe it's not the job. Maybe it's me. Chasing the wrong dream.

I thought of Dad—a man who gave everything to work, to us, to Mum. And now? He was alone, his own health fading. A shadow of his former self.

I love him for it. But I want more. Sorry, Dad.

And then, as if the universe had been eavesdropping on my existential crisis. Meg got a job offer. Huge. Life-changing.

And just like that, the treadmill stopped. For the first time in years, I stepped off—and saw it for what it was:

A chance to write a new story.

'Everyone has a friend during each stage of life. But only the lucky ones have the same friend in all stages of life.'
Unknown

Sixty Seven
The Breakfast Club

27th May 2023
London

Habits I'd toyed with for years finally locked into place. Routines became rituals. Excuses gave way to discipline.

Responsibility loomed, a quiet reminder to become someone worth rooting for. I look back at the stress I caused—how hard it must've been to watch me squander my life. That shame became fuel. I wanted to take revenge on the lazy bastard who'd worn my skin for so long.

I wanted to become the man my mum believed I could be.

Even in my mum's absence, I could still feel her. A quiet presence. A whisper in the dark: Don't let me down.

Dear Mama, I got this.

Four months into this new chapter, with my 46th birthday on the horizon, I felt stronger—mentally, physically, emotionally. What started as small, consistent changes had quietly transformed me. It wasn't just the habits. It was the mindset. For the first time in years, I could see a future worth leaning into.

The idea of a traditional birthday—booze-fuelled antics and hangovers—filled me with dread. But I wasn't doing this alone. The boys were my anchors. Barry was deep into his wellness kick. Wiggy was all gym routines and strict sleep windows. And Bobby? Our wildcard. He'd quit drinking, taken up wild swimming, and was a constant source of wisdom.

Instead of heading to the pub, I called the boys of The Breakfast Club

—my unofficial sponsors. We planned something different. Intimate. Honest. A spa retreat. Four middle-aged blokes in robes. A celebration without chaos. A reset disguised as a birthday.

Social connection had become my secret weapon. We often overlook it when we talk about health, but it's critical. Human connection builds resilience, strengthens mental health, anchors us when storms hit. Studies say people with strong social networks live longer—by as much as 50%. And loneliness? As damaging as smoking fifteen cigarettes a day. Which sounds mad. I'm assuming it's true, but how do you even measure that?

My past was full of bail-outs. Agreeing to plans, then ghosting. Cancelling last minute. Hiding in a dark room with weed and vodka. It felt easier than facing people.

But the new version of me had made a promise: reconnect or regress. The yes-man with boundaries.

It was awkward at first—like learning how to be human again. But it changed everything. Walks with Matt and his family. Coffee with Wiggy. Activities that didn't revolve around alcohol: food markets, outdoor galleries, hikes. My social calendar filled with soul-nourishing moments.

And above all, I rediscovered my true passion—live music.

Whether it was an open mic in a dingy pub or *Elton John's* farewell at the O2, live music became my medicine. Raw, immersive, shared—it healed me in ways nothing else could. It plugged me back in. To the world. To myself.

The more I said yes to meaningful moments, the more present I felt. My world expanded. My mood lifted. I started to feel... seen. And with that came something I'd long been searching for—purpose.

The Japanese call it ikigai—a reason for being. Where what you love, what you're good at, and what the world needs all meet. It became a direction. My compass. I wasn't there yet, but I was closing in.

Still figuring it out. Still chasing it. But I know one thing:

It's not facilities management.

Pretty sure that's nobody's ikigai.

With my newly rebuilt life taking shape, I prepped for the birthday retreat. This wasn't just about turning 46. I had a mission.

I pulled into the country spa just after 6 a.m. The air was crisp. Still. For the first time in years, I felt excited about my birthday. No pubs. No booze. Just four mates, herbal tea in hand, swapping massages and cucumber sandwiches. It felt surreal. Peaceful.

These weren't just mates. They were my chosen family.

Like the characters in *The Breakfast Club*, we each brought something different. Barry was Emilio Estevez—handsome, mysterious, quiet. Bobby was Brian—thoughtful, sharp, deceptively wise. Wiggy and I were a mash-up of the rest: nerdy, scarred, still a bit feral. But together, we worked.

Yet today felt different.

Beneath the banter and calm, I carried something heavy. I'd promised Rada I'd finally talk to Barry about the tsunami. I'd already waited too long to have that kind of talk with my mum. I wasn't making the same mistake twice.

Time was running out. I was moving away soon—leaving this crew, this support—and they needed to know. But first, I had to find the courage for one conversation I'd avoided for 19 years.

The sauna was warm, eucalyptus-scented. A glass wall opened onto the rolling Kent countryside. Light filtered through summer leaves, painting the room with shifting greens. Peaceful—almost too peaceful. I promised I wouldn't force the moment.

After twenty minutes, we slipped into the hot tub. Barry and Bobby drifted to the far end. Wiggy and I chatted about therapy. He understood. I told him about Rada, the breakthroughs, how my mindset had shifted.

It felt good. For a second, I thought: maybe that's enough for today.

But it wasn't. Not if I meant what I said.

Barry floated alone, arms on the pool's edge, eyes on the horizon. My chest tightened as I paddled toward him, nineteen years pressing down.

"Bazza," I said, voice thin.

He turned, curious.

"I need to talk to you. About... something. About Phi Phi."

No flinch. Just softened eyes. "Yeah," he said quietly. "I've thought about that day constantly."

The dam burst. I spoke of the fear, the bodies, the helplessness. The silence I'd lived in. The years pretending it hadn't happened. Barry didn't interrupt. Just listened.

When I stopped—gasping—he nodded. "For me," he said, "it was the bridge."

"The bridge?"

"Well, the pier really. When it started collapsing. People screaming, grabbing each other. That's when I thought, 'One of us ain't getting out.' I looked back and saw you. That was the image."

His words hit hard. I hadn't thought much about that part—it had barely registered in the hierarchy of horror.

"I almost forgot how terrifying that was."

"You didn't forget," Barry said. "You buried it."

We sat in silence. Then he added, "Do you remember calling your mum from the morgue?"

"I do."

"That sticks with me. My mum crying… trying to stay strong but breaking."

His voice cracked.

My own mind pulled me back to my mum's kitchen. The grief I swallowed. The tears I never let fall. She died, and I hadn't cried.

"I think I blocked everything out," I said. "For me, it was the baby. The bodies on the beach. That's all I saw."

"You were always stronger than me."

I shook my head. "I wasn't strong. I just shut it down. You dealt with it. I didn't. You talked—Lisbeth, your mum. I stayed silent. I didn't even speak to Tina."

Barry gave a sad smile. "Talking didn't feel like a choice. Lisbeth wouldn't let it go. She called me every day. Made me face it."

We talked more—the pier, the sunrise, the aftermath. Same event, different scars. He remembered the morning light. I remembered the stillness of death.

"We've never talked about this," I said. "Not in nineteen years."

"Life," Barry shrugged. "And fear."

"We should've. Maybe I wouldn't have carried it so long. I'm sorry."

"Maybe we weren't ready."

He was right. We were now.

"This," I said, gesturing between us, "is what I needed. Back then. And now."

Barry nodded. "There's more, isn't there?"

"Yeah. But this is a good start."

The water shimmered. Not everything had been said—but enough had. I felt lighter. Supported. Heard.

Friendship has always been my cornerstone. I've been lucky. Incredible people have shown up at every phase. Some brief. Some lifelong. But the boys? They're my constants. Through cities, continents, hangovers and heartbreaks. Most friendships fade. Drift. But this? This bond was forged in fire.

These men shaped me. Now they reflected me back—stronger, steadier, whole.

This wasn't just another birthday—it felt like the end of a story I'd been stuck in for years.

I could almost picture Eamonn Andrews handing me the big red book: *This is Your Life.*

Only now, I was ready for Act Two.

No longer the passive passenger. I was steering. From survival to intention. From flashbacks to stillness. From fear to purpose.

Transformation isn't sudden. It's a million small shifts—routine, rest, honesty, connection. A life built around who you're becoming, not who you've been.

That afternoon, we sat on the veranda in white robes, the forest glowing with spring light. Birds chirped. Pine and wildflowers drifted on the breeze. We sipped tea and laughed at how ridiculous we looked —middle-aged men swapping lagers for lemon balm.

I looked around at them. The moment held.

This was more than a birthday. More than a milestone. It was the line between old and new.

"Boys… I've got something important to tell you. I'm going away."

> *'The first step towards getting somewhere is to decide that you are not going to stay where you are.'*
> **J. P. Morgan**

Sixty Eight
Coming To America

10th August 2023
London

We were up far too early, sleep fractured by nerves and excitement. Meg gave up first, slipping out of bed at 4 a.m. I hung on, craving a few more minutes, but the hum of the hairdryer snapped me out of it. So much rested on today's decision. I sat silently, willing the right outcome into existence.

"What should I wear today?" I asked Meg, standing bollock naked in the dressing room, air cool on my skin.

"The instructions said to dress like a job interview. So something smart, please." Her voice was tight. Nervous.

I wasn't the only one feeling it.

Choosing an outfit wasn't as simple as it once was. Since COVID, my suits had become museum pieces. Smart-casual had taken over—chinos, polos, trainers. But today called for formality. Dress to impress, make a good first impression—my dad's voice echoed.

I had two suits. A black one from Mum's funeral—too sombre. And a blue one, last worn during my Michael Douglas meltdown, the day I walked away from the job I once loved. That suit had seen my lowest point. Still, it felt right. Or maybe necessary. Dry-cleaned and waiting —a reminder of what I'd survived. I paired it with a white shirt and Mum's cufflinks. Tied the Windsor knot the way my dad taught me, caught my reflection.

Battle gear. "Let's do this," I said to the mirror.

The journey to Nine Elms, London, was smooth—intentionally early, intentionally quiet. The Tube was near empty, just flickers of light passing through vacant stations. I'd planned it this way to control my environment. Calm mattered. Not just for me, but for Meg. For everyone in my orbit.

We rode the escalator to street level. Sunlight greeted us. Battersea Power Station stood nearby, reborn after decades of decay. Its chimneys once symbolised a dying age—now they loomed over luxury flats, office blocks, and artisan cafés. London reinventing itself again.

I felt an odd kinship with that skyline.

Meg smiled—nerves showing through the grin. I leaned in for a cheeky kiss, careful not to smudge her lipstick.

"Which way?" she asked.

"That way, near the river. Want to grab a coffee?"

We'd already had one on the Tube, but for me, coffee was more than habit—it was ritual. Since going sober, it had become my one indulgence. This morning's cup was a small victory: an independent café offering a Peru-Mexico blend with notes of caramel and cocoa. The first sip grounded me.

As we turned the final corner, the U.S. Embassy dominated the scene —an angular cube wrapped in sail-like panels, an architectural fortress. Naturally, I couldn't help myself. I snapped photos, Googled facts, mentally drafted an Instagram post. Anything to stay distracted.

Meg, patient as ever, queued up as I mumbled trivia. Thankfully, the doors opened before I got carried away.

Inside, the embassy felt more like an airport terminal than a fortress. Security was slick. We breezed through metal detectors and checkpoints. Meg stayed focused. I tried not to let the architecture and art pull me into distraction mode. Not today. This was her moment.

We'd spent over a year preparing for this—paperwork, legal calls, documents, appointments. Meg's company had offered her the chance to work in the U.S., and today was the final step: the interview at the

U.S. Consulate.

She was scared. Understandably. But I had no doubt she'd smash it.

I expected a grilling, Guantanamo-style. I'd rehearsed for intense scrutiny. Instead, it was… just a process. Polite. Efficient. Booth to booth. Form after form. The only tense moment? When I had to explain how I lost my passport in 2004.

"A guy ran off with it moments before the tsunami hit," I said.

The agent paused, looked up. "I've never heard that one before."

"Yeah… neither had I."

And that was it.

Ninety minutes later, we were outside again, blinking into the sun. The same building that had loomed so large in our minds now felt distant —almost anticlimactic.

"So that's it, then," I said.

Meg laughed. "Yeah. It's done. It's really happening!"

A smile spread across both our faces. That familiar stir returned—the one I hadn't felt since getting my Australian visa with Wiggy. A heady mix of freedom, relief, and anticipation.

"2026. Three years," I said, gripping Meg's hand. Then, slipping into my best Rodney Trotter impression: "Do you want to go first, or shall I?"

She smiled. "Let's go together."

"One, two, three…"

"Arrrggghhh!"

We roared with laughter—our own little *Only Fools* moment, shaking off months of stress in one joyful outburst.

As we strolled back toward the station, a flood of memories followed. The life we were leaving behind had been brutal and beautiful in equal measure.

South London. Violence. Gang culture.
World travel. The tsunami. Trauma.
Addiction. Isolation. Recovery.
Meg.
It had been a hell of a ride.

I'd survived one of the world's worst natural disasters. Battled depression. Fallen into substance dependence. Hid behind ego, anger, avoidance. And somehow, through all of that, found love—and a path out.

We were starting again—the American dream, reimagined. A clean page.

On the Tube home, my reflection stared back at me in the window. Same blue suit. Same tired eyes. But not the same man. That suit had seen me fall down. Today, it felt like a reckoning.

One twist? I'd be going back to the same company that once let me go. That still stung. But I owned my part in it now. *Extreme ownership.* I'd engineered that exit. It had been necessary.

Now, I was different.

Sharper. Honest. Clear. Ready.

"Wait till they get a load of me," I whispered, smirking at my reflection. Love, pain, redemption. It was more than a job—it was part of our story.

This time, I wouldn't just survive—I'd thrive. PTSD had broken me— but it had also rebuilt me.

More resilient. More empathetic. More… me.

I am ready.

Epilogue

A Better Tomorrow

Winter 2023
The Atlantic Ocean - Texas

A wall of water surrounds me—endless, merciless. No escape. It hammers the Queen Mary II with a fury that reverberates through every corridor. Waves reach for us like vengeful gods, fists pounding the windows in a relentless crescendo.

Up top, where the wind cuts like glass and the sky churns with fury, I find air—and with it, a strange sense of control. We're far from land. Thousands of miles of deep, violent sea in every direction. And yet, this voyage feels necessary. Symbolic.

I'm not here for the opulence of the crossing. I'm here because I had to be. Because Monty, my little Boston Terrier, can't fly. The only way for us to arrive as a family was by boat. A seven day voyage into the unknown.

Everyone had something to say. "You're brave, mate, you wouldn't catch me out there after what you've been through." "Fuck that for a laugh." Most brought up the tsunami. Then the Titanic. Like it hadn't crossed my mind.

Eventually, I beat them to it—Celine Dion jokes, arms outstretched on the bow, yelling, "I'm the king of the world!" Pretending helped. This was exposure therapy at sea. All or nothing.

Monty hated the kennel. Twenty-three dogs, one ancient cat named Sir Ivan, and a narrow walkway known—fittingly—as the poop deck. He trembled, too scared to piss. I wasn't much better. I'd stare at the roiling sea, locked in a silent duel with my oldest nemesis.

"How am I doing, Ma?"

I posted updates on Instagram. Everyone asked about Monty. No one asked about me. Maybe they didn't know what to say. Maybe they knew exactly what not to say. Either way, it helped. He became my reason to stay grounded.

There were calm days, too. I kept to routines—walk, read, breathe. But I'd still drift to the edge of the deck, overwhelmed by the sheer scale of the sea. It could swallow us whole if it wanted. And yet... here we were. Afloat.

On day four, the storm peaked—gale force 10. The ship groaned, and the wind nearly lifted me off the deck. I remembered a joke I'd made before we left: "If you don't hear from me by Friday, the ocean finally got me."

It wasn't funny anymore.

But on day seven, everything changed. We woke to Brooklyn Harbour. The Statue of Liberty rising through mist. We'd made it. I'd faced the ocean, and it let me pass.

It was emotional. Our dream had become real. Not through magic. Not fate. Through small choices. Hard lessons. And relentless perseverance.

Therapy made me face what I'd spent decades outrunning. I'm not "cured," but I'm more in control. The loose cannon still lives in me, but now, he answers to someone. Most of the time.

I've turned my PTSD from captor into companion. It's not easy. I still get blindsided. But I've learned to spot the warning signs. To intervene. Ignoring it isn't an option—it'll bite back. "It's a gift... and a curse." So I stay on my toes.

Gita would be proud. Where I once felt empty, numb, and unable to find joy, now I feel full—almost overwhelmed by how much there is to enjoy in this world.

My morning routine is my anchor: 5 a.m. wake-ups, lazy-man's yoga, sauna, reading, hydration. Simple. Sustainable. Each habit stacking on the next, like bricks in a wall. It started with a single push-up. A short walk. One glass of water. Change doesn't come in a burst.

I see you, my friend. I was you. I am you.

And if you need a nudge, just channel the immortal words of Arnold J. Rimmer: "You may think being a laid-back slob is fine and dandy, but when it all goes pear-shaped, it's the ones who follow the rules who come out on top."

Visualising my goals made them feel real. More than daydreams—they were plans. That gave me purpose. As Qui-Gon Jinn said, 'Your focus becomes your reality.' If it's good enough for a Jedi, it's good enough for me.

It's a strange thing—arriving in the future you used to dream about. A reward from the multiverse. By focusing on the version I want to be, maybe I dance across the realms—step into that version with grace.

The Prime.

Standing on the balcony at Southfork Ranch, I feel my mum again. I can still feel her arms around me as I drifted off on the settee. The iconic *Dallas* theme playing. I didn't know it then, but I was there to say goodbye.

Meg holds my hand in JR Ewing's bedroom. The grief catches up with me. What I swallowed down in her kitchen bursts forth now—not in tears, but in an overpowering sense of love, loss, and gratitude.

Boxing Day arrives. I wake early in Dallas. The air bites with cold. The weight of the date presses down on me. It's been 19 years. Next year, it'll be twenty.

Maybe I'll go back. Let myself grieve. As Rada suggested. Or maybe I'll go home to London, to the family that needs me more than the ghosts of strangers do.

Wherever I am, I'll carry this truth: I've built the life I once dreamed of. Through pain, through practice. Through saying yes.

New passions, New people. And, of course, at the heart of my existence, music.

Music has always been the thread. I didn't mean to give this book a soundtrack. But it wrote itself into the story, into my healing. Lyrics, albums, artists embedded throughout, shaping the story. Giving me the courage to push on when I thought I couldn't.

At a recent gig with Meg, hand in hand, listening to Counting Crows belt out "Mr. Jones," I realised something vital.

That chapter was finally over.

I wasn't lost in the past. I wasn't being transported back to dark moments by lyrics linked to my worst memories.

This chapter's over. But a new musical odyssey is beginning. New memories. New timestamps.

New purpose.

I ran my thumb over the broken clasp on the St. Christopher pendant Mum gave me at birth. Maybe it marked me before I understood why. Patron saint of travellers.

Marked for movement. For journeys. For survival.

Thanks, Mum.

Maybe this was always the path.

My Ikigai.

The ~~End~~ Beginning

'A truly brave man is never serene; he is never taken by surprise; nothing ruffles the equanimity of his spirit.

In the midst of catastrophes he keeps level his mind. Earthquakes do not shake him, he laughs at storms.

Who, in the menacing presence of danger or death, retains his self possession'

Inazo Nitobe

Acknowledgments:

Writing this book was a bit like surviving a tsunami all over again—waves of clarity followed by undertows of doubt, and the occasional embarrassing memory. I couldn't have made it through without some extraordinary people.

First to Meg—for your patience, your heart, and your fierce love. You saw me when I couldn't see myself.

To Barry—my trauma brother. You walked beside me through every kind of storm, literal and emotional. You never asked for recognition, but you deserve all of it.

To Mike and The Lads, and the many beautiful souls who left too soon—I carry your memory every day. This book is part tribute, part time machine. I hope you'd laugh at the dumb jokes and forgive the dark turns.

To Rada and Gita, who helped untangle decades of silence—thank you for giving me the tools to face the past without being buried by it.

And to my family, who taught me how to be strong even when we didn't always have the words.

To Lisbeth—Thank you, you helped me heal. From Orangutans to Enneagrams, the path was long but I wouldn't have found it without you.

To my people from Koh Phi Phi—I may not mention your names in this memoir but that in no way reflects the impact you made on my life.

To Bobby, Wiggy, Matt, Steve, Nick and Joey—My best friends. You've always been there for me and provided some of the best days of my life.

To Julie—Thank you for allowing me to monopolise your life during those dark years, you never once turned me away and always made me feel like part of your family.

To all my other friends, too numerous to mention. You know who you are. You know what you mean.

To Sam. Always an inspiration, and Ninja school may have just saved my life.

To the artists and creators that have dedicated their lives to producing content that means so much to so many. This book wouldn't be possible without the pop culture that has carried me through this strange life.

To every survivor I met, or never met, from Boxing Day 2004—this story belongs to all of us. You are not forgotten.

To my early readers and the angels who endured multiple drafts (and pop culture tangents): your notes made this sharper, funnier, and truer. Thank you for holding it with care.

And finally, to the reader: thank you for traveling through memory and mayhem with me. If you've ever felt broken or lost, I hope this book reminds you that healing isn't a straight line—but it's always possible. Sometimes, the wave that knocks you down is also the one that carries you forward.

More from John Bromfield:

 @tidesofresilience - Behind the book: the stories, struggles, and pop culture that shaped Tides of Resilience.

@footsteps_explorer - Travel. Experience. Escape. Repeat. Instagram is where I share the journeys that keep me grounded and the distractions that keep me sane

 Footsteps_explorer - Music carried me through the waves—past, present, and future. My taste is eclectic, my mission simple: keep listening, keep discovering.

 Footsteps Press publishes memoirs, travel narratives, and stories of resilience. Learn more @footstepspress